Scott Mann

THE EIGHT WITNESSES

JOSEPH SMITH
SEEKER AFTER TRUTH
PROPHET OF GOD

JOSEPH SMITH
From an early painting (about 1842)

JOSEPH SMITH
From an early Newspaper Illustration

JOSEPH SMITH

SEEKER AFTER TRUTH
PROPHET OF GOD

BY
JOHN A. WIDTSOE

B O O K C R A F T
SALT LAKE CITY, UTAH

1957

Printed in U.S.A.
DESERET NEWS PRESS
Salt Lake City, Utah

PREFACE

Joseph Smith has perplexed the world.

He taught a consistent authoritative theology, known only in fragments in his day, that answers satisfactorily the deep questions of the soul. He set up under this theology an understandable system of practices for human good. Besides, he left convincing evidences of the truth of his claims.

Was Joseph Smith a prophet of God?

The answer to that question lies in an honest, prayerful study of that which he taught and did. To help in such a study, a number of subjects have here been sketched simply and briefly, in the hope that they may awaken a desire for further and more profound study of the Prophet of the nineteenth century; also that they might help confirm the testimonies of his followers.

These sketches, built around a series of radio addresses, are written from the point of view of a believer. Unbelievers cannot object to that, provided the facts used are correct. Enemies who have written about Joseph Smith have been found too often to ignore facts. That destroys the value of the vast anti-Mormon literature. It is not safe to build conclusions on un-supported theories.

To help those unfamiliar with the subject, since time and places are here only briefly mentioned, a chronology of Joseph Smith's life, prepared by Dr. G. Homer Durham and published in his book, *Joseph Smith, Prophet-Statesman,* has been added. The sketches, however, follow in the main the chronology of Joseph Smith's teachings, with their resulting effects in works. Each of these sketches could well be expanded into a book.

This book was written at the suggestion of George Albert Smith, eighth president of the Church of Jesus Christ of Latter-day Saints. It was finished shortly before his death. He urged its early publication and wide circulation to aid, with other publications, in the establishment of the truth of the claims of the first prophet of this dispensation.

Prophetic blood ran strongly in the veins of George Albert Smith. His ancestor was the brother of Joseph Smith's father. His superb faith in Joseph Smith's mission was based on an intelligent examination and use of the principles of the restored gospel. To George Albert Smith the divine calling of Joseph Smith was the greatest event in the history of mankind since the days of the Savior. He was eager that anything new about Joseph Smith, in fact or presentation, provided it rests on truth, be given to the world. He knew that through the gospel alone would the great blessings of life come to the children of men. He was a worthy successor of Joseph the Prophet.

The commission given more than three years ago has guided the pen in the preparation of this volume.

Salt Lake City, Utah   JOHN A. WIDTSOE
July 24, 1951.

ACKNOWLEDGMENTS

Many friends have given help in the preparation of this book. Presidents Richard L. Evans and Milton R. Hunter of the First Council of Seventy; A. William Lund, Assistant Historian of the Church; Dr. G. Homer Durham of the Department of Political Science at the University of Utah; Mrs. Marba C. Josephson, Associate Managing Editor of the *Improvement Era;* Albert L. Zobell, Jr., Research Editor of the *Improvement Era;* Dr. Francis W. Kirkham and Ralph Bailey read the whole manuscript critically and made hundreds of helpful suggestions. The use of the Chronology of Joseph Smith's life by Dr. G. Homer Durham found in the book, *Joseph Smith, Prophet-Statesman* was kindly permitted by the publishers, The Bookcraft Company.

A. William Lund and the personnel of the Historian's Library, especially Lauritz G. Peterson, lightened the burden of preparation by finding and checking data, and by making helpful suggestions

Dr. Milton R. Hunter undertook the heavy and exacting work of seeing the volume through the press. The tedious proofreading was done by Mrs. Milton R. Hunter, who made numerous helpful suggestions; Mrs. Elizabeth J. Moffitt of the *Improvement Era* staff, Miss Ruth Peterson, Miss Elaine Pugmire, Mrs. Marion I. Mortensen, Mrs. Liliu D. Perry and Mrs. Vella H. Wetzel.

Dr. G. Homer Durham prepared the index, always an important part of a book.

Miss Eva Feik, my secretary, toiled through the manuscript repeatedly to prepare it properly for the printer.

Mrs. Leah D. Widtsoe, my wife, read the manuscript critically, made numerous valuable suggestions, often incisive, as the book grew towards completion. My debt to her is not easily expressed in words.

To all these, and to the many others who helped to make the book possible and printed, hearty and sincere thanks. Such friends make work easy.

CONTENTS

x   *CONTENTS*

ILLUSTRATIONS

CHAPTER 1

THE FIRST VISION

The remarkable story of Joseph Smith began with the astonishing answer to a boy's prayer for truth.

It came about in this wise:

Palmyra, a village in western New York State, near his home, was swept in the winter and spring of 1820 by a religious revival. Feelings ran high. Everybody wanted salvation. Which of the contending preachers had the right formula? That was the live, debated question of the community.

Joseph Smith, then between fourteen and fifteen years of age, was bewildered by the contending claims. Some members of his own family had joined one church, others were about to join another. He wanted to be sure before he joined any church.

In his own words:[1]

I was born in the year of our Lord 1805, on the twenty-third day of December, in the town of Sharon, Windsor County, State of Vermont. My father, Joseph Smith, Sr., left the State of Vermont and moved to Palmyra, Ontario (now Wayne) County, in the State of New York, when I was in my tenth year, or thereabouts. In about four years after my father's arrival in Palmyra, he moved with his family into Manchester, in the same County of Ontario.

Some time in the second year after our removal to Manchester, there was in the place where we lived an unusual excitement on the subject of religion. It commenced with the Methodists, but soon became general among all the sects in that region. Indeed, the whole district seemed affected by it, and great multitudes united themselves to the different religious parties, which created no small stir and division amongst the people, some crying, "Lo here!" and others, "Lo there!" Some were contending for the Methodist faith, some for the Presbyterian, and some for the Baptist.[2]

For notwithstanding the great love which the converts to these different faiths expressed at the time of their conversion, and the great zeal manifested by the respective clergy, who were active

---

[1]*History of the Church*, vol. 1, p. 2; *Times and Seasons*, vol. 3, p. 727.
[2]Peter G. Mode, *The Frontier Spirit In American Christianity.*

in getting up and promoting this extraordinary scene of religious feeling, in order to have everybody converted, as they were pleased to call it, let them join what sect they pleased—yet when the converts began to file off, some to one party and some to another, it was seen that the seemingly good feelings of both the priests and the converts were more pretended than real; for a scene of great confusion and bad feeling ensued; priest contending against priest and convert against convert; so that all their good feelings one for another, if they ever had any, were entirely lost in a strife of words and a contest about opinions.

I was at this time in my fifteenth year. My father's family was proselyted to the Presbyterian faith, and four of them joined that church, namely—my mother, Lucy; my brothers Hyrum and Samuel Harrison; and my sister Sophronia.

During this time of great excitement, my mind was called up to serious reflection and great uneasiness; but though my feelings were deep and often poignant, still I kept myself aloof from all these parties, though I attended their several meetings as often as occasion would permit. In process of time my mind became somewhat partial to the Methodist sect, and I felt some desire to be united with them; but so great were the confusion and strife among the different denominations, that it was impossible for a person young as I was, and so unacquainted with men and things, to come to any certain conclusion who was right and who was wrong.

My mind at times was greatly excited, the cry and tumult were so great and incessant.

In the midst of this war of words and tumult of opinions, I often said to myself, What is to be done? Who of all these parties are right; or, are they all wrong together? If any one of them be right, which is it, and how shall I know it?

While I was laboring under the extreme difficulties caused by the contests of these parties of religionists, I was one day reading the Epistle of James, first chapter and fifth verse, which reads: "If any of you lack wisdom, let him ask of God, that giveth to all men liberally, and upbraideth not; and it shall be given him."

Never did any passage of scripture come with more power to the heart of man than this did at this time to mine. It seemed to enter with great force into every feeling of my heart. I reflected on it again and again, knowing that if any person needed wisdom from God, I did; for how to act I did not know, and unless I could get more wisdom than I then had, I would never know; for the teachers of religion of the different sects understood the same passages of scripture so differently as to destroy all confidence in settling the question by an appeal to the Bible.

At length I came to the conclusion that I must either remain in darkness and confusion, or else I must do as James directs, that is, ask of God. I at length came to the determination to ask of God, concluding that if He gave wisdom to them that lacked wisdom, and would give liberally, and not upbraid, I might venture.

So, in accordance with this, my determination to ask of God, I retired to the woods to make the attempt. It was on the morning of a beautiful, clear day, early in the spring of 1820. It was the first time in my life that I had made such an attempt, for amidst all my anxieties I had never as yet made the attempt to pray vocally.

After I had retired to the place where I had previously designed to go, having looked around me, and finding myself alone, I kneeled down and began to offer up the desires of my heart to God. I had scarcely done so, when immediately I was seized upon by some power which entirely overcame me, and had such an astonishing influence over me as to bind my tongue so that I could not speak. Thick darkness gathered around me, and it seemed to me for a time as if I were doomed to sudden destruction.

But, exerting all my powers to call upon God to deliver me out of the power of this enemy which had seized upon me, and at the very moment when I was ready to sink into despair and abandon myself to destruction—not to an imaginary ruin, but to the power of some actual being from the unseen world, who had such marvelous power as I had never before felt in any being—just at this moment of great alarm, I saw a pillar of light exactly over my head, above the brightness of the sun, which descended gradually until it fell upon me.

It no sooner appeared than I found myself delivered from the enemy which held me bound. When the light rested upon me I saw two personages, whose brightness and glory defy all description, standing above me in the air. One of them spake unto me, calling me by name, and said, pointing to the other—"This is my Beloved Son, hear Him!"

My object in going to inquire of the Lord was to know which of all the sects was right, that I might know which to join. No sooner, therefore, did I get possession of myself, so as to be able to speak, than I asked the Personages who stood above me in the light, which of all the sects was right—and which I should join.

I was answered that I must join none of them, for they were all wrong and the Personage who addressed me said that all their creeds were an abomination in His sight, that those professors were all corrupt; that "they draw near to me with their lips, but their hearts are far from me; they teach for doctrines the commandments of men, having a form of godliness, but they deny the power thereof."

He again forbade me to join with any of them; and many

other things did He say unto me, which I cannot write at this time. When I came to myself again, I found myself lying on my back, looking up into heaven.[3]

He was also promised that "the fulness of the gospel should at some future time be made known unto me."[4]

It was an extraordinary experience. Never before had God the Father and God the Son appeared to mortal man. It was the more astonishing in that it came to a half-grown boy. Certainly it was most astonishing to the lad, who had asked which of the contending religions was right, to hear that they had all fallen into error; that the true church was to be re-established on earth; and that he was to be the instrument through whom this would be done.

There was of course nothing impossible or improbable in the event. In the Christian faith lies imbedded the doctrine that God is the framer of the heavens and the earth, the creator of man on earth. Such a personage cannot be divested of the right to come on earth, to show himself to his children, or to set his work in order. He has done so before; he may do so at his pleasure, or at any time. It is a type of blasphemy to say that he cannot do so.

The far-flung teaching among Christian sects that the day of revelation has ended is not supported by evidence, nor is it logically acceptable. It is a sad commentary on human frailty that the sentence at the end of the Bible, clearly belonging to the last book of the Bible, has been heralded as proof of the end of revelation. God's revelation to man is in various ways continuously present in every earnest human life. The Book of Moses ends with a similar challenge;[5] and Christ as he hung on the cross said, "it is finished."[6] These statements really imply the coming of a new period or philosophy.

---

[3]On another occasion, in the famous Wentworth letter, Joseph Smith told of his First Vision, *Times and Seasons*, vol. 3, pp. 748-749, 753-754, March, 1842; *History of the Church*, vol. 4, pp. 535-536.
   [4]*Times and Seasons*, vol. 2, pp. 706-707; *History of the Church*, vol. 4, p. 536.
   [5]Deuteronomy 4:2.
   [6]John 19:30.

CHAPTER 2

THE CHALLENGE OF THE FIRST VISION

The First Vision was a challenge to the religious vagaries of the day. It shattered many a false doctrine taught throughout the centuries. Yet it was plain and simple to the human understanding. There was no mysticism about it. Joseph saw, in full light, the personages of the vision and heard their words. The vision was beyond philosophic quibbling.

The vision struck first at atheism. The man-made definitions of God, inadequate for clear human thinking, had made atheists of many persons and near atheists of many more. Most of these people felt that there must be a moving power behind all natural phenomena, but many preferred to believe that the universe is driven by unknown, probably unintelligent, mechanistic forces. To such a conception, the vision made emphatic answer. God the Father with his Son stood before Joseph and instructed him. God, an intelligent being, does exist! That was the witness of the vision. Upon the certainty of the existence of God, the life labors of Joseph Smith were built.

Further, the vision challenged the contradictory and confusing conceptions of the nature of God. For centuries men had thought, talked and philosophized about the nature of God, not only his powers but the essence of him, without reaching an agreement. Some of the ablest minds on earth, from Socrates to Ralph Waldo Emerson, had engaged in the discussion. The result was unutterable confusion to the rational mind.

A few, and a very few, had conceived God to be a person, not merely a personage. This view had ordinarily been laid aside, since it made God more nearly like man in body and powers. Men had held up their hands in horror at an anthropomorphic God, whatever that may have meant.

In early Christian days, more thinkers had accepted God as a personage, but one wholly different from man, usually a tenuous entity, indefinable, and incomprehensible.

Others, many of them Christians, taught that God was neither a person nor a personage, but a force, much like electricity or magnetism, permeating the universe, dealing impersonally with men as with all other things and beings, a world spirit, a first cause, an unknowable source of all things, the immovable mover of the universe, pure energy, the spirit filling all men, the sole independent substance of the universe, a thought in the human mind, a spiritual substance, a monad, man's highest idea, universal reason and intelligence, and other equally useless and incomprehensible definitions![1]

The First Vision clarified this whole matter. It set these philosophic guesses at rest. It answered the centuries' old query about the nature of God. The Father and the Son had appeared to Joseph as persons, like men on earth in form. They spoke to him as persons. They were persons, not mental aberrations. To Joseph Smith, God was thenceforth a living, personal Being.

From the early days of Christianity, the erroneous doctrine of the nature of God had led to other equally false conclusions. Jesus of Nazareth had declared himself to be the Son of God. So he was accepted by his followers. He had also taught the existence, powers, and mission of the Holy Ghost. The Son and the Holy Ghost possessed godlike powers. Christian philosophers, departing from the simple truth in Christ's teachings, began to ask if there could be more than one God. Out of their thinking came the conception that the Father, the Son, and the Holy Ghost, the Godhead, were One, a unity. Therefore, though God is One, he is also Three Persons, or as some philosophers preferred to say, three emanations. Through the following centuries, this doctrine, in one form or another, led to any number of absurd and mystical conclusions.

---

[1] S. E. Frost, *The Basic Teachings of the Great Philosophers.*

This false doctrine was laid low by the First Vision. Two personages, the Father and the Son, stood before Joseph. The Father asked the Son to deliver the message to the boy. There was no mingling of personalities in the vision. Each of the personages was an individual member of the Godhead. Each one separately took part in the vision.

There was also the current heretical belief that God, whatever he was, was a faraway figure, who no longer had direct concern with earth. Any contact with him was by long distance, imperceptible to human senses. He had placed men on earth and had no further concern with them until after death. In answer to the teaching that the day of revelation had ended, the First Vision was a declaration not only of the possibility of revelation but of a continuity of revelation. God is the framer of the universe and its contents. He would not forget his children on earth, nor can he be divorced from the right to come on earth, to show himself to his children, or to set his work in order. He had done so before, in earlier times, according to the Holy Scriptures. He showed himself to Abraham, Samuel and others. Why not in our day, to carry his work forward? Surely he may do so at his pleasure. That was the message of the vision. (It taught that it is a type of blasphemy to say that God cannot or will not reveal himself to his children on earth.)

It was astonishing to the lad, who had asked which of the contending religions was right, to hear that they had all fallen into error, that none had the full gospel. This might of course have been foretold. The simple gospel, left by Jesus Christ, was broken into hundreds of sects, each clamoring for support. Certainly only one, if any of them, was right. In the vision none was right.

So, a restoration of the ancient truth, in doctrine and organization, was necessary. Indeed, the Personages in the First Vision declared that the true Church was to be re-established on earth. He, Joseph Smith, was to be the instrument through whom this was to be done. But he was to wait for further commands from the Lord. He was not to do it of himself.

This was another challenge to the practices of the world. Men who felt that they had an "inward call," had thought themselves at liberty to organize a church. This was not proper in building God's church. The authority must come directly from the Lord or his appointed agents. Though Joseph was called to effect the restoration, he would have to wait until the actual call came from the Lord by revelation, and then for full preparation.

The First Vision thus offered challenges at least to some existing dogmas: God exists as a glorious Personage; God and Christ are personal Beings; members of the Godhead may act individually as separate beings; all churches on earth had departed more or less from the pure gospel of Christ; God may reveal himself to man at any time; the church of God would be restored, but only by direct spoken authority of the Lord. These challenges aimed at one or another of the many dogmas of the confusion of churches. The challenges were upsetting to minds trained in the traditions of the past. Naturally, the priests, professional teachers of religion, resented Joseph's claims, and proceeded to try to destroy the new invader of the field which they had so long cultivated and maintained as their own.

Astonishing as all this was in light of the teachings of the day, probably the most astounding to Joseph Smith was the statement that he, a boy untaught in the schools of the world, a toiler on his father's farm, had been chosen to be the instrument for accomplishing the restoration of the gospel of Jesus Christ.

Joseph did not understand at the time the full import of the First Vision, but he treasured it and its message in his mind. As he approached maturity, it became the foundation fact upon which his work was built. His later career was but an amplification of the truths revealed in the First Vision. We can only surmise the long thoughts of this healthy, wholesome country boy, after the shattering of the dogmas of the day by the First Vision.

He joined no church. The Palmyra revivalists were unsuccessful so far as he was concerned. Instead, had men only understood, the First Vision of the boy was the biggest event connected with the revival.

In the grove at Palmyra on the sun-bathed spring day of 1820, the new age of continuous revelation of God's truth had dawned.

Chapter 3

TRUTH SEEKERS MAY FIND THE WAY

The First Vision was the beginning of a process of education under direct divine supervision of a boy destined in God's hands to be the instrument through which the restoration of gospel truth and authority was to be accomplished.

The education was gradual, as it should be. Three years elapsed before he had another spiritual experience and further instructions. It was ten years after the First Vision before he was authorized to organize the Church, the real objective of his coming work.

Nevertheless, amidst his farm labors, Joseph must have pondered the many universal lessons that the First Vision taught—lessons that every truth seeker must know, and lessons which Joseph was to use henceforth in his work.

Joseph's desire for certain truth was the key that unlocked the door to heavenly visions. It was not conceivable that God would impose a knowledge of himself upon any person who cared indifferently for truth. Desire must precede any great accomplishment. Men may always be judged by their desires.

God deals only in truth and cannot palliate untruth. Error is always abominable. The sorrows of the world may be traced to untruth masquerading as truth. The noble spirit of truth seeking has in all ages brought light out of darkness.

The truth seeker is neither doubter, skeptic, nor unbeliever. The truth of a statement is not denied until it has been examined. The truth seeker always holds his judgment in abeyance until he has accumulated sufficient evidence on which to base a conclusion. He has an open mind; above all else he desires to know truth. The authority of superior knowledge or position is respected, but only after a full personal conviction that it is real authority and that it is properly exercised. In the end, truth followers must rest their convictions on personal experiences.

It was knowledge of God's truth that Joseph desired. Complying with the scriptural injunction that had inspired him, as well as the use of common sense, the boy proceeded to ask of the Lord. Every great work begins with a prayer to a master. The spirit of prayer runs through the whole accumulation of learning, profane and sacred. Every student in school may be said to be an asker for truth. Every leader of thought teaches only answers to the questions that he and others have asked.

Prayer, "the soul's sincere desire," must accompany the seeker in quest of truth. Without prayer he fails. Joseph's prayer was heard. It seemed in earlier days a great mystery that God could hear all the prayers of his children. To our generation, trained in the wonders of communication through space by telephone, telegraph, radio, television, and the fixation of speech upon waxen surfaces, or magnetized metallic wires, it is easy to conceive of a higher intelligence capable of recognizing and answering the spoken and unspoken prayers of his children.

Not only was Joseph's prayer heard, it was also answered. Every prayer of man is answered, provided it is uttered in full faith in the goodness and power of God. The way of communication between man and God is always open to the sincere soul. The answer may not come at the time or in the form expected, but it does come. It may be that the economy of heavenly things makes it impossible for a prayer to remain unanswered.

The boy was hardly upon his knees in the quiet grove before he was attacked by the power of evil, the contending, untruthful force in the universe. The ordeal must have been fearfully trying. Before the battle was over, the boy felt that his very life was in danger. This was only to be expected. From within came disturbing questions.

Was it not a preposterous thing to ask God about something that the ministers were supposed to know? Would God answer? How would the answer come? Would he, Joseph, recognize the message if one came? The darkness and fear of an unsteady faith seized upon the boy. Every person who has set out in search of truth has had his prejudices, preconceived notions, doubts of success, and all sorts of apparently logical antagonisms rise up against him and his venture. Men all too often fail to realize the vast opposition heaped up within their own minds to anything contrary to their traditions and false teachings. Once these inward doubts are overcome, progress may be expected. But they are always to be reckoned with and to be feared.

In Joseph's case, however, more important opposition came from without. The forces of evil, angels of darkness, lie everywhere in waiting. Joseph's love of truth, his determination to find truth, and his willingness to follow the appointed way to truth, were challenges to evil. Here was a human being to be feared by the minions of the devil. Into what godlike power might he not grow! Therefore, he was obliged to learn that the powers of darkness were real. The terrific struggle was not of an imaginary character, but he says, as "the power of some actual being from the unseen world—which had such marvelous power as I had never before felt in any being." He was almost ready to give up his quest and "abandon myself to destruction." This contest with evil was necessary. Knowledge comes by comparisons and contrasts. By light we know darkness, by good we know evil; by successive, comparative steps man moves into a larger knowledge. A person does not need to practise evil to know good. Evil is recognized by its effects without practising it. Everyone must oppose it as Joseph did in the Sacred Grove. There was fine pedagogic purpose in Joseph's battle with evil, as it gave him a contrast with the glory he was about to experience. Every seeker for truth must expect to battle with untruth.

The praying boy won. He vanquished the powers of darkness. Praying men are always victorious. Light triumphs over darkness, good over evil; truth is revealed if the seeker fail not in his search. Faith, courage, effort, and persistence lead to conquest. Joseph exerted all his powers to call upon God for help; and truth issued from her secret chambers.

When the youthful prophet had fought off evil, the vision began. An effulgent light gradually filled the grove, until every leaf, twig, and branch stood out distinctly against the bright light. So it must be. Truth cannot dwell with mystery and superstition and darkness. Truth can always be recognized by the accompanying clearness of vision and peace of mind. Fear and doubt retreat from truth. Truth and light always travel together.

God the Father and God the Son stood before the prostrate boy. The Father pointed to the other and said, "This is My Beloved Son, hear Him."

The Father is the supreme ruler of the universe, but his Son had been commissioned to care for this earth. It was an eloquent lesson to the coming prophet with respect to law and order. Orderliness makes the present universe possible and pleasant to dwell in. The universe is under a reign of law. Chaos, the opposite of law, is unnatural and abhorrent, for it confuses the mind and makes progress impossible.

When the heavenly beings had departed, Joseph found himself lying on his back, looking into heaven, with his physical strength largely spent.

It was his first realization of the fierce cost of truth. Knowledge does not come unsought or without effort on the part of the learner. Only by tremendous self-effort does great knowledge come. It required terrific effort to fight away the evil powers that sought to keep knowledge from him. It required an intense concentration of body and spirit to keep in tune with Divinity so that the heavenly message could be understood. Naturally, the boy was exhausted in body and in mind. But who would not gladly pay any price for such an experience?

The vision was over. The boy who had communed with the Gods stood in the humble home by the fireplace. The mother was moving about with her homely duties. In answer to his mother's anxious question concerning his welfare he answered, "Never mind, I am well enough off," and added, "I have learned for myself that [your church] is not true."[1] He had sought and found truth. There was neither place nor feeling for many words.

The whole career of Joseph Smith was the use of these universal lessons of the First Vision in a lifelong search for truth; to ask of God with a certain feeling that the prayer will be heard and answered, and to be armed to defeat the evil one who opposes any sincere prayer to God.

Many lessons came out of the First Vision for Joseph's future guidance, such as: the desire for truth unlocks heavenly visions, a sincere prayer is always heard and answered, the seeker for truth must be ready to battle with the forces of untruth, and the seeker for truth must pay a great cost in effort. Truth is often known by contrasts.

Every truth seeker could profitably learn the lessons which came out of Joseph's First Vision. In one form or another they are always present when a person sets out to find truth.

---

[1]*History of the Church*, vol. 1, p. 6.

CHAPTER 4

PERSECUTION RAISES ITS HEAD

The First Vision spared no false tradition, however ancient and honored. It challenged the long-held beliefs of multitudes. It held up as false many of the teachings of the ministerial class.

In self-defense, if for no other reason, the clergy protested. Their parishioners also, who saw the cherished beliefs of childhood slipping away, frowned upon Joseph's story. The protests grew into persecution.

In Joseph Smith's own words:[1]

It seems as though the adversary was aware, at a very early period of my life, that I was destined to be a disturber and an annoyer of his kingdom; else why should the powers of darkness combine against me? Why the opposition and persecution that arose against me, almost in my infancy? Some few days after I had this vision, I happened to be in company with one of the Methodist preachers, who was very active in the before mentioned religious excitement; and, conversing with him on the subject of religion, I took occasion to give him an account of the vision which I had had. I was greatly surprised at his behavior; he treated my communication not only lightly, but with great contempt, saying it was all of the devil, that there were no such things as visions or revelation in these days; that all such things had ceased with the apostles, and that there would never be any more of them.

I soon found, however, that my telling the story had excited a great deal of prejudice against me among professors of religion, and was the cause of great persecution, which continued to increase; and though I was an obscure boy, only between fourteen and fifteen years of age, and my circumstances in life such as to make a boy of no consequence in the world, yet men of high standing would take notice sufficient to excite the public mind against me, and create a bitter persecution; and this was common among all the sects—all united to persecute me.

It caused me serious reflection then, and often has since, how very strange it was that an obscure boy, of a little over fourteen years of age, and one, too, who was doomed to the

---

[1]*History of the Church*, vol. 1, p. 6; et seq.

necessity of obtaining a scanty maintenance by his daily labor, should be thought a character of sufficient importance to attract the attention of the great ones of the most popular sects of the day, and in a manner to create in them a spirit of the most bitter persecution and reviling. But strange or not, so it was, and it was often the cause of great sorrow to myself.

However, it was nevertheless a fact that I had beheld a vision. I have thought since, that I felt much like Paul, when he made his defense before King Agrippa, and related the account of the vision he had when he saw a light and heard a voice; still there were but few who believed him; some said he was dishonest, others said he was mad; and he was ridiculed and reviled. But all this did not destroy the reality of his vision. He had seen a vision, he knew he had, and all the persecution under heaven could not make it otherwise; and though they should persecute him unto death, yet he knew, and would know to his latest breath, that he had both seen a light and heard a voice speaking unto him, and all the world could not make him think or believe otherwise.

So it was with me. I had actually seen a light, and in the midst of that light I saw two Personages, and they did in reality speak to me; and though I was hated and persecuted for saying that I had seen a vision, yet it was true; and while they were persecuting me, reviling me, and speaking all manner of evil against me falsely for so saying, I was led to say in my heart; Why persecute me for telling the truth? I have actually seen a vision, and who am I that I can withstand God, or why does the world think to make me deny what I have actually seen? For I have seen a vision; I knew it, and I knew that God knew it, and I could not deny it, neither dared I do it, at least I knew that by so doing I would offend God, and come under condemnation.

I had now got my mind satisfied so far as the sectarian world was concerned; that it was not my duty to join with any of them, but to continue as I was until further directed. I had found the testimony of James to be true, that a man who lacked wisdom might ask of God, and obtain, and not be upbraided.

The preacher to whom he told his story was Reverend George Lane,[2] who was the leader of the Palmyra revival and who had quoted the saying from James, which had so deeply affected the lad.

It is only reasonable to suppose that Reverend Lane

[2]John A. Clark, *Gleanings By The Way*, pp. 216-232; *Journal History*, January 20, 1894, p. 2.

told others of Joseph's story. They in turn would tell it
to friends. Soon, it became part of the village gossip. The
Palmyra population was a small community with little
new material for street corner and parlor discussion. To
the gossipers, Joseph's story was a welcome addition to
their available material. Thus Joseph Smith became a
marked boy. More than likely, those who had heard the
gossip said or thought when they saw Joseph, "There is
the boy who says he saw God." Of course, no one took
his story seriously. It was only a boy's dream, they explained. But it was a dangerous dream, they felt, insulting
to ministers of the gospel and overthrowing the beliefs of
centuries, the beliefs by which men had lived and died.
The story of the vision did not add to Joseph's popularity.
The story grew among the people.

When some years later, Joseph had other spiritual
experiences, enemies resorted to the story of the First
Vision for the basis of their persecutions. They used their
imaginations to explain how the story of the vision had
come about. Distorted versions of the story appeared. It
was even said that Joseph had dealt in necromancy; he
had consorted with evil spirits; he was a crystal gazer; he
was in league with the devil, and so forth.

Only after the Book of Mormon plates were seen,
however, did the wildest tales to blacken Joseph's character
appear. People drew upon the ugly gossip concerning the
First Vision. Further stories were invented to malign
Joseph's character. When the Book of Mormon became
an issue, Joseph's persecutors were compelled to explain
him and his claim. His own story was unacceptable to
them. In the beginning of his career the only explanation
of enemies was that he lied about the vision and the
things that followed. His opponents, detractors of his
character, brought together every village gossip and laid
it upon the shoulders of the young man who stubbornly
insisted that he had had heavenly communications.

Then his enemies said that all this was only to be
expected, for they added that he came of a dishonest,

shiftless family. His traits and taints were inherited!
This brought the whole Smith family into the controversy,
really to the discomfiture of the persecutors, for the Smith
ancestry was known through three hundred years to have
been honest people and good citizens.

There were of course a few kindly souls who thought
that Joseph was honest enough but was deceived by a
dream he had had. Even they could not believe the vision
as told by Joseph Smith.

Persecution began early in his life. It was to continue
with increasing vehemence until his persecutors murdered
him. His life story could be told as a record of continued
persecution.

CHAPTER 5

DID JOSEPH SMITH HAVE THE FIRST VISION?

The First Vision of 1820 is of first importance in the history of Joseph Smith. Upon its reality rest the truth and value of his subsequent work.

Professed enemies of Joseph Smith and his work, have felt themselves helpless in their efforts to destroy the reality of the First Vision and have said little about it. However, a few have brazenly declared in their books that Joseph invented the story of the First Vision in 1838, eighteen years after it occurred.[1] This charge, supported by no confirmatory facts, but circulated industriously by recent defamers of Joseph Smith, deserves comment.

The earliest available written official account of the First Vision dates from 1838 when Joseph Smith began to write the history of the Church. It was first printed in 1840.[2] Nearly a century later, enemies have set up the theory that the vision was then concocted by the Prophet. This far-fetched charge implies not only that Joseph Smith lied about his First Vision but also that facts of history to be acceptable must be written at the time of their occurrence. This is a preposterous claim, a new guide for historians. If that were true, the historicity of Jesus the Christ would vanish, for there are no available documents dealing with his life until many years after his crucifixion.

Whether the story of the First Vision existed in written form in the early days of the Church is not known. The Church attempted from its beginning to keep careful records of its history.[3] Many manuscripts of that time have, however, been lost. In some cases secretaries deliberately carried records away from Church possession.[4] But even were they all available, minutes of meetings as

---

[1]G. B. Arbaugh, *Revelation Among the Mormons*, pp. 34, 35, 238; W. A. Linn, *The Story of the Mormons*, p. 30; Fawn M. Brodie, *No Man Knows My History*, pp. 21-25.
[2]Orson Pratt, *An Interesting Account of Several Remarkable Visions, and of the Later Discovery of Ancient American Records*, p. 5.
[3]*Doctrine and Covenants*, Section 21.
[4]*History of the Church*, vol. 3, p. 15.

they are usually kept might seldom mention the First
Vision, for familiar and repeated things are usually taken
for granted.

Moreover, the followers of Joseph Smith thought
primarily about the restoration of the simple teachings of
Jesus Christ. The miraculous foundation of the work,
except the Book of Mormon, seldom found its way into
the printed records of the Church. The missionaries to
England were specifically so instructed.

> My instructions to the brethren were, when they arrived in
> England, to adhere strictly to the first principles of the gospel and
> remain silent concerning the gathering, the vision, and the Book of
> Doctrine and Covenants until such time as the work was fully estab-
> lished and it should be clearly made manifest by the spirit to do
> otherwise.[5]

Knowledge is usually first carried from person to
person by word of mouth. The writers who have set
up the theory that the Prophet did not mention the First
Vision until 1838 have to prove that the vision was not
mentioned before that time. Therein they fail, for there
is ample and sufficient evidence that it was mentioned
before that time. The refusal by enemy historians to accept
sure evidence of the mention of the First Vision before
1838 throws doubt upon the accuracy of nearly all their
historical accounts.

The Book of Mormon, printed in 1830, became at
once the storm center of the claims of Joseph Smith. All
other issues were forgotten when friend or foe held the
printed Nephite record in his hands. The coming forth
of this volume and of the Church soon after established
became tangible things which could be argued about.
The vision of a boy, ten years earlier, whether true or
false, could not be attacked in the same way.

Meanwhile, many persons living at the time of the
Prophet, before 1838, have spoken of the First Vision
as a spiritual experience had by the Prophet, before the

---

[5]*Ibid.*, vol. 2, p. 492.

coming forth of the Book of Mormon was revealed to him.[6]

Pomeroy Tucker, the proprietor and editor of the Wayne *Sentinel* and the owner of the press on which the Book of Mormon was first printed, knew most of the persons and events connected with the early days of the Church. He was deeply prejudiced against the divine claims of Joseph Smith and looked upon them as hoaxes. Nevertheless he had reason to know the succession of events, even if he did not believe their authenticity. He writes:

About this time[7] [he places the date about 1823] Smith had a remarkable vision. He pretended that, while engaged in secret prayer, alone in the wilderness, an "angel of the Lord" appeared to him . . . and proclaimed further that "all the religious denominations were believing in false doctrines and consequently that none of them were accepted of God as His Church and Kingdom," and also that he received a "promise that the true doctrine and the fullness of the gospel should at some future time be revealed to him." Following this, soon came another angel, (or possibly the same one,) revealing to him that he was himself to be "the favored instrument of the new revelation"; "that the American Indians were a remnant of the Israelites, who, after coming to this country, had their prophets and inspired writings; that such of their writings as had not been destroyed were safely deposited in a certain place made known to him, and to him only; that they contained revelations in regard to the last days, and that, if he remained faithful, he would be the chosen prophet to translate them to the world."[8]

Despite the errors in dates and detail, this statement repeats in essence the First Vision as told by the Prophet himself, and sets the time of its occurrence before the coming forth of the Book of Mormon. That is, the Prophet had a vision before he received the revelations about the Book of Mormon.

Professor J. B. Turner, a non-Mormon, one of the

---

[6]George A. Smith, the Prophet's cousin, said that "In the fall of 1828, my grandfather received by letter from my uncle Joseph Smith, Senior, the information that his son, Joseph had received several remarkable visions." *Deseret News*, August 11, 1858, p. 1.

[7]Pomeroy Tucker, *Origin, Rise and Progress of Mormonism*, 1867 edition, p. 28, D. Appleton and Company.

[8]*Ibid.*, p. 28.

early writers on Mormonism, published a book on the
Mormons in 1842. His version of the First Vision, though
containing errors of date, corroborates the Prophet's story.
He writes:

> In the year 1823, when our prophet was about seventeen
> years of age, his mind became, for the first time, deeply excited on
> the subject of religion by Mr. Lane, a devoted and talented elder
> of the Methodist Church, under whose preaching there was a "great
> awakening."
>
> After the revival ceased, the usual strife for proselytes between
> the several sects commenced. This resulted in leaving Joseph as
> he states, "in disgust with all the sects, and almost in despair of
> ever coming to the knowledge of the truth amid so many contra-
> dictory and conflicting claims." He resorted to prayer for a "full
> manifestation of divine approbation" and "for the assurance that
> he was accepted of him." This occurred sometime in the winter of
> 1823.
>
> On the memorable evening of the 21st of September following
> . . . a form stood before him . . . [who] proceeded to inform Smith . . .
> the Lord had chosen him to bring forth and translate the Book of
> Mormon.[9]

This early author, though confusing dates, also confirms the claim of Joseph Smith that the First Vision
antedated the promise by the angel Moroni of the Book
of Mormon.[10]

One Obediah Dogberry, an avowed enemy, published
in 1831 several articles on Joseph Smith's claims. He says:

> It is well-known that Joe Smith never pretended to have any
> communication with angels until a long time after the pretended
> finding of his book.[11]

This proves that in 1831, seven years before his
history was begun, Joseph Smith did claim to have had
visions before the knowledge of the Book of Mormon
plates were obtained. Otherwise Dogberry would have
had no reason to write as he did.

----

[9]J. B. Turner, *Mormonism In All Ages*, p. 15. The work of Reverend Lane in
Palmyra is well known, and occurred in the early twenties of the last century, as set by
Joseph Smith. Oliver Cowdery in his letters confirms the story of Reverend Lane and
the date of his work in Palmyra.
[10]Reverend Lane himself confirms the dates of the revival. It was in 1820, not 1823.
[11]Francis W. Kirkham, *A New Witness For Christ in America*, p. 291.

The *History of Wayne County*, New York, the County in which Joseph lived, and in which the history would be well-known, states: "Smith announced a vision wherein an angel had appeared and promised the revelation of a true and full gospel, which should supersede all others." Again, the angel appeared to Smith and revealed "That the American Indians were a remnant of the Israelites, who, after coming to this country had their prophets and inspired writings," etc.[12]

Most writers on the Mormons accept without question Joseph Smith's own story as to time and date. In fact, proof of the occurrence of the vision in Joseph Smith's early years could, if needed, be established wholly from non-Mormon sources.[13]

Mormon writers and speakers who lived in the days of Joseph Smith believed without exception that the First Vision occurred in the early life of the boy, before the Book of Mormon visitations. His mother accepted her son's own story in full, including the First Vision in 1820, and added more about his early spiritual experiences.[14]

Elder Edward Stevenson of the First Council of the Seventy who knew the Prophet, wrote:

> In . . . 1834 in the midst of many large congregations, the Prophet testified with great power concerning the visit of the Father and the Son.[15]

In his old age, only two weeks before his death, William Smith, brother of the Prophet, confirmed the story of the First Vision. He said:

> Hyrum, Catherine and mother were members of the Presbyterian Church. My father would not join. He did not like it because of Reverend Stockton. He had preached my brother's [Alvin's] funeral sermon and intimated very strongly that he had gone to hell, for Alvin was not a church member. . . . What caused Joseph

---

[12]*History of Wayne County*, New York (1877) p. 150.
[13]For example, J. H. Kennedy, *Early Days of Mormonism*, pp. 23-24; T. B. H. Stenhouse, *Rocky Mountain Saints*, p. 15; I. W. Riley, *The Founder of Mormonism*, p. 66; Ellen Dickinson, *New Light on Mormonism*, p. 33; Doris H. Bays, *Doctrines and Dogmas of Mormonism*, p. 19; E. Meyer *Ursprung und Geschichte der Mormonen*, pp. 16-17.
[14]Lucy Mack Smith, *Joseph Smith the Prophet*, 1902 edition, pp. 73-77; 1945 edition, pp. 69-74.
[15]Edward Stevenson, *Reminiscences of Joseph, the Prophet*, p. 4.

to ask for guidance as to what church he should join? Why there was a joint revival in the neighborhood between the Baptists, Methodists and Presbyterians and they had succeeded in stirring up quite a festing, and after the meeting the question arose which church should have the converts. Reverend Stockton was the president of the meeting, and suggested it was their meeting and under their care, and they had a church there and they ought to join the Presbyterians, but as father did not like Reverend Stockton very well, our folks hesitated, and the next evening Reverend Mr. Lane of the Methodists preached a sermon on "What church shall I join?" And the burden of the discourse was to ask of God, using as a text, "If any man lacks wisdom let him ask of God who giveth to all men liberally." And of course when Joseph went home and was looking over the text he was impressed to do just what the preacher had said, and going in the woods with a childlike simple trusting faith believing that God meant what He said, he kneeled down and prayed; and the time having come for the reorganization of His church, God was pleased to show him that he should join none of these churches, but if faithful he would be chosen to establish the true church.[16]

Isabella H. Horne, who first met the Prophet in Canada in 1837, says that she "heard him relate his First Vision when the Father and the Son appeared to him."[17]

Joseph Smith himself relates in his journal that in a council meeting held February 8, 1834, he spoke as follows:

"The office conferred upon me by the ministering of the angel of God, by His own voice, and by the voice of this Church."[18] Here the distinction between the angel and the voice of God certainly refers to the First Vision.

In 1835 he told one Erastus Holmes of his "First Vision which was when I was fourteen years old."[19] Clearly the story of the First Vision was common knowledge among members of the Church. The proponents of the theory that the Prophet invented the First Vision in 1838 doubt the accuracy of the Holmes and similar references, because they hold that the *Church History*, the journal of Joseph Smith, has been tampered with by later workers. It is

---

16*Deseret News*, January 20, 1894.
17*Young Women's Journal*, vol. 32, p. 212; *Relief Society Magazine*, vol. 38, p. 158.
18*History of the Church*, vol. 2, p. 25.
19*Ibid.*, vol. 2, p. 312; *Journal History*, Saturday, November 14, 1835.

sad when a drowning man does not even have a straw to which he may cling! That seemed and seems to be the need of these critics.

Orson Pratt, who lived for some time in the Prophet's home, issued a pamphlet in 1839, in which the First Vision is described, and it is there placed in 1820.[20] Later in life, Orson Pratt said, "I have often heard him [the Prophet] relate it!"[21] Orson Pratt joined the Church in 1830, and became a member of the first Quorum of Apostles. It is most improbable that he would say that "I have often heard the Prophet relate it," and fix the date in 1820, if he had heard it for the first time in 1838.

Brigham Young, who often spoke about the Prophet and his early experiences, said on one occasion:

> The Lord called Joseph Smith, called upon him at fourteen years of age, gave him visions, and led him along, guided and directed him in his obscurity, until he brought forth the plates and translated them.[22]

Brigham Young knew the Prophet from 1832. He also was one of the first Quorum of Apostles; and one of the leaders of the Church, in close communion with the Prophet. It passes belief that he would so speak of the First Vision, had he heard it for the first time in 1838.

Heber C. Kimball, Wilford Woodruff, John Taylor, George A. Smith, and numerous others who lived in the days of the Prophet and knew the Prophet intimately, have spoken of the First Vision as a fact accomplished in 1820, and before the Prophet saw the Book of Mormon plates.[23]

These men were among the early converts to Mormonism. They were hardheaded men, who wanted to be certain about things. If they had heard for the first time in 1838 of the Prophet's First Vision, Joseph Smith would

---

[20]Orson Pratt, *Remarkable Visions*, pp. 4-5.
[21]*Journal of Discourses*, vol. 7, pp. 220-221; vol. 11, pp. 65-66; vol. 12, p. 302; vol. 14, pp. 140-141; vol. 15, pp. 18-82; N. B. Lundwall, *Masterful Discourses* and *Writings of Orson Pratt*, pp. 235-236.
[22]*Journal of Discourses*, vol. 8, p. 354.
[23]Heber C. Kimball, *Journal of Discourses*, vol. 6, p. 29; John Taylor, *The Gospel Kingdom*, p. 121; Wilford Woodruff, *Leaves from my Journal*, first edition, p. 86; George A. Smith, *Journal of Discourses*, vol. 12, p. 334; vol. 13, p. 78; vol. 11, pp. 1-2.

have had to do some explaining! They were not men to follow a deceiver.

If Joseph Smith had told the story of the First Vision for the first time in 1838, it would have been a precious find for the waiting enemies of that day. Apostates from the Church would have pounced upon it. The days of 1838 were trying days for the Prophet. Foes were lying in wait to destroy him. Books about him were being penned. Nevertheless, no mention of such an invention is mentioned. All accept Joseph's story as told for eighteen years, that he had a vision of the Father and the Son in 1820.

Joseph Smith was not a fool. He would have known the effect of such a major invention in 1838. His enemies were wise enough not to allow so juicy a morsel to escape them in their persecutions.

All acceptable evidence within and beyond the Church confirms the Prophet's story that his First Vision occurred when he was between fourteen and fifteen years of age in the year 1820 and before the Book of Mormon revelations occurred.

The attempt to make the First Vision of 1820 an afterthought, a fiction invented in 1838, shows that some historians, usually so self-styled, who are guided by their prejudices rather than by facts, go far afield from truth to deceive their readers. They represent the type of opposition with which Joseph Smith and his followers have long had to deal. However, it is the kind of opposition that falls before truth. The story of the First Vision need only to be studied from original sources to assure the seeker not only of its truth, but also of the time of its occurrence.

CHAPTER 6

MORONI'S VISIT

From the spring of 1820 when he had the First Vision to September, 1823, from his fourteenth to his seventeenth year, Joseph Smith continued to help his father on the farm and to accept other obtainable employment. He said that he was "doomed to the necessity of obtaining a scanty maintenance by his daily labor."[1] He lived as did other farm boys in the region, a clean, wholesome life of humble labor and enjoyments.

At seventeen, Joseph Smith was practically full grown. Blue-eyed, brown-haired, nearly six feet tall, with a trim and symmetrical body, he was a fine specimen of manhood, good to look upon. He was not bookish, but a lover of sports and outdoor life, a wrestler and jumper. He had the power to attract his fellow men. He was popular and good company.

Nothing distinguished him from his fellows during these years, except that he continued to affirm that he had had a vision of God the Father and God the Son. This story was usually received with cool unbelief and often with active contempt.

He had a very sensitive conscience. In his autobiography he confesses that during this youthful period some of his experiences were as follows:

I frequently fell into many foolish errors, and displayed the weaknesses of youth, and the foibles of human nature which I am sorry led me into diverse temptations offensive in the sight of God ...[But]...no one need suppose me guilty of any great or malignant sin. A disposition to commit such was never in my nature. But I was guilty of levity, and sometimes associated with jovial company, etc., not consistent with that character which ought to be maintained by one who was called of God, as I had been.[2]

There can be no doubt that during these years, Joseph

---
[1]*History of the Church*, vol. 1, p. 7
[2]*Ibid.*, vol. 1, p. 9.

thought long and often about the vision he had had, the
lessons it taught, and the commission given him. His
adolescence was approaching maturity. Deep thoughts
and heavy ones often filled his mind.

His high commission to restore the Church of Jesus
Christ was always in his mind. He was waiting for the
call to begin the work. Therefore, he tried in his boyish
way to keep himself fit for the great task before him.

At length, in the evening and night of September 21,
1823, more than three years after the First Vision, the
expected call came. His education and training began.

That night after retiring, he sought the Lord in earnest
prayer to forgive his follies, and to give him further light.
While he was thus praying, the room became filled with
light until it was "lighter than noon day."

A glorious personage appeared at his bedside, who
declared himself to be a heavenly messenger, Moroni by
name, an ancient American resurrected prophet, sent by
God, he said, to prepare Joseph further for the work he
was to do.

He confirmed the message and call of Joseph's First
Vision. Joseph was to initiate God's work in these days.
He quoted and explained to the lad many passages of
scripture which prophetically referred to the coming work.
He warned Joseph that his work was of such a nature
that his name would be known for good and evil the
world over. It was not to be an easy commission.

Among the scriptural passages confirming the coming
work, he specifically quoted part of the third chapter
and the last part of the fourth chapter of Malachi; the
eleventh chapter of Isaiah; the third chapter of Acts,
twenty-second and twenty-third verses, saying that the
prophet there mentioned was Christ; and the second chapter of Joel, twenty-second verse to the last.

The quotations were made as they stand in King
James' translation of the Bible excepting the fourth chapter
of Malachi. This chapter was quoted with apparently
slight variations which form a remarkable evidence of

Joseph's prophetic power, and they set forth also the essential nature of the work Joseph was about to initiate. (See chapters 16 and 38.)

The messenger also told Joseph, to his utter astonishment, that he was to translate a book written upon gold plates, "giving an account of the former inhabitants of this continent, and the source from which they sprang. He also said that the fulness of the everlasting gospel was contained in it, as delivered by the Savior to the ancient inhabitants of America."[3]

Along with the plates, he said, were the Urim and Thummim, which would serve as helps to him in the translating of the engravings upon the plates.

The location of these plates, buried in a neighboring hill, was told him. In a vision, he saw the place. He was to uncover them the next day and then go to see them annually on the anniversary of this visit but not to secure possession of them for a period of four years. He was further instructed how to care for them when he received them. He was warned not to allow himself to try to secure and use these golden plates for mercenary purposes, to supply the needs of himself and his family, then in an impoverished condition.

After this long and detailed explanation and instruction, the messenger and the accompanying light vanished, Joseph lay "musing" on the extraordinary event. But not for long, for soon the room became light again, the messenger reappeared, and rehearsed all that he had said on his first visit "without the least variation," but followed by a description of the grievous judgments soon to be poured out upon the earth. The messenger again vanished but reappeared and repeated his message for the third time.

Soon after the third visit, the cock crew, morning broke. The whole night had been spent in impressing the messages upon the young man's mind.

So great however had been the strain of the night

---

[3]*Ibid.*, vol. 1, p. 11.

that when Joseph went to work in the field that morning, he found his strength gone. His father noted this and sent him home. On the way to the house, in attempting to cross a fence, he fell helpless to the ground. While Joseph was in this condition, the messenger of the night before, surrounded by the vivid light, appeared again, repeated the messages of the night for the fourth time, and commanded Joseph to tell his father of the night's experiences.

Joseph obeyed. He returned to his father in the field and "rehearsed the whole matter to him." The father replied that it was of God, that Joseph should do exactly as Moroni had commanded and visit the hill where the plates were said to be buried.

Near the village of Manchester, New York, is a hill of considerable size, the most elevated in the region, known to Latter-day Saints as Cumorah, to others as "Mormon Hill." On the west side of the hill not far from the top, under a stone, that had to be pried up, "lay the plates" in a stone box. In the box were also the promised Urim and Thummim.

Moroni, the messenger, who was present, forbade the young man to take the plates with him. The time had not yet come.

Year after year on September 22 Joseph visited the hill and viewed the plates. Moroni was always there, giving further instructions concerning the coming restoration of the gospel. It is not known whether Moroni visited the young man between the annual visits.

Four years elapsed before Joseph was allowed to possess the plates and begin the translation. It seemed a long wait, but it was a period of education. To make memory lasting and understanding clear, Moroni, on his first visit, repeated his message four times. During the four annual visits to see the plates Moroni was present to rehearse the story, and to give new instructions. These were years of thinking about the work to come. It was the correct method of education. He needed preparation for the work he was to do; and few men have had such an education as this from a heavenly visitor. Education is a slow process for human beings, and the Lord respects the nature of his children on earth. He himself has placed them on earth under the limitations of flesh and blood.

Joseph was ripening in maturity, and every year he became more fitted to undertake the divine task before him. His career, short as it was, is marked by constant, steady growth. He was called as a boy; made to wait ten years for the beginning of his mission—the organization of the Church; every step onward was taken after periods of preparation. It is not enough to have divine communication. One must grow, progress, increase, to become fitted to do the Lord's work. Sound educational practice, as men understand it, was followed in making Joseph Smith a restorer of the gospel.

Moroni's visitation was in full harmony with Christian belief. There is an unseen world, a spiritual world, in which God the Father and God the Son reside. In that world unnumbered others dwell, among them those who have finished their work on earth. When the time is right, as on this occasion when the everlasting gospel was to be restored on earth, the Lord may send any of this great family to carry messages to earth, or to perform any other appointed task. No one who claims faith in Christ can deny that the Lord has this power and may and does exercise it. From the evidence at hand no one can deny the possibility of Moroni's visit; all may know that it really occurred.

CHAPTER 7

WAITING TO RECEIVE THE PLATES

Joseph Smith first saw the golden plates from which the Book of Mormon was translated, on September 22, 1823. He was not to receive them until four years later.

This period, from his eighteenth to his twenty-second year, was an important interval in his preparation. It gave opportunity for serious consideration of Moroni's instructions. They were always in the mind of the young man. Gradually, the work he was to do became clearer to him; and he learned to comprehend the vastness of his mission.

This was perhaps the first lesson from the visits of the Nephite prophet. Truth should be examined, pondered upon, before put into execution. It takes time to explore the depths of truth.

Joseph learned again the power of prayer. The first visitation of Moroni came in answer to prayer. So came the First Vision. The Lord is ready to give, but he requires that his children ask. It would not be natural or wise to force blessings on anyone. The power of prayer is inestimable. One prays for little; usually much comes in answer. If men would only approach the Lord, what great gifts might not be vouchsafed them!

When the visitation occurred, Joseph was praying for more light. He was also confessing his minor follies—he had committed no major ones. For his careless actions Joseph was sincerely repentant. That gave him strength. Repentance, clean, sincere, and continued, blots out the sins of men from the eyes of the Lord. Then prayer becomes doubly powerful. Men with the seeds of greatness in them do not defend their errors.

It was significant that this vision, like the first one, came in full light. Truth always comes in light. Truth and light are eternal companions. The errors and superstitions that enslave men are forged in darkness. In the Church organized by Joseph Smith under divine direction, candor, openness, and enlightenment prevail. Its work is sacred, not secret.

Moroni warned Joseph that in the coming work he would have to pay the heavy price of persecution from those who love error more than truth, and from those who will not tread new paths. Usually, work well done receives praise. It was not to be so in Joseph's case. If praise did come, it would be blended with hatred. His name ". . . should be both good and evil spoken of among all people." It was not an inviting prospect; yet he did not flinch.

This prophecy has been literally fulfilled. Joseph Smith was loved by his people, held in contempt by others, and misunderstood by the majority of men. Often he was hunted as if he were an animal. Arrest, imprisonment, trial followed one another until his death. It is said that about fifty times charges were made against him in the courts, yet, so the records prove, he was never found guilty of a violation of the law.[1]

Moroni also warned him against the temptation of using the golden plates to alleviate the period of poverty through which the Smith family were then passing. Covetousness carries with it real danger. He whose heart is set upon gold for its own sake can seldom find time or place for the things of God. The covetous man cannot hear divine messages.

The most marvelous part of the message to the young man, lying upon his wakeful pillow, was that he, Joseph Smith, was the chosen instrument in the hands of the Lord to inaugurate the great work planned for the last days of the world. It was astonishing! It was wonderful!

During the four years following Moroni's visit Joseph Smith engaged in hard physical work for his support. Sometimes he worked by the day; sometimes his work

[1]Andrew Jenson, *Biographical Encyclopedia*, vol. 1, p. 7; *History of the Church*, vol. 7, p. 403; Lyman O. Littlefield, *The Martyrs*, p. 106.

took him away from home for days or weeks. The distances that he traveled were not great, perhaps in no
case more than one hundred and fifty miles and usually
much less. Most of the places visited by him in those
early days were in the same neighborhood, closely associated with one another.

In October of 1825 he was employed by one Josiah
Stoal who lived in Chenango County, State of New York.
Thereby hangs an important tale. Mr. Stoal had heard
that a Spanish silver mine was supposed to exist in the
neighborhood. Thereupon he put his men to work, trying
to find the lost treasure. This was done by Mr. Stoal before
Joseph Smith was employed. When Joseph arrived, he
was put to work with the others and so labored for about
a month. This employment started the rumor that he
had been a money digger. He freely admitted this event
in his life. He says:

> After I went to live with him [Josiah Stoal], he took me among
> the rest of his hands to dig for the silver mine, at which I continued
> to work for nearly a month without success in our undertaking, and
> finally I prevailed with the old gentleman to cease digging after it.
> Hence arose a very prevalent story of my having been a money
> digger.[2]

He adds that it was not profitable to him as he
received only fourteen dollars a month for the work.[3]

Enemies have suggested, and widely circulated the
suggestion that Stoal employed Joseph because he was
said to have a peepstone by which lost treasure could be
located. The suggestion is of course based upon his
claim of having had communications with heavenly beings.
In fact, shortly after the Church was organized, Hiram
Page, who claimed to have a stone by which revelations
from the Lord could be obtained, was sternly rebuked by
the Prophet.[4]

While working for Mr. Stoal the Prophet boarded

[2]*History of the Church*, vol. 1, p. 17.
[3]*Elders' Journal*, July, 1838.
[4]*Doctrine and Covenants* 28:11.

with the family of a Mr. Isaac Hale.[5]   Mr. Hale's daughter, Emma, was an attractive personality, a brunette with luminous eyes, intelligent, and capable.   Joseph and Emma met frequently.   A courtship developed.   This was vigorously opposed by the Hale family, for Joseph Smith was a poor lad, without financial promise, and therefore seemed unfitted to care for their beloved daughter.   Besides, he had the reputation of being a visionary, for he said that he had had visitations from heavenly beings.

Oliver Cowdery, telling the story of Joseph Smith, remarks that "an officious person" had Joseph arrested; but the charge was found groundless, and the case dismissed.[6]   It is not improbable that this occurred while Joseph was employed by Mr. Stoal, and that it was done to get him out of the country and away from Emma.   It is interesting to remember that members of the Hale family joined the Church later organized by Joseph Smith. Some became prominent in the Cause.

Emma Smith, at that time, was past twenty-two years old, having been born July 10, 1804.   Joseph Smith was more than a year younger.   Since both were of legal age, they did not need their parents' consent to the marriage.   Therefore they went to a neighboring village where the local justice of peace performed the ceremony on January 18, 1827.

Emma Smith, in course of time, became an important factor in Joseph's history. He was very loyal to her; undoubtedly he loved her devotedly.

The persecutions that Joseph Smith had to endure during his short career were many, but Emma, who shared them, faced them bravely with him.   She stood by her husband in all the exigencies that arose from time to time.   She bore him eight children, four of whom died in infancy.   At the time of his martyrdom, on June 27, 1844, he left her with three sons.   Another son was born six

---

[5]*History of the Church*, vol. 1, p. 17.
[6]Francis W. Kirkham, *A New Witness for Christ in America*, p. 105.

months after the martyrdom. These children she raised
to honorable maturity.

On one occasion he wrote in his journal:

> With what unspeakable delight, and what transports of joy
> swelled my bosom, when I took by the hand, on that night, my
> beloved Emma—she that was my wife, even the wife of my youth,
> and the choice of my heart. Many were the reverberations of my
> mind when I contemplated for a moment the many scenes we had
> been called to pass through, the fatigues and the toils, the sorrows
> and sufferings, and the joys and consolations, from time to time,
> which had strewed our paths, and crowned our board. Oh what
> a commingling of thought filled my mind for the moment, again
> she is here . . . undaunted, firm, and unwavering—unchangeable,
> affectionate Emma![7]

Emma in turn appeared to have loved Joseph. She
sought as best she could to support him in his extraordinary
calling. Under divine revelation she selected the first body
of hymns to be sung by Latter-day Saints.[8] She also
served as the first president of the Relief Society, when it
was later organized, which was made up of the mature
women of the Church.[9] When Joseph finally obtained
the plates of the Book of Mormon, she assisted for a short
time in taking his dictation. She helped in various other
ways to carry forward his work.[10]

Meanwhile, during the four years following Moroni's
visit, Joseph waited patiently for the beginning of the
great work assigned to him. Patience is a noble virtue;
it conquers in the end. Unless patience is learned, unhappiness often enters the heart.

---

[7]*History of the Church*, vol. 5, p. 107.
[8]*Doctrine and Covenants* 25:11-12.
[9]*History of the Church*, vol. 2, p. 273; vol. 4, p. 17.
[10]*Ibid.*, vol. 4, p. 510.

LUCY MACK SMITH
Mother of Joseph Smith

LUCY MACK SMITH
Joseph Smith's mother

HYRUM SMITH
Patriarch to the Church martyred with his brother Joseph.

THE SMITH HOME
Near Palmyra, New York

CHAPTER 8

THE BOOK OF MORMON IS TRANSLATED

After four years of waiting Joseph Smith received permission to remove the Book of Mormon plates from their resting place and to take them home.

At length the time arrived for obtaining the plates, the Urim and Thummim, and the Breastplate. On the 22nd day of September, 1827, having gone as usual at the end of another year to the place where they were deposited, the same heavenly messenger delivered them up to me with this charge: "that I should be responsible for them; that if I should let them go carelessly, or through any neglect of mine, I should be cut off; but that if I would use all my endeavors to preserve them, until he, the messenger, should call for them, they should be protected."[1]

Joseph was then nearly twenty-two years of age. It was a great day for him. With both fear and joy he climbed Hill Cumorah where the plates were buried, fear that he might fail the Lord, joy in the great privilege that had come to him!

Moroni, the ancient Nephite prophet who visited and instructed Joseph and was present when he received the plates, warned the young man to take the greatest care of them, and to show them to no one except by divine permission. The report had gone forth that they were of gold, which indeed they were. Cupidity had led evil and designing persons to plan to steal them from the Prophet. They were on the alert continually to obtain them, to steal them if necessary.

The plates themselves were a little larger than an average book, six inches wide by eight inches high and about six inches thick. Three rings at the inner margins held them together. A piece of solid, pure gold of that size would weigh in the neighborhood of two hundred pounds. Gold however is very soft, easily bent, and would

---

[1]*History of the Church*, vol. 1, p. 18.

not be an ideal substance in its pure condition on which to preserve writings. It is more likely that the gold had been hardened by alloying it with copper as is done by gold-smiths today.[2]

If it be assumed that enough copper had been added to make the alloy an eight carat gold, the plates would be hard and stiff enough to preserve inscriptions made upon them. If the plates were of such an alloy, and if about ten per cent were allowed for the spaces between the leaves, the weight of the plates would be in the neighbor-hood of one hundred pounds. This would not be an excessive weight for a young man of the strength of Joseph Smith.[3]

A part of the plates, said to be about two-thirds, was sealed.[4] The Prophet had instructions not to break the seal nor attempt to use the writings on the sealed portion. The unsealed third he was to translate for the benefit of the coming cause of the Lord.

The records were engraven on plates which had the appearance of gold, each plate was six inches wide and eight inches long, and not so thick as common tin. They were filled with engravings, in Egyptian characters, and bound together in a volume as the leaves of a book, with the rings running through the whole.

The volume was something near six inches in thickness, a part of which was sealed. With the records was found a curious instrument, which the ancients called "Urim and Thummim" which consisted of two transparent stones set in the rim of a bow fastened to a breastplate.[5]

The characters upon the plates were in reformed Egyptian, so the book itself says.[6] The language itself was probably Hebrew.[7]

After receiving the plates, the Prophet first devoted some days to transcribing or copying characters from the plates. It was his way of becoming acquainted with the

[2]*Ibid.*, vol. 1, p. 18.
[3]John A. Widtsoe and Franklin S. Harris, Jr., *Seven Claims of the Book of Mormon,* pp. 37-38.
[4]*Journal of Discourses,* vol. 3, p. 347.
[5]*History of the Church,* vol. 4, p. 537.
[6]*Book of Mormon,* Mormon 9:32, p. 478.
[7]Sidney B. Sperry, *Our Book of Mormon,* p. 28.

work to be done. On February 28, 1828, Martin Harris, a prosperous farmer of Palmyra, friendly to Joseph, took one of these transcripts to New York City. There two eminent students of ancient languages, Doctors Anthon and Mitchell, examined them. In later years both of these men acknowledged that the characters were presented to them. Martin Harris declared that the "experts" said the characters were a mixture of ancient alphabets.[8] However when they learned how the characters had been obtained and that part of the "book" or plates was sealed, they repudiated their first positive statement. Egyptology was in its early infancy at that time. The visit and the statements of the two men were sufficient, however, to induce Harris to become a scribe for the Prophet, and later when the Book of Mormon was to be published, to mortgage his farm for $3000.00 with which to pay the printer.[9]

Fortunately, one of the slips of paper taken by Harris to New York was reproduced in periodicals near the Prophet's day and has been reproduced many times since.[10] It is now in the possession of the Reorganized Church. Lately, (1942,) it has been given careful, scholarly study by Ariel L. Crowley, who has shown that every character said by the Prophet to be copied from the plates has been used at some time in Egyptian writing.[11] This is a notable confirmation of the truth of the Prophet's story, and an answer to those who have said that the characters were only the childish scrawls of an ignorant person.

Not long after receiving the plates, April 12, 1828, Joseph began the translation, with Martin Harris as scribe.[12] The first 116 pages of the manuscript were completed by June 14 but were lost through the disobedience of the scribe, who wanted to show them to his wife and friends. Thereupon, Joseph, under divine displeasure because he had vigorously importuned the heavenly guar-

[8]Francis W. Kirkham, *A New Witness for Christ in America*, pp. 27, 414.
[9]*Ibid.*, p. 172, chapter 14.
[10]*Ibid.*, p. 247.
[11]Ariel L. Crowley, "The Anthon Transcript," *Improvement Era*, vol. 45, pp. 14, 76, 150; vol. 47, p. 542.
[12]*History of the Church*, vol. 1, p. 20.

dian to satisfy his friend's urgent request, lost the power
of translation for a while and went in search of work. The
pages taken by his scribe were lost and have never been
recovered.

It must be remembered that at this time Joseph had
no knowledge of any foreign language. Such worldly
knowledge as he had gave no clue to the meaning of the
characters on the plates. He was wholly dependent on
spiritual help to perform his commission. This he freely
admitted, for he declared that he accomplished the translation by "the gift and power of God." Time was needed
to qualify him through proper concentration to receive
and understand the story recorded on the plates.

A year and a half after receiving the plates, he began
at last the serious translation of them.[13] This is another
luminous testimony of the proof of the truth of the claims
of the Prophet. Undoubtedly, at first he felt that all he
had to do was to use the Urim and Thummim in order for
the meaning of the characters on the plates to be made
plain to him.

This is not the normal nor natural manner of obtaining
any kind of information. Learning requires effort, application, and toil. Any great work makes severe concentration demands upon the powers of man. Especially would
this be so when receiving divine messages. Men must
be prepared to receive them.

The use of the Urim and Thummim was provided
to assist the young man in the work, not to do the work
for him. The use of this instrument required concentration of thought, and intense concentration at that. The
translation of the Book of Mormon was no doubt a part
of Joseph's preparation for the task of organizing and
establishing the Church. The concentration of mind
required in the translation from the plates trained the
young man for the important task which lay before him.
Step by step as the Church grew, he had to be in close
communion with the Lord. Question after question was

---

[13]Kirkham, *op. cit.*, pp. 28, 71, 212, 219.

propounded, and he must be in the right condition to receive the answer. The work he had to do could not be accomplished superficially. It required all the strength of the man, coupled with divine help.

When the translation was finished, the most important procedure in preparing for the reception of divine communication had been learned. That alone would justify as a part of Joseph's mission the coming forth of the Book Mormon.

When he resumed the translation, after the loss of the first 116 pages of the manuscript, his wife, Emma Smith, served as scribe. However, they worked on the translation only a very short time. She had many other duties. Again it was laid aside. Then at length, on April 5, 1829, Oliver Cowdery, a schoolteacher who had been boarding with the Smith family in Palmyra, came to Joseph, who then lived at Harmony, Pennsylvania, to converse with him and to investigate the reality of his claims.

Within two days, April 7, 1829, Oliver Cowdery became Joseph's scribe and continued so until the translation was completed. Upon Oliver Cowdery's own testimony, he wrote every word of the Book of Mormon, save a few, as they fell from the lips of the Prophet.[14]

From the testimony available, Joseph and Oliver occupied the room of translation. Joseph had been forbidden by Moroni to show the plates to anyone except designated witnesses. He therefore sat behind a curtain, with the plates and the Urim and Thummim before him. This also secured concentration of thought. As he dictated, he uttered the words slowly, clearly, and distinctly. His dictation was taken down by Oliver Cowdery. Then Oliver read back what had been said by the Prophet, to make sure that the dictation had been taken down correctly.[15] All this however is in the nature of hearsay.

There were no further changes, additions, or revisions.

---

[14]*Ibid.*, p. 71.
[15]David Whitmer, "An Address to all Believers in Christ," 1887, p. 12.

This is really marvelous. Authors correct and rewrite many times before they go to press. Before the manuscript was sent to the printer, a copy of it was carefully made.

However, it was not a word-for-word translation. As nearly as can be understood, the ideas set forth by the characters were revealed to the Prophet. He then expressed the ideas in English as best he could; that is, the language of the English Book of Mormon is to a large degree the language of the Prophet as used in his every day conversation on religious subjects, but brightened, illuminated, and dignified by the inspiration under which he worked. It must be said, however, that the vocabulary of the Book of Mormon appears to be far beyond that of an unlettered youth.[16]

In some respects, the most remarkable thing about the translation of the Book of Mormon by Joseph Smith is that the work was accomplished within about ninety days, perhaps less. It was completed toward the end of June, or early July, 1829, for it was in the hands of the printer in the month of August of that year.[17] The book has five hundred and ninety pages in the original edition, and several hundred thousands of words. It contains hundreds of ideas and episodes.

After more than a century of careful study by friend and foe, no contradictions have been found within the book. Probably no known writer has composed so large a book of such a nature, without corrections or rewritings, in so short a time. More than human power, as we know it, is evidenced in the translation.

While the translation was going on, the Prophet or his representatives went to various places to discuss the matter of printing; among them the printing establishment of Thurlow Weed in Rochester.[18] The job of printing five thousand copies was finally, in August, 1829, given to the press of Egbert B. Grandin who ran a printing office in Palmyra, New York.

---

[16]Widtsoe and Harris, Jr., *op. cit.*, p. 20.
[17]*Millennial Star*, vol. 43, p. 423; Kirkham, *op. cit.*, p. 223.
[18]Life of Thurlow Weed, *Autobiography*, vol. 1, pp. 358-359.

As the printing progressed, several difficulties and interruptions arose. The printing plant was small. It took, therefore, longer than otherwise would have been required to print and bind the book.

The one unpleasant episode during the time of the printing was the attempt of one Cole, apparently an agent for Obediah Dogberry, editor of the Palmyra *Reflector*, to secure surreptitiously the proofs of the Book of Mormon as it was set up, and to publish them, after changing them, in the *Reflector*. The subscribers could then get the book before its publication without cost and have a chance of ridiculing the book and Joseph Smith at the same time.

Before this pilfering was stopped, Joseph Smith himself had to come to Palmyra and demand, as the copyright owner, that no one tamper with the proofs of the book.[19] The book was finally published March 26, 1830.

One can imagine the feelings of the Prophet when he held the first copy of the Book of Mormon in his hands. He looked back to 1820 when he had his First Vision. The decade had been years of toilsome preparation. But now the book was published. He had kept his covenant with the Lord. His heart thrilled to the memory of his experiences and to the promises of the work to come.

One wonders if he saw with the vision of a prophet, that the Book of Mormon was destined to become one of the most notable in the history of man's literature and one of the great helps in humanity's search for truth and joy.

To those who ask why the Lord did not dictate the message of the Book of Mormon directly, without the intervention of the plates, the first answer is that the ways of the Lord are not the ways of man. Those who want the Lord to do things their way are usually frigid believers in divinity.

To us, more than a century removed, the events connected with the translation of the Book of Mormon form unanswerable evidences for the truth of the Prophet's

---

[19]Lucy Mack Smith, *History of the Prophet Joseph*, chapter 33, pp. 148-151.

claims. They need only to be carefully examined by an unprejudiced mind. The book was translated by the gift and power of God.[20]

---

[20]*Book of Mormon*, Title Page.

CHAPTER 9

WHO SAW THE BOOK OF MORMON PLATES?

The extraordinary spiritual experiences of Joseph Smith are challenges to faith. They provoke immediately two questions: First, were such things possible? Second, did they really happen?

Of course, the experiences of Joseph Smith were possible. That is known to every Christian. God has the power to show himself and speak to man, to send messengers from his domain to his children on earth, or to uncover buried records of a past civilization. That was all that Joseph claimed. To deny that God has such power is blasphemy.

The answer to the second question is also simple. Nothing is required of man beyond his natural power to do or understand. Therefore, material evidences, proofs of reality for other human minds accompany divine manifestations. Faith is strengthened and supported by tangible evidence. It should be the concern of man to seek for and to accept such evidences.

This was the method of Jesus the Christ. He always provided a material background for his spiritual teachings. When the people refused to believe him, he said, ". . . believe me for the very works' sake";[1] and on another occasion, ". . . the same works that I do, bear witness of me, that the Father hath sent me";[2] and he laid down the law that "If any man will do his will, he shall know of the doctrine whether it be of God, or whether I speak of myself."[3] He took three of his apostles into the Mount where they had discourse with Moses and Elias, translated beings, long since passed from mortal existence.[4] Peter, James, and John saw these personages and became living mortal witnesses of that experience. Their testimony we must

[1]John 14:11.
[2]Ibid., 14:11; 5:37.
[3]Ibid., 7:17.
[4]Mark 9:2-8; Matthew 17:1-8; Luke 9:28-36.

believe, unless we reject their veracity, and with it Christianity.

In the history of religion since Christ until Joseph Smith came, witnesses to spiritual experiences had become most unusual. They of the past, Mahomet, Buddha, Luther, and many others, had their experiences alone. In that respect, Joseph Smith is a unique figure.

Much of the life-work of Joseph Smith was in the spiritual field, yet his experiences were so presented that mortal men could test them with their natural powers. In nearly all of the fundamental events of his life, mortal companions shared the experiences with him. They became living witnesses, direct or indirect, to his divine manifestations. This adds greatly to the veracity of all his claims.

The events connected with the Book of Mormon plates were no exception. Mortal men, other than Joseph Smith, saw and handled them. Upon the testimonies of these men, we of a later day may rest a part of our faith.

In March, 1829, the Lord declared to Joseph that three men should have the privilege of seeing the plates and bearing witness to their existence.[5] A similar prediction was found also in the Book of Mormon itself.[6] Oliver Cowdery, David Whitmer, and Martin Harris were later designated as these witnesses. In full conformity with the prediction, in June, 1829, when the translation of the plates was approaching the end, this promise was realized.

Joseph and his three friends at the Peter Whitmer, Sr., home in Fayette, Seneca County, New York, went into the nearby woods one day, and there engaged in earnest prayer that the plates might be shown to them. Before they returned to the house, all three had had a glorious experience and had seen the plates shown to them by Moroni.[7] To this they testified in a written and published statement. This event is related by Joseph Smith in his history, and published while the witnesses were living.

---

[5]*Doctrine and Covenants*, Section 5; *History of the Church*, vol. 1, p. 52.
[6]2 Nephi 11:3; Ether 5:3.
[7]*History of the Church*, vol. 1, pp. 52-59.

Sometime later, divine permission was given to show these plates to eight other men.[8] To have more witnesses was making the assurance of the reality of the plates doubly sure. The corroboration of the testimony of the three men, by the eight under different conditions, and at different times, certifies immeasurably to the truth of the events. The men, Christian Whitmer, Jacob Whitmer, Peter Whitmer, Jr., John Whitmer, Hiram Page, Joseph Smith, Sr., Hyrum Smith, and Samuel H. Smith unitedly signed a testimony in which they describe the plates and the engravings on them, and further declare that they actually handled and "hefted" the plates. There are no generalities in these testimonies; they are specific.

The signed statement of the experiences by the three witnesses and the eight witnesses are printed in every edition of the Book of Mormon published by the Church.[9]

THE TESTIMONY OF THREE WITNESSES[10]

Be It Known unto all nations, kindreds, tongues, and people, unto whom this work shall come: That we, through the grace of God the Father, and our Lord Jesus Christ, have seen the plates which contain this record, which is a record of the people of Nephi, and also of the Lamanites, their brethren, and also of the people of Jared, who came from the tower of which hath been spoken. And we also know that they have been translated by the gift and power of God, for his voice hath declared it unto us; wherefore we know of a surety that the work is true. And we also testify that we have seen the engravings which are upon the plates; and they have been shown unto us by the power of God, and not of man. And we declare with words of soberness, that an angel of God came down from heaven, and he brought and laid before our eyes, that we beheld and saw the plates, and the engravings thereon; and we know that it is by the grace of God the Father, and our Lord Jesus Christ, that we beheld and bear record that these things are true. And it is marvelous in our eyes. Nevertheless, the voice of the Lord commanded us that we should bear record of it; wherefore, to be obedient unto the commandments of God, we bear testimony of these things. And we know that if we are faithful in

---

[8]*Ibid.*, vol. 1, p. 57.
[9]Lucy Mack Smith, *History of the Prophet Joseph*, 1902 edition, p. 139; 1945 edition, p. 152.
[10]*Book of Mormon.*

Christ, we shall rid our garments of the blood of all men, and be found spotless before the judgment-seat of Christ, and shall dwell with him eternally in the heavens. And the honor be to the Father, and to the Son, and to the Holy Ghost, which is one God. Amen.

OLIVER COWDERY
DAVID WHITMER
MARTIN HARRIS

THE TESTIMONY OF EIGHT WITNESSES[11]

Be It Known unto all nations, kindreds, tongues, and people, unto whom this work shall come: That Joseph Smith, Jun., the translator of this work, has shown unto us the plates of which hath been spoken, which have the appearance of gold; and as many of the leaves as the said Smith has translated we did handle with our hands; and we also saw the engravings thereon, all of which has the appearance of ancient work, and of curious workmanship. And this we bear record with words of soberness, that the said Smith has shown unto us, for we have seen and hefted, and know of a surety that the said Smith has got the plates of which we have spoken. And we give our names unto the world, to witness unto the world that which we have seen. And we lie not, God bearing witness of it.

CHRISTIAN WHITMER	HIRAM PAGE
JACOB WHITMER	JOSEPH SMITH, SEN.
PETER WHITMER, JUN.	HYRUM SMITH
JOHN WHITMER	SAMUEL H. SMITH

Thus there were eleven men witnesses besides Joseph Smith himself who had seen the plates. It is possible that Joseph's mother and Mrs. Whitmer, mother of the Whitmer boys who played such an important part in the early history of the Church, also saw the plates. This, however, cannot be verified.

Joseph, whose word was being doubted, had great joy in having others testify to the existence of the plates. His mother related that after the three witnesses had beheld the plates the following occurred:

He threw himself down before me, and exclaimed, "Father, Mother, you do not know how happy I am.[12] The Lord has now caused the plates to be shown to three more besides myself. They have seen an angel, who has testified to them, and they will have

---

[11]*Ibid.*
[12]Lucy Mack Smith, *op. cit.*, p. 152; 1902 edition, p. 139.

to bear witness to the truth of what I have said, for now they will know for themselves that I do not go about to deceive the people, and I feel as if I were relieved of a great burden which was almost too heavy for me to bear, and it rejoices my soul that I am not any longer to be entirely alone in the world."[13]

The importance of the statements of these eleven men in establishing faith in the divine mission of Joseph Smith has been recognized by all students of the restored gospel. To Latter-day Saints these testimonies have been and are a source of faith. To unprejudiced investigators of Joseph Smith's life they carry convincing proof of the existence of the plates and the truth of Joseph's whole story.

On the other hand, unbelievers in the divine origin of the Book of Mormon continue to stand baffled and perplexed before the sober testimonies of eleven sane, reputable, vigorous men in good health who would be competent witnesses to testify in any court of law.

These eleven men, whose careers are well-known, were very different in temperament. They all had minds and doubts of their own. They had heard Joseph's story from his own lips and wanted to make sure for themselves that it was true. They were given this privilege and maintained to the last the truth of their experience.

From the human point of view, it was a daring if not a dangerous thing for Joseph Smith to predict before the book was finished that men should see the plates as he did while translating them. One cannot well foretell what others will do or what the Lord will do. However the prediction was not Joseph's but the Lord's. Therefore he felt certain it would come to pass. And it did. There exists a published detailed account of the events. Deceivers deal in few details and many generalities. Moreover, the events occurred in full daylight. The participants were together. Hallucinations or delusions were impossible. The testimonies were published while the witnesses were living, and the witnesses offered no corrections. If human

[13]*Ibid.*, p. 139; *History of the Church*, vol. 1, pp. 55-56.

experience can be believed, the testimonies of these eleven men must be accepted.[14]

Some of the witnesses left the Church; others were excommunicated; but their testimonies that they saw the plates of the Book of Mormon remained unchanged.

Of the three witnesses, Oliver Cowdery and David Whitmer were severed from the Church by local councils for being out of harmony with the Church officials in the trying days of the Missouri period. Martin Harris drifted away. Both Cowdery and Harris returned and were again baptized into the Church. Whitmer, hugging old grievances, remained unaffiliated with the Church but bore frequent testimony to the truth of the translation of the Book of Mormon from the Nephite plates which he insisted he had seen. All three remained firm in their testimony that they had seen the plates.

The lives of the eight witnesses tell similar stories. One, John Whitmer, was excommunicated from the Church; two, Jacob Whitmer and Hiram Page, withdrew from the Church; the other five, Christian Whitmer, Peter Whitmer, Jr., Joseph Smith, Sr., Hyrum Smith, and Samuel H. Smith, remained faithful, useful members of the Church during their lives. The eight witnesses, all of them, whether in or out of the Church, maintained to their last breath that they saw and handled the plates from which the Book of Mormon was translated.[15]

The facts connected with the Book of Mormon witnesses are so unanswerable that they have been and remain disconcerting stumbling blocks to unbelievers.

Joseph's enemies, non-plussed over this evidence, have preferred to ignore it or to explain it by some impossible theory. That is a poor approach to knowledge.

So evident is the truth of these testimonies, that unfriendly critics have usually tried to draw attention away from them as being of little significance or have attempted two feeble explanations of the events.

---

[14]John Henry Evans, *Joseph Smith, An American Prophet*, p. 388.
[15]*Journal of Discourses*, vol. 18, pp. 156-161.

The first explanation is that the witnesses were in collusion with the Prophet and therefore lied in their testimonies; that is, the whole story of seeing the plates was invented by Joseph and his friends and had no basis in fact. It was fraudulent. That explanation has admittedly long since fallen to the ground through the persistent testimonies of the men themselves.

The well-attested life histories of the witnesses show every one of them to have been honest and honorable in their dealings with their fellow men. If their testimonies had been untrue, one or the other would have revealed the perfidy. Many opportunities to do so were given them. Instead, they remained true to their testimonies. Even anti-Mormons have conceded that collusion among Joseph Smith and the witnesses is an improbable, if not impossible, hypothesis.

The second explanation, conceived in desperation by those who will not believe the truth, has been that Joseph Smith was endowed with great hypnotic power, which enabled him to make the eleven witnesses think they saw things which did not exist. This is much like a drowning man clutching at a straw. This far-fetched explanation actually asks us to believe that eleven very dissimilar men, all questioning the claims of the Prophet, could be made to see, hear, and touch alike, figments of nothingness. It is an absurd test of the credulity of intelligent people.

The testimonies of the witnesses rest upon three senses: seeing, hearing, touching. Even the confirmed believer in any form of hypnotism or its related cults would hardly dare cover so large a territory or make such vast claims. Moreover, though it is conceded that the Prophet had an appealing personality, there is nothing in his well-documented life to credit him with hypnotic power.

We of the later generations, it is to be hoped, are as honest, intelligent, and truth-loving as were the men who testify that they saw the plates of the Book of Mormon. Then we must accept with a clear conscience the attested

statements of the witnesses. It would be a species of dishonesty not to do so.

The testimonies of the witnesses to the Book of Mormon are among the certain proofs of the existence of the
plates of the Book of Mormon and of the divine mission
of Joseph Smith the Prophet.

CHAPTER 10

WERE THE WITNESSES HONEST?

The lives of these eleven men should furnish the answer.

Martin Harris (1783-1875), was the first of the witnesses to appear in the story of Joseph Smith. He was acquainted with the Smith family and, it is said, employed the boy Joseph on his farm.[1] Martin Harris was a religiously minded, prosperous farmer. He appears to have been a rather wilful but honest man, who wanted to be sure of everything he undertook. It was he who took the transcript of characters from the Book of Mormon plates to Professor Anthon for verification. He was the one of the three witnesses who had most difficulty on the occasion when the plates were shown to them. He was not easily led. But so certain was he at last of the claims of Joseph Smith that he advanced $3,000.00 for the publication of the Book of Mormon. In a mistaken allegiance to Joseph Smith after the martyrdom he did not go westward with the Church. In his old age, however, he sought out the Church, bore to the members, in the valleys of the mountains, his oft-repeated testimony of the truth of Joseph Smith's claims, and died a faithful member of the Church.[2]

No blemish of dishonesty has been found in his life. Therefore, some enemies have resorted to the charge that Harris helped to publish the Book of Mormon purely to make money; and others have held him up as a fanatical, simple ignorant man, whose stupidity became a help to the "knavery" of Joseph Smith. Neither cupidity nor stupidity is accepted by fair-minded historians to explain the actions of Martin Harris who was really a good, intelligent businessman. Honesty marked the course of his life.

---

[1]*Millennial Star*, vol. 55 p. 794
[2]*Improvement Era*, vol. 29, pp. 468-472; Andrew Jenson, *Biographical Encyclopedia*, vol. 1, pp. 271-276.

Oliver Cowdery (1806-1850), one of the three witnesses, came next into the Prophet's life. He became an intimate associate, shared with him most of the early spiritual experiences, and stood next to him in the organization of the Church.

Oliver Cowdery came from Vermont, where he received a good common school education. He came to Palmyra as a schoolteacher and, according to the custom of that day, boarded with the families of the district. Thus he became acquainted with the parents of Joseph Smith and heard them relate the extraordinary events in young Joseph's life. He became interested and went to Harmony, Pennsylvania, where the Prophet was then living, to investigate for himself the truth of Joseph's claims. Convinced at last of Joseph's prophetic calling, he joined him as the scribe in the work of translation. At the organization of the Church he was sustained as its second elder. He headed the first westward missionary party, built up the Church in Kirtland, Ohio, and helped explore the Missouri territory.

During the later Missouri days charges were made against him, chiefly of ambition and disloyalty to the Prophet. They were substantiated and he was excommunicated from the Church. Wounded in his self pride, and expecting Joseph to make the first step toward reconciliation, he remained aloof from the Church for ten years. During that time he studied and practised law in Ohio, Michigan, and Missouri. During this long absence from the Church which he helped establish, he always bore testimony to the divine origin of the Book of Mormon.

It is related that in a court case the opposing attorney chided Oliver for signing his name as a witness to the Book of Mormon. Oliver in reply declared that he knew the work founded upon Joseph Smith's visions was true and that he could not retract.[3] When the Church was

—————
[3]*Improvement Era*, vol. 46, p. 8

moving westward, he rejoined it, bore a humble testimony, asked for membership, and was baptized.[4]

Oliver Cowdery was not the type of man to be imposed upon by Joseph Smith. In the history of Seneca County, Ohio,[5] the author speaks of Oliver Cowdery as unusually intelligent, a student of Greek and "Chaldee," (undoubtedly from the School of the Prophets in Kirtland) kindly and friendly, who did not speak ill of anyone, and never complained. "His addresses to the court and jury were characterized by a high order of oratory with brilliant forensic force."

David Whitmer (1805-1888), the third of the three witnesses, was an early associate of Joseph Smith and was a prominent figure in many of the early events of the Church. He was intelligent—like Martin and Oliver—a person who also wanted to know things for himself. He was so closely associated with Joseph Smith from early days that he had every opportunity to discover any charlatanry, if any existed, in the life and work of the Prophet.

In Missouri where he was called to preside, conditions arose which led a Church council to excommunicate David Whitmer. He was deeply wounded in his feelings. To what extent pride and ambition played a part in his later actions can only be surmised. He never rejoined the Church nor did he join any other church, but he bore frequent and eloquent testimonies during his long life to the truth of the work of Joseph Smith. His own following of disciples were called Whitmerites. He did not falter in declaring that he had seen and handled the plates from which the Book of Mormon was translated. His defense for his failure to rejoin the Church was that Joseph Smith was a Prophet up to a certain time; then he became a fallen Prophet.[6]

His life was one of probity, his temperament such as

[4]*Liahona*, vol. 8, p. 161
[5]P. W. Lang, *History of Seneca County*, p. 364.
[6]Richmond (Mo.) *Conservator*, March 25, 1881; Andrew Jenson, *Historical Record*, pp. 210-212.

to gainsay the charge that he was ever under the hypnotic influence of Joseph Smith.

Critics, faultfinders and enemies have failed to prove any one of the three witnesses dishonest in his life or of such nature as to "fall for" a fraud. They were sane, honorable men.

The eight witnesses fall into two groups.

In the first group were the Prophet's father, Joseph Smith, Sr., and two of his brothers, Hyrum and Samuel Harrison Smith. No question has ever been raised about the honesty of these men. They were near enough to the Prophet to have discovered any deceit.

Joseph Smith, Senior (1771-1840),[7] was a capable man who weathered misfortune nobly, and reared despite the vagaries of fortune, an honorable family. He entered fully into the work of the Church in which he became the first patriarch. His recorded blessings are abundant evidences of his intelligence and sincere acceptance of the work which his son was commissioned to do. He also took active part in the changing fortunes of the Church. None has charged Father Smith with dishonesty.

Hyrum Smith (1800-1844), the elder brother of Joseph the Prophet, was a devoted believer in the restoration of the gospel through his brother. He was called into prominent positions in the Church. He succeeded his father as Patriarch to the Church. With his brother he suffered martyrdom for his faith. No one has questioned the honesty of Hyrum Smith.

Samuel H. Smith (1808-1844), a younger brother of the Prophet, was enthusiastic in his belief in his brother's work. In fact he was one of the earliest converts to his brother's divine calling—the first man baptized after Joseph and Oliver. Soon after the Church was organized, he set out eastward to proclaim the glad message. Out of the labors of this twenty-two year old youth many persons, later important in Church government, joined

---

[7]Andrew Jenson, *op. cit.*, vol. 1, p. 181

the Church. So apparent was the honesty of Samuel H. Smith that it has not been questioned by friends or foe of the Church.

The remaining five of the eight witnesses belonged to one family, the Whitmer family. Four were sons of Father Whitmer, and one, Hiram Page, was a son-in-law. Oliver Cowdery, one of the three witnesses, was also a son-in-law. At the time of the translation of the Book of Mormon, Joseph Smith had only a handful of friends. The Whitmers were among the few who looked with kindly eyes upon his work. Indeed, some of the translation was done in the home of Peter Whitmer, Senior; there some important revelations were received, and there the Church was organized. It was only natural that the plates would be shown to these people.

The Whitmer family came of Pennsylvania Dutch stock—sturdy, honorable farmers. Peter Whitmer, Senior, was a strict Presbyterian and maintained a religious household. The members of his family were held in high repute among their neighbors. They had business integrity and were not inclined to fanaticism. No evidence against their character has been found.

Father Whitmer's sons grew to be farmers and businessmen. Some were very fortunate in their enterprises. All maintained to the end a high reputation for honesty, diligence, and integrity.

Christian Whitmer (1798-1835), the eldest, took part in the early trials of the Church and remained faithful to the end.

Peter Whitmer, Jr., (1809-1836), remained ever faithful to his testimony and maintained his membership in the Church.

John Whitmer (1802-1878), became a valuable helper in building the young Church. He likewise maintained his testimony throughout his life. Because he later fell into error, he was excommunicated from the Church.

Jacob Whitmer (1800-1856), likewise was valiant

in helping to build the Church. He became disaffected and withdrew from the Church. Nevertheless throughout his life he bore witness to the truth of his testimony regarding the Book of Mormon plates.

Hiram Page (1800-1852), appears to have been somewhat fanatical. He found a stone through which he claimed to receive revelations, often contrary to those received by Joseph Smith. For this he was reprimanded. At last he withdrew from the Church but, as with the others, courageously and sturdily maintained that he had seen the plates, and that Joseph Smith was a Prophet of God.[8]

On one occasion, at a conference of the Church, the Prophet and at least most of the eleven witnesses were all present. With uplifted hands they unitedly bore witness to the truth of their testimonies.[9]

Eleven men state that they saw the plates from which the Book of Mormon was translated. While closely associated, some by blood, others by sympathy, these men were of differing temperaments. They had their own approach to truth. All were, however, seekers after truth. These eleven men, whose lives fell into different channels, never denied their testimony. All insisted to the end of their lives that it was true.

Had it not been true it would have been easy for those who were excommunicated or who seceded from the Church to modify the story. They might have said that they thought they saw the plates, or that Joseph's influence overcame them, or that they were trying to help the young man. Any number of explanations might have been concocted.

None of the witnesses did so. Unitedly they stand to witness to all the world that Joseph Smith's claims were and are true.

The critics must also bear in mind that in the coming forth of the latter-day work, Joseph Smith surrounded

---

[8]Andrew Jenson, *op. cit.*, vol. 1, p. 277.
[9]*History of the Church*, vol. 1, p. 220.

himself by intelligent, honest men. Mormonism was not born in ignorance or out of uncontrolled fanaticism, as some would have us believe. Honesty, honor, and integrity have ever marked the Church and her people.

CHAPTER 11

EVIDENCES FOR THE BOOK OF MORMON

The Book of Mormon is essentially a history of some of the early inhabitants of the American continent. It records three migrations from Asia to America, two of them from Palestine. The earliest of these took place at the time of the Tower of Babel. The second and third just before and after the fall of Zedekiah, king of Judah, about six hundred years before Christ.

The history of these peoples on the American continent as contained in the Book of Mormon is mainly a condensation by the Prophet Mormon of larger and more comprehensive records. Hence, it is called the Book of Mormon. Yet the condensation sets forth in considerable detail much political history and many religious beliefs and practices of the people who descended from the three migrations.

It also recounts the visit, after his resurrection and ascension, of the Lord Jesus Christ to the American continent; and reports in some detail his teachings to the people there at that time. The history ends about four hundred years after Christ, when a series of civil wars destroyed the majority of the people.

For more than a century the Book of Mormon has been discussed by tongue and pen, by friend and foe. Friends have searched for its strength, enemies for its weaknesses. Both sides have given wide publicity to their findings. The book is well-known.

Today, all intelligent people, except those ruled by their prejudices, concede that the book stands upon firmer ground than when it was first published. As knowledge has advanced, and more careful study has been given the book, the questions that the book provokes have found more and more acceptable answers. Indeed, the questions it raises may be used as tests to establish its authenticity.

Was the Book of Mormon really of divine origin?

This is the first and most difficult question for unbelievers. The answer is in the book itself.

The known life and training of Joseph Smith do not warrant the conclusion that the Book of Mormon was a product of his mind.

Note that it was translated and written in a remarkably short time, about three months; that it is coherent throughout; that it does not anywhere in its more than five hundred pages of narrative and multiplicity of doctrinal material, contradict itself; that it is filled with rich ideas far beyond the power of Joseph's maturity or experience; and that the plates from which it was translated were seen by several mortal men. To make Joseph Smith the creator demands too many hypotheses. The unbeliever stands perplexed as he tries to answer the question. If he resents the truth and becomes angry, he has to resort to the old, illogical comment that Joseph Smith lied. It is easier to accept Joseph's words that the book is of divine origin than to place the authorship on him. He was only the translator.

Was the book really translated from plates of gold on which the contents were engraved? That is another common question. This question is simply and easily answered. The first answer is that competent witnesses saw the plates and the engravings on them. That should be sufficient. Moreover writing on metal plates has been shown to be an ancient practice.

In the British Museum are twenty-five silver plates, approximately eighteen by two inches, bound together by thongs, a Pate manuscript on which a sermon by Buddha is beautifully engraved. Nearby in the Museum lies a gold plate two by nine and one half inches on which is inscribed a letter from one native prince to another. In the Evkaft Museum in Turkey are some inscribed silver plates, about four and one half by three inches and about one inch thick. Dr. Franklin S. Harris, Sr., relates that during his sojourn in

Persia in the cornerstone of an ancient building a box was found containing metal plates on which were written messages.[1]

The ancient writing on plates is a well substantiated fact. No reader of the Book of Mormon needs to stumble over the use of metallic plates in writing.

Was the book written in Egyptian characters? The book says reformed Egyptian. The final answer to this question is that still existing characters, more than two hundred, copied from the plates by Joseph, have been shown definitely to be Egyptian. Historical research has pointed out the close association of Israel with Egypt. Lehi, the first personage in the Book of Mormon, did business with Egypt. There is no reason why Egyptian symbols used in writing could not have been in possession of Book of Mormon peoples.[2]

Was the book written, as it says, by a succession of historians? If so, the style and manner of writing, and the ideas treated should vary somewhat with different writers. In fact, as any student may verify, the English and the emphasized ideas of the Book of Mormon vary greatly, indicating different writers. The English of the book shows unmistakable relationship to the Hebrew idiom—suggesting that the book was written in Hebrew, with the use of Egyptian characters.[3]

The book says that there were populous civilizations in ancient America. For answer one needs only refer to the vast knowledge of American archaeology gathered since the Book of Mormon was published. Remains of great cities and of gigantic irrigation canals, evidences of large populations possessing a high culture in many fields including astronomy, have been found.[4]

It is almost a waste of time to defend the Book of Mormon claim that there have been populous civilizations

---

[1]*Improvement Era*, vol. 43, p. 714.
[2]Sidney B. Sperry, *Our Book of Mormon*, chapter 3, p. 28.
[3]*Ibid.*, pp. 28-38; Sjodahl, *An Introduction to the Study of the Book of Mormon*, p. 74.
[4]Hubert Howe Bancroft, *Native Races*, vol. 2, pp. 116-117.

in ancient America. In this connection it should be remembered that in 1830, when the book was first published, knowledge of prehistoric America was very limited. There was then no clear conception of the extent of the civilizations in ancient America. Therefore, the answer to this claim becomes increasingly important in proving the truth of the book.

Are some of the American aborigines, American Indians, of Hebrew descent? The book so states. Students are not all in agreement on the answer. Without question there are Hebrew elements in many of the American native languages, customs, and beliefs. The American aborigines have traditions of leading Hebrew personalities and events before the time of Christ. Some tribes have blood factors like the present-day Hebrews.[5]

In their religious beliefs and practices they have followed and follow with astonishing similarity corresponding beliefs and practices of the Hebrews of that day. This claim of the book cannot be lightly set aside. Indeed, every new discovery tends to confirm it.[6]

Did Jesus the resurrected Christ visit the American continent? This is the astonishing assertion of the Book of Mormon. In confirmation of this claim is the fact that the Christ story was common among the natives of the two Americas before the coming of Columbus. This might have come through a knowledge of the Hebrew religion, which looked forward to a coming Messiah, but the American tradition declares that a personage like Jesus did come to the people on the American continent.

So extensive and so thoroughly ingrained in the historical and traditional life of the people is the Messiah story that one must either accept the coming of Christ to America as a fact or the coming of some other great man who was mistaken for Jesus the Christ.

This latter supposition disappears, however, in view

[5]Daniel G. Briton, *The American Race*, p. 18; John A. Widtsoe and F. S. Harris, Jr., *Seven Claims to the Book of Mormon*, pp. 91-124.
[6]Milton R. Hunter and Thomas Stuart Ferguson, *Ancient America and the Book of Mormon*.

of the many Christian ordinances and beliefs as taught by the Savior which survive among American aborigines. Modern scholarship stands confused before the beliefs of the aborigines of America. The Book of Mormon offers the simplest answer: The resurrected Jesus did visit America.[7]

Perhaps the most remarkable proof of the divine origin of the Book of Mormon is the inspiration in the book felt by every honest, unprejudiced reader. The contents are manifestly beyond the power of an ordinary man to produce.

Note the striking evidences. The book, produced by an unlettered young man on the western frontier of New York, deals with the leading theological world controversies of the past and the present and offers such clear solutions for them as progressive thinkers within other churches have attempted during the last century. The book has a definite message, the one that runs through the Old and New Testaments. It presents an astonishing doctrinal harmony with the Bible.

The summary of Book of Mormon doctrines presents the gospel of Jesus Christ in plainness and simplicity beyond limitations placed upon the gospel by the churches of that or the present day. There are also in the book many striking statements of beauty and deep import that could scarcely fall from the lips of an untrained youth without inspiration from above.

In addition, prophecies are uttered in the book, many of which have been fulfilled. The claim of inspiration for the contents of the Book of Mormon, like the other claims, presents such an array of evidence that it commands belief among all who accept truth wherever it may be found.[8]

The Book of Mormon itself presents a test of its truth, a simple test that all, high or low, may apply. It runs as follows:

---

[7]*Book of Mormon*, 3 Nephi, chapter 11
[8]B. H. Roberts, *New Witness for God*, (Y.M.M.I.A. Manuals 1903-1906) pp. 430-452.

When ye shall receive these things, I would exhort you that ye would ask God, the Eternal Father, in the name of Christ, if these things are not true; and if ye shall ask with a sincere heart, with real intent, having faith in Christ, he will manifest the truth to you, by the power of the Holy Ghost.[9]

Hundreds of thousands of people have tried this test and have found it effective. Rich and poor, learned and unlearned, mighty and humble have used this test to satisfy their seeking after truth. By the use of this test the followers of Joseph Smith have increased to a multitude.

In view of these and other evidences of truth which converge upon the Book of Mormon, does anyone have the right in this day of truth-seeking and truth-loving to lay aside the Book of Mormon without applying fully and without reservation the test proposed by the ancient Prophet Moroni?

Let us restate the problems: Is the book of divine origin? Was it written on metallic plates? Was it written in Egyptian characters? Was it written by a succession of historians? Are some of the American Indians of Hebrew descent? Were there populous civilizations in ancient America? Did Jesus visit the American continent? Is inspiration from divine sources evident in the book?

To these questions even unbelievers in view of modern knowledge and logical thinking must answer yes, and admit the evidence is in favor of the book. Indeed the book itself offers a test of its truth.

The answers to other questions suggested by the Book of Mormon only add to the mass of evidence for its truth. Those here presented are startling in confirming Book of Mormon claims.

Had there been flaws in the book they would long since have been discovered under the intense scrutiny of unfriendly students. Professional men, as well as laymen, have undertaken to find weaknesses in the book. The

[9]*Book of Mormon*, Moroni 10:4.

objections raised are of the kind to which men are driven when they find themselves without logical support of the things that they expected to discover. They are trivial, superficial, unsound, and based on insufficient knowledge or of preconceived notions. The book has withstood successfully the assaults of its enemies. It is more than ever a mystery to them.

The probability of the truth of the Book of Mormon is daily being more firmly established in the minds of thinking people. In fact all that is needed is to read the book and examine the circumstances surrounding its origin. It is its own best witness.

One by one the evidences at hand lead to the convincing conclusion that Joseph Smith's story is true; that the Book of Mormon is just what it claims to be—a record written by ancient men under divine inspiration, and preserved and translated in this day by the gift and power of God; and that it offers knowledge, comfort, and solace to a troubled world, which is man's great need today.

CHAPTER 12

THE VOCABULARY OF JOSEPH SMITH

Joseph Smith's mother wrote that of all her children he was the least inclined to give his time to the reading of books.[1] He was fond of outdoor life, and physical games. His history mentions wrestling matches, jumping, and ball playing. Children grown to manhood related the story of games with the Prophet.[2]

He grew up used to hard work. His father was chiefly a farmer in the Palmyra days.[3] Joseph had to take his share in the labors on the farm. When their farm labors permitted he sought employment elsewhere. Josiah Stoal employed him to dig for a lost mine,[4] Clark Chase to dig a well.[5] He writes in his journal that he was obliged to earn a scant living by the toil of his hands.[6]

His school education was very meager. He could read, write an imperfect hand, and knew enough arithmetic for his needs. In the words of Orson Pratt who lived in his house, and became his great defender:

His advantages for acquiring scientific knowledge were exceedingly small, being limited to a slight acquaintance with two or three of the common branches of learning. He could read without much difficulty, and write a very imperfect hand; and had a very limited understanding of the elementary rules of arithmetic. These were his highest and only attainments; while the rest of those branches, so universally taught in the common schools throughout the United States were entirely unknown to him.[7]

However, he had a fine mind. All who knew him, friend and foe, conceded that his mental ability was high. Under favorable circumstances he would have used educational opportunities to the full. In his later years he

---

[1]Lucy Mack Smith, *History of the Prophet Joseph*, 1902 edition, p. 84.
[2]*Juvenile Instructor*, vol. 27, p. 172.
[3]Lucy Mack Smith, *op. cit.*, 1902 edition, p. 54.
[4]*Ibid.*, 1902 edition, p. 91.
[5]B. H. Roberts, *Comprehensive History of the Church*, vol. 1, p. 129.
[6]*History of the Church*, vol. 1, p. 28
[7]Orson Pratt, *Remarkable Visions*, p. 1.

sought learning in many fields—languages, law and others. From his earliest association with the Church, after the translation of the Book of Mormon he urged education upon the people.

In short, Joseph Smith was not better educated than the average boy of his pioneer period, from a family reduced to poverty, inured to toil with little chance for an education. His training came from his observation of nature about him, and the people whom he met.

His was a Bible reading family. In those days on the frontier, the Bible was the chief book of the household. Joseph was a Bible-reader. That of itself would aid much in the education of the boy. The writings that he left behind him show his fine Bible versatility from Genesis to Revelation. In that sense he grew up a well educated man; but it would not be suspected that he had a large or technical vocabulary.

Enemies who have read the Book of Mormon have found its contents to be beyond the capacity of a boy with such meager training for writing. Therefore they have set up the theory that some competent person, hiding behind Joseph Smith, was the real author of the Book of Mormon.[8] Sidney Rigdon, a man of some education, a reader, a student, and an orator was picked by many defeated antagonists, but unsuccessfully, to be the unknown man who really wrote the Book of Mormon.[9]

If a man of superior learning wrote the Book of Mormon, it would be reflected in the extent and character of his vocabulary. If the vocabulary should be small and simple it would be another evidence for the truth of Joseph Smith's claim that he translated the book from engravings on golden plates. Every translator catches the idea in the old language, and reports it in the new manner according to the manner of his own speech.

The English language has a multitude of words borrowed from many tongues. So large is this collection

[8]E. D. Howe, *Mormonism Unvailed,* 1834 edition, p. 290.
[9]Francis W. Kirkham, *A New Witness for Christ in America,* 1947 edition, p. 299.

that it has been estimated that in ordinary use, in speech and writing, not more than one tenth or one twentieth of English words are employed, even by the most learned. Many books and articles on this subject have been published. Recently a competent author declared that with one thousand English words all ordinary ideas could be expressed, and that the common man seldom uses more than five thousand words.

Milton's vocabulary was between seven thousand and eight thousand words.[10] Some double this number. The translators of Homer's Iliad and Odyssey, linguistic scholars, used about nine thousand words.[11] Four thousand and eight hundred in the New Testament; five thousand six hundred forty-two in the Old Testament. The varying number depends in part on whether inflected forms of words are included. There are those who think that the Bible has twenty thousand words, everything counted; and Shakespeare follows with eighteen thousand words. Any translation of any book depends of course primarily upon the vocabulary of the translator, since a good translation deals with ideas, not with words.

Many studies have been made to discover the number of words used by the average man. Naturally every man uses a number depending on many factors such as the parental vocabulary, kind and amount of thinking, companions and reading habits. It is pretty generally agreed, however, that on the average a fairly well educated man uses about eight thousand words in his daily conversation.[12]

Joseph Smith used only between two thousand and three thousand words in his written publications. This smaller number would be expected from a knowledge of his educational opportunities.

An actual count shows (leaving out all inflected forms of words) the following vocabulary for the Book of Mormon:

---

[10]Mrs. Clark's Concordance.
[11]*The Nation*, September 12, 1912.
[12]Henry Louis Mencken, *The American Language*, p. 4.

General Words	2,896
Persons' Names	245
Place Names	166
Total	3,307

This indicates that the Book of Mormon translator was a person of little education, and with little facility in the use of unusual words. This checks precisely with Joseph's story of the origin of the Book of Mormon. It should help lay low the charge that someone other than Joseph Smith himself wrote the Book of Mormon.

It is interesting to note whether a similar vocabulary was used by Joseph Smith in other writings. It is somewhat unusual for a man to change his vocabulary very much after maturity unless he is professionally in literary labors. To answer this question the Prophet's vocabulary in the revelations he received was examined. In the Doctrine and Covenants there are the following:

Ordinary Words	2,445
Persons' Names	230
Place Names	47
Total	2,722

This indicates a grade of vocabulary similar to that in the Book of Mormon. It furnishes additional proof of Joseph's truthfulness in telling his story. None has doubted that the revelations were written by Joseph. The two vocabularies are of the same order.

There are about four hundred and fifty-one more words used in the Book of Mormon than in the Doctrine and Covenants. That is accounted for no doubt in the larger Book of Mormon movements as recorded over a thousand year period, drawing more heavily upon his vocabulary to make the ideas and events clear. In that book are also fifteen more persons' names; and one hundred nineteen more place names.

But, the totals are such as to show that the Book of Mormon and the Doctrine and Covenants were written by a man of limited education.

Whenever the life of Joseph Smith is touched truth comes forth.

CHAPTER 13

SOURCES OF CHARACTER CHARGES

Joseph Smith was subjected to steady opposition, often persecution, from the time of the First Vision, though they were not of wide extent. Only the immediate community heard of it. After all, a farm boy simply said that he had had a vision in which he saw God. People shrugged their shoulders and made caustic comments or looked upon him with contempt.

Nearly all the serious character charges against him refer to the period between the visit of the ancient American Prophet, Moroni, three years after the First Vision, and the obtaining of the golden plates four years later; that is, from his eighteenth to his twenty-second year.

Before the coming of Moroni Joseph appears to have had a good reputation. After the plates were secured, his everyday life became well-known, but little has been said about it in print. It is upon this four year interval that his enemies have directed their fury of hatred. This casts serious doubt upon the sincerity of the charges. Men do not usually become evil overnight, and after a few years return to their former normal condition.

It is to be remembered that the charges against Joseph were not formulated and put into general circulation until a year or more after the Church had been organized; that is, ten years after the first divine visit, the First Vision. By that time religious intolerance had had time to burst into a living flame. A new church had been organized by Joseph Smith, claiming to be the restored Church of Jesus Christ, therefore, a threat to existing churches! Every effort even to exaggeration must be made to destroy the newcomer—so, many people thought. Many believed, of course, that Joseph Smith had had no vision or plates but that his story was a colossal lie. To fortify this new

conception of his character, unfounded charges against
the Prophet were bandied about.

He was said to be a crystal or peepstone gazer, a
digger for lost treasure, and a devotee of the black arts.
He came of a low ancestry, they said, and was reared in
a superstitious, untruthful family. Moreover, some held
that the Book of Mormon was written, not by him, but by
some ally that he had duped into helping him. The charges
were many and varied.

He had to meet men who charged him with some
breach of the law in the courts of the day but he was
never convicted. Significantly, no charges of immorality
were hurled against him until polygamy was introduced.
Liars themselves to save their own skins dare not go too
far.

In fairness it should be said that while he was hounded
and persecuted by enemies, usually inspired by ministers,
many friends not members of the Church stood by and
helped him. The attorneys whom he employed to defend
him became his lifelong friends. They became convinced
of his high character. He tells of these early persecutions
in his own history, while most of the personalities mentioned were then living. They had the chance to correct
an untruth.

A small branch had been formed in Colesville, Broome
County, New York. Vicious opposition developed there.
Joseph was arrested, charged with "being a disorderly
person, of setting the county in an uproar by preaching
the Book of Mormon, etc." This was only a few months
after the organization of the Church. The court found
the Prophet innocent and discharged him. He was again
arrested on the same charge and again discharged for
want of evidence.

The attorneys "spoke like men inspired of God." Mr.
Reed, one of the attorneys, made a public address in Nauvoo, on the 17th of May, 1844, in which he corroborated
the unfounded persecutions of Joseph Smith. Among
other things, he said:

The first acquaintance I had with Joseph Smith was about 1823. He came into my neighborhood, being then about eighteen years and resided there two years; during which time I became intimately acquainted with him. I do know that his character was irreproachable; that he was well known for truth and uprightness; that he moved in the first circles of the community, and he was often spoken of as a young man of intelligence and good morals, and possessing a mind susceptible of the highest intellectual attainments.[1]

It is notable that the local newspapers from 1823 to 1827, covering the period in question, were silent as to any charges against Joseph; yet enemies, who have written books on the subject, would have readers believe that he was engaged in nefarious practices, treasure hunting, divining, and so forth, to such an extent as to keep the whole community in a state of tension.

It was common knowledge in his neighborhood that Joseph Smith said that he was to obtain hidden plates from which he would translate a book about the American Indians. This is proved by newspaper articles printed before the Book of Mormon was published.[2] Many people waited in curiosity to see the forthcoming book. There were no character charges accompanying such announcements of the forthcoming book.

Moreover, it is remarkable that during the translation of the plates and after the Book of Mormon had been published and the Church organized, there are no real character charges that appear against the Prophet. His work was always done with the full knowledge of the communities in which he lived.

No one has made a defensible charge of questionable behavior against him during his active life from the coming forth of the Book of Mormon until his death. True, he was brought into court many times, not on moral charges, but was never found guilty.[3]

Not one of the charges against Joseph is of itself sufficient to blacken a man's character. Men are not

[1]*Times and Seasons*, vol. 5, pp. 549-552; *History of the Church*, vol. 1, p. 94.
[2]Francis W. Kirkham, *A New Witness for Christ in America*, pp. 146-152.
[3]*Journal History*, April 24, 1845.

necessarily of bad character because they claim to have had spiritual or supernatural experiences. For centuries men have sought treasure supposed to be lost. One hundred years after Joseph's death people of good reputations are outfitting expeditions to find lost mines or treasures buried by pirates. Today there are many who claim to see things beyond the power of the normal eye. Yet they are not supposed to be evil men.

The supposed evidences of the charges against Joseph Smith used by nearly all unfriendly authors over a century, follow the same pattern and are drawn from two doubtful sources, unacceptable in a reputable court of law.

The first source of the charges against Joseph Smith's character comes from a series of articles written and published in 1831 by one Obediah Dogberry, editor of the Palmyra *Reflector*. These articles were republished in the Painesville *Telegraph* edited by E. D. Howe. It must be kept in mind that they were published after the Church had been organized, and seven to eight years after the events were said to have occurred.

These articles make charges, more specifically, of money digging, peepstone use, that the Book of Mormon was a fiction, and that the Smith family were ignorant and stupid. However, the author appears to believe firmly that Joseph Smith was the author of the Book of Mormon; and the charges against the Smith family were founded upon their supposed beliefs in such things. Immoral conduct or dishonesty in community or personal affairs are not suggested. No proofs are given of the charges made. They are personal opinions, based no doubt upon Joseph's employment with others to dig for a silver mine for a short time, by Josiah Stoal, and his own claim that he dug golden plates from the ground. It does not take long in the mouth of an enemy to transform any human action to suit the purpose in mind.

It is curious that, while the Book of Mormon was being translated, to the full knowledge of the community, neither Dogberry's own paper nor any other paper said anything derogatory about Joseph or his family.

There is good reason to believe that this same Dogberry was the man who attempted, until stopped by Joseph Smith himself, to purloin the printer's proofs of the Book of Mormon, and to print them before the publication of the book.[4]

There is an element of hate in the Dogberry papers, probably dating from this failure. They have no value in an unprejudiced study of Joseph Smith, and, indeed, most writers have not used them.

The second source of these charges, which has been read and used most extensively in anti-Mormon literature, is a series of affidavits in the book *Mormonism Unvailed*,[5] published in 1834 by E. D. Howe,[6] a printer who assumed authorship because of the unsavory reputation of one Philastus Hurlburt, the real author of the book. This book also contains the original Rigdon-Spaulding theory of the origin of the Book of Mormon, to be discussed later.

Hurlburt, a convert to the Church, had been excommunicated for adultery. Upon his pleading he was forgiven and restored to membership. Again he fell into sin and was again excommunicated. The refusal of the Church to receive him back made him an enemy, villainous in his opposition.[7]

In the preparation of a book against the Church he secured from upwards of a hundred people in Palmyra and vicinity unfriendly affidavits as to the character of Joseph Smith and his family. This was done in 1833, eight or ten years after the period discussed in the affidavits.

They contain no specific charges beyond saying that the Smith family, especially Joseph and his father, were of low character. The affidavits are weak and watery,

---

[4]*History of the Church*, vol. 1, p. 76; Lucy Mack Smith, *History of the Prophet Joseph Smith*, 1945 edition, p. 164.
[5]E. D. Howe, *Mormonism Unvailed*, 1834 edition, p. 290.
[6]Illegitimate author, "The Prophet Calls Him", *History of the Church*, vol. 2, p. 270.
[7]B. H. Roberts, *Defense of the Faith*, vol. 2, p. 125; *History of the Church*, vol. 1, p. 352-354; Kirkham, *op. cit.*, p. 129.

general in statement. No person making an affidavit says that Joseph Smith stole from him or lied to him. No one accuses Joseph of immorality. No names of people who were "injured by the Smiths" are given.

The spirit of religious intolerance which ran high in those days explains these affidavits. It had become current knowledge that Joseph Smith had set up a church. Since it claimed to be the only true Church of Jesus Christ restored in opposition to their own churches, people would stretch their memories to report any gossip that might prevent the spread of such a movement, to them evil. The book is an excellent example of what has come to be called muckraking, instead of the product of historical research. Men, pronounced but honest enemies of Joseph, have been obliged to lay them aside as being untrustworthy.

E. D. Howe, publisher of the Painesville *Telegraph* had a personal motive in publishing the book. His wife and other members of the family had been converted to the truth of the restored gospel and had joined the Church. Despite Howe's insistence, they refused to leave the Church.[8] In furious anger, Howe bought and used the morbid manuscript which Hurlburt had offered him. These two men, fierce enemies of Joseph's work, produced the book which has been as a "bible" to every anti-Mormon writer since that day. Honest historians would accept with much caution statements made by such a combination. In *Mormonism Unvailed* hate and the lust for money stand out primarily

These two sources, the articles of Obediah Dogberry, and the affidavits collected by Hurlburt, are unsatisfactory, wobbly, inacceptable evidence. Yet upon them Joseph Smith has been publicized by his enemies as being an unworthy personage, untruthful, dishonest, and deceiving. Thinking people cannot accept conclusions resting upon such insecure foundations.

---

[8]Inez Smith Davis, *The Story of the Church*, p. 5; Fawn M. Brodie, *No Man Knows my History*, 1945 edition, p. 103.

Two other "sources" appear fifty years later, which have been used by a few distraught thunderers against Joseph Smith. These are two supposed records that differ in important assertions of proceedings of a supposed trial of Joseph Smith, held before a justice of the peace in 1826 in a time when county justices of the peace were not required to record and did not record the testimonies of those who came before their courts. This is proved by records of 1820 to 1830 in the New York State Library at Albany, New York.[9]

In one of these supposed records, known as the "Tuttle record," Joseph Smith is made to confess to all his errors, including treasure hunting, peepstone practices, etc., etc. In fact, it is such a complete self-confession as to throw immediate doubt upon the genuineness of the document. Joseph Smith was not a fool. This alleged court record was brought to Utah in the 1870's[10] by a woman who said that she had torn the pages from her father's record book. It seems to be a literary attempt of an enemy to ridicule Joseph Smith by bringing together all the current gossip of that day and making him appear to confess to it.

The other so-called "record" of the supposed trial is by one W. D. Purple, who in 1877, fifty years later in his published reminiscences, gives an account of the charges of that day against Joseph Smith. This was written at the height of later Utah persecution, when no one was expected to speak well of the Latter-day Saints or their Prophet.

Neither of these reports carries the seal of authenticity. The first is clearly the invention of an enemy; the second, the babblings of an old man who retailed the popular gossip of a past day to support that of a later day. There is no existing proof that such a trial was ever held. It is remarkable that enemies in Joseph's day hunting desperately for evidence against him have said noth-

---

[9]Kirkham, *op. cit.,* 1947 edition, p. 467.
[10]*Ibid.,* p. 489-492.

ing about this supposed trial. Apparently they had not heard of it. It is mentioned in only one history, and not until 1876.[11] Had such a trial been held, with such confessions as are cited, it would have been a choice morsel for the enemies, Dogberry, Hurlburt, and Howe, who were hunting for evidence against Joseph. There is no probability that it would not have been discovered and circulated among the community and made known generally. There is something ludicrous in the sober use made of these "records" by recent writers against the character of Joseph Smith.

Only one arrest of Joseph Smith has been found between his eighteenth and twenty-second year. While working for Josiah Stoal, "some very officious person complained of him, Joseph Smith, as a disorderly person, and brought him before the authorities of the county. There being no cause of action, he was honorably acquitted."[12] This may be the event upon which the supposed "records" were built. It is a credible guess that this charge was made by the Hale family to get Joseph out of the county and away from Emma Hale, who later became his wife, whom he was then courting against the wishes of her family.[13]

Philastus Hurlburt is a pathetic figure. Benjamin Winchester, in whose home young Hurlburt occasionally stayed, wrote a brief biography of the man.[14] He tells that E. D. Howe paid Hurlburt five hundred dollars for the manuscript of his book and then dared not publish it under the real author's name, for his reputation was "too rotten." Winchester closes his story as follows:

Mr. Hurlburt with his ill-gotten gains, went to Erie County, Pennsylvania, in the township of Girard Miller settlement, and bought a farm, and married a wife, soon became a drunkard, spent every cent of his inglorious gains, was reduced to beggary, took to stealing for a livelihood, was detected in stealing a log chain, fled

---

[11]*Ibid.*, pp. 377-378.
[12]Oliver Cowdery, *Messenger and Advocate*, 1835.
[13]Kirkham, *op. cit.*, p. 387.
[14]B. Winchester, *The Spaulding Story*, 1840 edition, p. 11, Philadelphia.

the country, to escape justice and that is the last of him, so far as I know.

Ellen E. Dickinson sought out Hurlburt in 1880 and, when talking about the book, found him nervous and contradictory in his answers.[15]

The famous affidavits in Howe's book are remarkably alike in composition. One hand must have written them. They have little to say about "peepstones"; much about treasure hunting and the deluded nature of the Smith family. One affidavit, signed by fifty-one persons, charges the Smith family with treasure hunting, being visionary, and "destitute of the moral character which ought to entitle them to the confidence of any community."[16]

These are all general charges, with no background of facts, wholly unworthy of intelligent people. They might well be placed against testimonies of other people who lived in Palmyra at that time, which state that the Smith family were respectable people.[17] None can read the literature of that day without laying aside Dogberry and Howe as untrustworthy witnesses.

The charge of "crystal gazing" came of course from Joseph Smith's use of the "Seer Stone" (though there is no evidence that he used the Seer Stone in sacred work,) and the Urim and Thummim, and from his treasure hunting in his employment by Josiah Stoal to dig for treasure, and from Joseph's story that he found golden plates, buried in a hill.

It is a marvel that authors writing against Joseph Smith's spiritual claims would stoop to mull over interminably, charges evidently manufactured by admitted enemies to suit their purposes. Even in a contest, fair play should be recognized. Joseph Smith was but a human being, with the frailties of men. The muckrakers past and present have made desperate, dishonest, but un-

---

[15]Ellen E. Dickinson, *New Light on Mormonism*, 1885 edition, pp. 63-76, 272.
[16]E. D. Howe, *op. cit.*, pp. 261-262.
[17]J. H. Kennedy, *Early Days of Mormonism*, pp. 1-275.

successful attempts to destroy Joseph Smith and his work. There is a grim humor in the failure of their splashing in garbage pails to prove Joseph a false prophet. The test of Joseph Smith's veracity is in his work and teachings. They are convincing to all who will apply the test of truth sincerely.

After the Church was organized and had won hosts of converts, the fury of enemies grew. In New York, Ohio and Missouri unbridled talk led to persecution often with terrible consequences. At length in Illinois, the hatred of truth, because it differed from tradition, became so ugly that Joseph Smith was murdered.

CHAPTER 14

DID JOSEPH SMITH WRITE THE
BOOK OF MORMON?

To ask if Joseph Smith produced the Book of Mormon seems unnecessary. Of course, he was the translator unaided by mortal man. Yet, it may be worth while to examine into the widespread theory of anti-Mormon writers that Joseph wrote the book and that he stole his ideas from others.

When the Book of Mormon was first published, no question was raised about its authorship or authenticity. Over several years Joseph Smith had told the story of the visitation of Moroni, the promise of the golden plates, when he received them, and how he devoted time to their translation.

The earliest writers in opposition to the Church accepted Joseph Smith as the author of the book; for example, Alexander Campbell, the leader of the Church of Disciples, who had lost to Joseph Smith some capable followers, wrote in 1831 that Joseph Smith was the author and that the Book of Mormon contained only the gossip of the neighborhood, in which every religious problem of the day was discussed in crude language.

However, after people had had time to give the book more careful examination, and thousands had joined the Church, doubts began to arise in the minds of many as to whether Joseph Smith, the plowboy, was indeed the author of the book. Its language was found not to be crude but generally beautiful and inspiring. The book was found to present religious ideas in full harmony with the doctrine of the Lord Jesus Christ. Important religious problems were given a simple, understandable explanation. It was, in its own words, a witness for Christ. The book seemed to be beyond the power of Joseph Smith to produce.

So the theory was advanced that Joseph must have had help to produce the book. Some enemies went so far as to suggest that it was wholly written by someone else! This was just what the unbelievers wanted, apparently without recognizing that such a theory would, without supporting facts, be a powerful evidence of the truth of Joseph's story. He acknowledged that he had received help from divine sources! Careless writers in their enmity of Joseph Smith have said for a century or more that Joseph Smith was helped in the writing of the book by mortal men.

From the book *Mormonism Unvailed,* published in 1834, nearly all anti-Mormon books have drawn their material. The theory was there advanced that Joseph Smith had had a silent partner in his work. It was implied that this person was Sidney Rigdon, a close friend of Alexander Campbell, and an associate founder and preacher of the Campbellite Church.

After a careful and searching inquiry into the truth of Mormonism, Rigdon joined the Church in November, 1831, more than a year after the Church was organized. He was an eloquent preacher of some learning and an outstanding man wherever he went.

It was suggested in the Howe book that Rigdon had written the theological or religious portions of the Book of Mormon, and that the historical setting of the book was also furnished by him by plagiarizing an unpublished novel written nearly twenty years earlier by one Solomon Spaulding, declared atheist, about the ancient peoples of America. Rigdon was supposed to have purloined the manuscript from the printer with whom it had been deposited.

The Book of Mormon, according to this theory, was nothing more than this Spaulding story, ornamented with Rigdon's religious emanations. This theory was as a raft at sea for the helpless enemies of Joseph Smith, and it has been peddled industriously by anti-Mormon writers for the delectation of unwary readers.

The Spaulding tale is a story of a party of Romans who came to America and an account of their life there. The story was read by Mr. Spaulding to his family and some friends. Several persons who had heard the story read fifteen or twenty years earlier were induced to sign a statement that the language and the characters in the story fitted in with the contents of the Book of Mormon. This was enough to set up and circulate the theory that the Book of Mormon was based upon the manuscript story of Solomon Spaulding.

Unfortunately for the Rigdon-Spaulding theory, the manuscript of the Spaulding story was discovered in 1884 among the possessions of Mr. L. L. Rice of Honolulu, who had secured Spaulding's literary remains,[1] when he purchased the printing effects of E. D. Howe. The discovered Spaulding story has since been published in two editions. It bears no resemblance in language, style, names, or subject matter to the Book of Mormon.

In utter despair, the enemies of the Church fled for cover. A few proceeded to set up another theory, that Spaulding had written more than one story and that the one found was not the one that resembled the Book of Mormon.[2]

However, the discovered Spaulding manuscript was identified with the one set up in the book *Mormonism Unvailed.* The names of the people who thought that the Spaulding story as read by them many years before and the Book of Mormon story were similar, were found endorsed on the discovered manuscript as those who knew it in Spaulding's day. This was destructive of the theory that the Howe book had used another manuscript than that found in Honolulu.

The Spaulding theory of the origin of the Book of Mormon has been thoroughly demolished. Anyone who teaches this theory today betrays deliberate dishonesty or pitiful lack of knowledge concerning the whole matter.

---

[1]Francis W. Kirkham, *A New Witness for Christ in America*, pp. 344-345.
[2]Charles A. Shook, *The True Origin of the Book of Mormon*, p. 71.

HILL CUMORAH, NEAR MANCHESTER, NEW YORK

Where the plates from which the Book of Mormon was translated were found

CHARACTERS COPIED BY JOSEPH SMITH
From the Book of Mormon plates (taken by Martin Harris to Dr. Anton)

WRITING FROM THE ORIGINAL MANUSCRIPT
Of the Book of Mormon

That Sidney Rigdon ever saw the Prophet Joseph Smith before the Book of Mormon was published has been disproved. His activities and whereabouts are pretty well-known from November 2, 1826, to November 14, 1830, the years during which the Book of Mormon was being translated and printed.[3] His first visit to Palmyra was nine months after the organization of the Church and after the Book of Mormon was given to the world. At that time he had his first meeting with the Prophet Joseph Smith. Printed non-Mormon contemporaneous reports of Rigdon's acceptance of the gospel do not mention or hint of any previous meeting of Joseph Smith and Rigdon. Historical evidence fails to prove any earlier connection between Sidney Rigdon and Joseph Smith.

Die-hard anti-Mormon writers have suggested that to help produce the Book of Mormon Sidney Rigdon traveled incognito over long distances and as a mysterious stranger unknown to the community met Joseph Smith. That theory is not only unlikely, and unproved, but absurd, lodged only in the minds of those who refuse any evidence that Joseph Smith told the truth.

Sidney Rigdon himself testified time and again that the first time he saw the Book of Mormon was in Mentor, Ohio, near Kirtland, after the Book of Mormon was published and the Church organized. Then, Parley P. Pratt, a former colleague in the Disciples Church gave him a copy. Elder Pratt was one of four Mormon elders traveling through the Kirtland territory to do missionary work among the Indians.

The missionaries stopped for some time in and near Kirtland to preach and to bear witness of the restored gospel. They held long conferences with Sidney Rigdon who declared this to be the first time that he had ever seen the Book of Mormon or known of its contents. His son, John W. Rigdon, who joined the Church long after Joseph's death, testified that when his father, Sidney Rigdon, lay upon his deathbed, he, John W. Rigdon, put the

---

[3]Fawn M. Brodie, *No Man Knows My History*, pp. 413-432.

question of the origin of the Book of Mormon to his father. The result is best told in his own words:

> You have been charged with writing that Book of Mormon and giving it to Joseph Smith to introduce to the world. You have always told me one story, that you never saw the book until it was presented to you by Parley P. Pratt and Oliver Cowdery. That all you ever knew of the origin of that book was what they told you, and what Joseph Smith and the witnesses who have claimed to have seen the plates have told you.
>
> Is this true? If so, all right. If it is not, you owe it to me and to your family to tell it. You are an old man, and you will soon pass away, and I wish to know if Joseph Smith in your intimacy with him for fourteen years has not said something to you that led you to believe he obtained that book in some other way than that which he has told you. Give me all you know about it that I may know the truth.
>
> My father looked at me a moment and raised his hand above his head and slowly said with tears glistening in his eyes, "My son, I can swear before high heaven that what I have told you about the origin of that book is true. Your mother and sister, Mrs. Obega Robinson, were present when that book was handed to me in Mentor, Ohio, and all I ever knew about the origin of that book was what Parley P. Pratt, Oliver Cowdery, Joseph Smith, and the witnesses who claimed they saw the plates have told me.
>
> And with all my intimacy with Joseph Smith he never told me but one story, and that was that he found it engraved on gold plates in a hill near Palmyra, New York, and that an angel had appeared to him and had directed him where to find it and I have never to you nor to anyone else told but the one story and that I now repeat to you." I believe him and now believe he told me the truth. He also said to me after that, "Mormonism is true, that Joseph Smith was a Prophet, and this world would find it out some day."[4]

The Rigdon-Spaulding explanation of the Book of Mormon, now thoroughly disproved, has no historical foundation but was clearly manufactured by a dishonest writer in hate of Joseph Smith. It remains an evidence of the ugly dishonesty that may enter the mind of hate.[5] In the face of intense, long continued research, the theory

---

[4]Mrs. John W. Rigdon, *Life of Sidney Rigdon; History of the Church,* vol. 1, p. 123; Kirkham, *op. cit.,* pp. 327-329
[5]Daryl Chase, *Sidney Rigdon, Early Mormon,* unpublished thesis, University of Chicago.

has been thoroughly discredited by competent historians. It is now used only by those who love their prejudices more than truth, but often enough to disturb the uninformed.

After a century of fruitless hunting, Sidney Rigdon is really the only person who has been charged with being a helper to Joseph Smith in the writing of the Book of Mormon. In view of the proof that Rigdon did not help him, Joseph Smith remains the sole producer of the book, unaided by any mortal person, except the scribes who wrote after his dictation.

Those who cannot or will not believe that Joseph Smith produced the Book of Mormon have then had only one other theory to fall back upon. I. W. Riley in his book, *The Founder of Mormonism,* a "psychological" study of Joseph Smith, accepts the Book of Mormon as a product of Joseph Smith's mind but believes that it was written by him while he was in an epileptic state.

If that be accepted, Joseph Smith must have been seized by such fits, regularly, forenoon and afternoon, possibly during meals, during the ninety days in which the Book of Mormon was translated and then was free from such fits the remainder of his life. That theory, smacking of *Arabian Nights* fables, is so strained as to be an insult to the credulity of intelligent people.

It is merely an admission that students of Joseph Smith stand helpless before the interpretation of the work he did, unless they accept the statements of Joseph Smith himself. His own frank admission is that the Book of Mormon was produced by the "gift and power of God."

A variation of these theories has recently appeared. Gasping for breath, the opponents of Joseph Smith now assert that he possessed tremendous mental power which enabled him to write the Book of Mormon but also that he was so deficient in moral sense as to palm off his work as coming from God. That is old stuff! Joseph's life of rectitude is a sufficient answer. The theory is probably the death rattle of the defeated critics of Joseph Smith.

That Joseph Smith had the Book of Mormon plates, and translated from them the Book of Mormon is confirmed by Oliver Cowdery, who acted as Joseph's scribe while the Prophet dictated. At one time, after Cowdery had been severed from the Church, he was contemptuously charged by an attorney that he claimed to have seen the plates from which the Book of Mormon was translated. Oliver Cowdery answered:

> May it please the court and gentlemen of the jury: my brother attorney on the other side has charged me with connection with Joseph Smith and the golden Bible. The responsibility has been placed upon me, and I cannot escape reply.
>
> Before God and man I dare not deny what I have said, and what my testimony contains as written and printed on the front page of the Book of Mormon. May it please your honor and gentlemen of the jury, this I say: I saw the angel and heard his voice—how can I deny it? It happened in the daytime when the sun was shining brightly in the firmament; not at night when I was asleep. The glorious messenger from heaven, dressed in white, standing above the ground, in a glory I have never seen anything to compare with—the sun insignificant in comparison—told us if we denied that testimony there is no forgiveness in this life or in the world to come.
>
> Now how can I deny it—I dare not; I will not.[6]

Later, when Oliver Cowdery asked to be rebaptized, he spoke to the people as follows:

> I wrote with my own pen, the entire Book of Mormon (save a few pages) as it fell from the lips of the Prophet Joseph Smith, as he translated it by the gift and power of God, by the means of the Urim and Thummim, or, as it is called by that book, "Holy Interpreters."
>
> I beheld with my eyes and handled with my hands the gold plates from which it was translated. I also saw with my eyes and handled with my hands the "Holy Interpreters."
>
> That book is true! Sidney Rigdon did not write it; Mr. Spaulding did not write it; I wrote it myself as it fell from the lips of the Prophet. It contains the everlasting Gospel, and came forth to the children of men in fulfillment of the revelations of John, where he says he saw an angel come with the Everlasting Gospel to preach to every nation, kindred, tongue, and people. It contains the principles of salvation; and if you, my hearers, will walk by its light

---
[6]*Liahona*, vol. 8, p. 163.

and obey its precepts, you will be saved with an everlasting salvation in the kingdom of God on high.[7]

What more can honest men ask?

After examining the long shelves of books on Mormonism, a wearisome and thankless task, there is but one conclusion: Joseph Smith wrote the Book of Mormon unaided by mortal man. That is also the verdict of history.

---

[7]*Millennial Star*, vol. 27, p. 57.

CHAPTER 15

EARLY WRITINGS ABOUT THE MORMONS

The publication of the Book of Mormon and the organization of the Church were followed by a steady flow of newspaper stories, pamphlets, and books, dealing chiefly with Joseph Smith and the creditability of his claims.

Few of these publications gave serious consideration to the doctrine and system of organization of the restored Church. None gave critical consideration to the Mormon movement. Nearly all aimed primarily to destroy belief in Joseph Smith and his claims. Nearly all rested their whole case upon statements made in Howe's book *Mormonism Unvailed*. The few which did not do so set up personal unproved opinions about Joseph Smith and his work. This was the method of writers about Mormonism in Joseph's day, and unfortunately during the century since his martyrdom.

Eight or more pamphlets and eight or more books, including Howe's *Mormonism Unvailed*, discussed in a previous chapter, form the bulk of non-Mormon and anti-Mormon literature from 1831 to 1844. There are a number of other pamphlets mostly published in England, but relying chiefly on doctrinal points. A simple examination of this literature shows how untrustworthy it is.

Alexander Campbell made the earliest attempt, after the Dogberry articles, to prove Joseph Smith a false prophet, but Campbell later changed his explanation. Campbell first wrote a review called *Delusions* of the Book of Mormon which was published in his *Millennial Harbinger* on February 7, 1831, ten months after the organization of the Church. This article was republished in a pamphlet of sixteen pages with a foreword by Joshua V. Himes, in 1832, under the title "Delusions." Mr. Campbell was greatly vexed because prominent members of his congregation, Sidney Rigdon, Parley P. Pratt, Edward Partridge, and others, had accepted the gospel as taught by Joseph Smith. This vexation runs through the whole pamphlet.

The booklet is essentially "an analysis of the Book of Mormon, with an examination of its internal and external evidences, and a refutation of its pretenses to divine authority." After the analysis he sets up several points of refutation. Essentially, he objects to the Book of Mormon doctrine that the gospel did not begin with Christ on earth, that priesthood can be held by others than Levites, and that temple worship and other ordinances may be performed elsewhere than in Jerusalem. He calls attention to two questionable historical statements and two quotations he thinks originated after Book of Mormon times. These "refutations" have long since perished, under critical study, even by non-Mormons, and are used only by extreme enemies of the cause of Joseph Smith. He contends, however, but in unbecoming language, that Joseph Smith was the author of the book: "Smith, its real author, as ignorant and impudent a knave as ever wrote a book."[1]

He admits that the Book of Mormon deals with "every error and almost every truth discussed in New York State for the last ten years," yet declares it to be the "meanest book in the English language—it has not one good sentence in it."[2] The language of the book which scholarship has found to be good, he contends is so crude as to prove Joseph Smith the author. The witnesses to the Book of Mormon he dismisses as "interested retailers."[3] He would not have noticed the book, he says apologetically, "had not several hundred persons of different denominations believed in it."[4]

The pamphlet is a pitiful, superficial venture, by a man of great parts. He must later have scourged himself for running prematurely, not fully informed, into the

---

[1]Alexander Campbell, *Delusions*, pp. 11-12.
[2]*Ibid.*, pp. 13-15.
[3]*Ibid.*, p. 15.
[4]*Ibid.*, p. 11.

controversy, when he saw his arguments one after the other torn to shreds. Truth must be loved above all else, to accept it.

However, two things are to be noted: he felt certain that Joseph Smith wrote the Book of Mormon; and though he hurled invective against Joseph Smith, whom he had probably never seen, he seems to have heard nothing derogatory about the Smith family. Such was the first book published in Joseph's day against himself and the Book of Mormon.

By 1836 the Mormons had found their way into a statistical survey of the land. True, the author[5] places the Mormons in an appendix, where he can give them special attention. He announces that they are mostly in Ohio and Missouri, though there are many in Canada. In telling the story of the "Mormonites," he draws on the authority of Howe's book, but ventures no opinion of his own. He publishes the creed of the Church as presented by Joseph Young.

By 1838 many pamphlets began to appear about and usually against the Mormons. Origen Batchelor[6] felt it his duty to warn the public about the worst "liars and impostors, who ever breathed." He becomes eloquent in his anger, as he denounces the foundation of the Church as a "fable," "the most ridiculous, the most imbecile, the most contemptible concern" ever palmed off as revelation. "Its author was a quiz or a blockhead, but no ingenious impostor." He follows almost slavishly Campbell's *Delusions* and Howe's *Mormonism Unvailed*. He accepts without question the affidavits and the Rigdon-Spaulding theory in that book.

Richard Livesey,[7] a minister of the Methodist Episcopal Church at Winchester, Massachusetts, on a visit to the old country found that news of the Mormons had reached his native England. To answer questions and

---

[5]John Maynard, *The Religious Creeds and Statistics of Every Christian Denomination in the United States and British Provinces*, 1836 edition pp. 1-156.
[6]Origen Batchelor, *Mormonism Exposed*, 1838 edition, p. 48, Boston.
[7]Richard Livesey, *Exposure of Mormonism*, 1838 edition, p. 12, Preston, England.

to protect the public he wrote a pamphlet. He frankly admits that he has compiled it from American books on the subject. He swallows without reservation the Howe book with its affidavits and the Rigdon-Spaulding theory. The witnesses to the Book of Mormon are explained as being a collusive family affair. Mormonism to him is a system of money making. This pamphlet appeared in England before the missionaries arrived and curiously enough in the town (Preston) where the English work of the Church began.

James McChesney,[8] also a Methodist minister, whose home was in Brooklyn, New York, heard that two Mormon elders, Curtis and Parley P. Pratt, had won converts in New York and Brooklyn. He notes that there are fifty thousand in the United States and four thousand in England. He saw that it was a "battle of extermination" and "a desperate combat." So he challenged the elders to debate, but too late, for they had left for another appointment. But to satisfy his conscience he wrote a tract, pointing out the iniquities of the Mormons who "drink and secure money unlawfully." As he went along he became lost in Biblical arguments against Mormon doctrine and finally admitted that it contained some truth. He swallowed the Howe book with relish. He also adds to our knowledge by saying that the word Mormon is derived from the Hebrew, and means apostate, rebel against God, or an infidel!

John Corrill,[9] who withdrew from the Church, wrote in temperate and moderate language the history of the early Church. He left the Church, he said because of its many afflictions which proved to him that it was not being led by God. He paid no attention to the scurrilous writings against the Church. He made careful personal investigation of Joseph Smith and felt assured that the Prophet and none other wrote the Book of Mormon. He

---

[8]James McChesney, *An Antidote to Mormonism*, 1838 edition, p. 60, New York, Supplement, 1839.
[9]John Corrill, *A Brief History of the Church of Latter-day Saints*, 1839 edition, p. 50.

also met the witnesses to the book, but was not able to impeach them.

John Simon,[10] follower of Richard Livesey, knew little about the subject, but echoed what he had heard. England must be protected! Howe's book was used. Joseph Smith and Martin Harris were called the Gold Bible Company. The whole thing, he thought, was a deep-laid scheme of swindling.

Dr. Adrian Orr [11] was a minister in Palmyra in Joseph Smith's day. His pamphlet was really compiled from notes on a debate between him and E. H. Davis, a Mormon elder. He told of a visit in 1827 of Martin Harris. Notably, he did not quote Howe, nor did he mention Rigdon. He did say that Joseph Smith came of a shiftless family. He devoted himself almost wholly to supposed disagreements between the Bible and the Book of Mormon. Mormonism to him was the latest "scheme of hell."

William Harris,[12] a former member of the Church reviewed the history of the Church, dwelling especially on the Missouri period. He quoted from John A. Clark, which meant that he accepted Howe's theories. As for the early events, Joseph lied and the witnesses were deceived, so he says.

Daniel F. Kidder[13] frankly admitted that his work was based upon information gathered from the books of Howe and Corrill, and deplored the "want of material" for his use. He trotted out the Howe affidavits to prove the vicious character of the Smith family, and accepted without further consideration the genuineness of the Sidney Rigdon-Spaulding Theory. He called Joseph Smith an impostor, hypocrite, and liar, with Martin Harris second in importance in the "fraud." He went so far as to say that the witnesses to the Book of Mormon might have seen some plates, but they had no ability to discover the deception practised upon them.

[10]John Simon, *A Few More Facts*, 1840 edition, p. 18, Ledbury, England.
[11]Dr. Adrian Orr, *Mormonism Dissected*, 1841 edition, p. 12, Bethaina, Pennsylvania.
[12]William Harris, *Mormonism Portrayed*, 1841 edition, p. 61, Warsaw, Illinois.
[13]Daniel F. Kidder, *Mormonism and the Mormons*, 1842 edition, p. 342, New York.

In passing, he estimated that the Church had at that time (1841) eighteen thousand members, eight thousand five hundred in Nauvoo, three thousand in the United States and Canada, six thousand five hundred in Great Britain.

Dr. John A. Clark[14] was a minister in Palmyra during the early years of Joseph Smith. He was inclined to accept the Rigdon-Spaulding theory advanced in *Mormonism Unvailed*. He did not of course accept the divine origin of Joseph's work. He vacillated much in coming to this conclusion.

In 1842 appeared also the almost unspeakable book by John C. Bennett.[15] He joined the Church and professed great love for the restored gospel. It was soon discovered that not only was he disloyal to the Church, but was also suspected of immoral practices. After eighteen months in the Church he was excommunicated. Then he set about, much as Philastus Hurlburt, to destroy the Church.

Bennett confessed that he had never believed in the restored gospel but joined the Church to discover its inner conditions. He excused himself for this contemptible action in a religious organization by reminding his readers that Napoleon in Egypt became a Mohammedan! Then he branched into an unorganized body of affidavits, clippings, letters, and presentations, all contributing to prove that "I, John C. Bennett, is the great I am," without adding a whit to what had been told and printed over and over numerous times. He swallowed everything that could mar the Mormons and decorated it with his own brand of hate. Untruth after untruth, self-praise after self-praise, litter the book. Naturally the book has received scant notice by writers on Mormonism, whether for or against the work of Joseph Smith. It is a pitiful exhibition by a man trying to hide his own sins.

The life of John C. Bennett has recently been studied. His career was that of an uncertain, changeable individual,

---

[14]Rev. John A. Clark, D.D., *Gleanings By the Way*, 1842 edition, pp. 216-352,– Philadelphia–New York.
[15]John C. Bennett, *History of the Saints*, 1842 edition, p. 344, New York.

who did not anywhere succeed in satisfying his ambitions.[16] At the end of his life, as chicken raiser, he had little of merit to look back upon.

Professor J. B. Turner,[17] a Presbyterian minister, was a member of the faculty of Illinois College in Jacksonville, Illinois. He stated that the sources of his information were the Book of Mormon, Doctrine and Covenants, and early Church publications, in addition to *Facts Relative to the Expulsion of the Mormons from Missouri*, by J. P. Greene; *History of the Church* by John Corrill; *Biography of "Dr." Hurlburt*, by Winchester; *Letters* by Booth; *Mormonism Portrayed* by William Harris. He was of the opinion that Mormonism was the "most dangerous and violent enemy to our political and religious party." He classed Mormonism with atheism and Romanism. He considered Joseph Smith's attempt to "translate" the Bible ridiculous.

Professor Turner was one of the few writers on Mormonism who attempted to discuss the principles of the new faith. He classed speaking in tongues, visions, etc., as evidences of mental, emotional instability.

The testimonies of the witnesses of the Book of Mormon he held of little value because no details were given.

While he did not mention Howe's book, he used the affidavits in that book. However, he set up an entirely new theory of the origin of the Book of Mormon. Sidney Rigdon and Parley P. Pratt he thought were the "original founders." As early as 1827, three years before the Church was restored, these men, with Joseph Smith as a tool, began to plan Mormonism. Rigdon was long accustomed to play upon people's beliefs; and the doctrines announced by the Church were his cherished doctrines.

In passing, Turner says that seven months after its organization the Church had about eighty members. Like

[16]*History of the Church*, vol. 5, pp. 67-82; *Life of John C. Bennett* (Manuscript) Historian's Office.
[17]J. B. Turner, *Mormonism in all Ages, or the Rise, Progress, and Cause of Mormonism*, 1842 edition, p. 304, New York, and London.

other writers on this subject he informed the reader that his work was done "in a few weeks of leisure."

Reverend Henry Caswall,[18] M.A., an Englishman, a Professor of Divinity in Kemper College, St. Louis, Missouri, spent three days, in 1842, in civilian dress, in Nauvoo, after seeing in St. Louis three hundred English converts on their way to Nauvoo. He told about the sport he had in fooling Joseph Smith and the people whom he met into believing that a Greek psalter he had with him was a new find, perhaps a lost scripture for the Prophet to decipher. He attributed to the Prophet the appearance of a knave and a clown, using exceedingly coarse language.

In reporting his talk with Joesph Smith, he forgot that the Prophet and many other Church members had studied, Greek, Hebrew, and other languages, sufficiently to recognize Greek script. Such mistakes are often made by those who fail to tell the truth. Caswall's bitter opposition to Mormonism was revealed in the book he wrote a year later.

After meeting the Mormons, attending a Sunday meeting in the grove and talking with many people, he concluded that the success of the Church lay in the "system and discipline" maintained.

He noted that the population of Nauvoo was shrinking. A year later Reverend Caswall[19] published a book on the Mormons. He did not list the Howe book among his authorities but followed J. B. Turner, who accepted Howe. He used the Howe affidavits and the Rigdon-Spaulding theory of the coming forth of the Book of Mormon. He concluded that Mormonism was a product of fanaticism and "Campbellism." He suggested that Joseph Smith's own story as published was fabricated to satisfy inquirers.

These are the major contributions to Mormon literature by anti-Mormons, during the lifetime of Joseph Smith. Nothing new was produced. In the main, they repeated

---

[18]Henry Caswall, *The City of the Mormons,* 1842 edition, p. 82, London.
[19]Henry Caswall, *The Prophet of the Nineteenth Century,* 1843 edition, p. 277, London.

endlessly the charges made in the Dogberry articles and Howe's book, *Mormonism Unvailed*. Some of the writers revealed their hate of Mormonism by their distortion of events and facts, as for example, Caswall, in his report of his conversation with Joseph Smith about the Greek psalter. If Joseph called attention to the similarity of a letter in the psalter to an Egyptian symbol, it became at once in Caswall's memory evidence of the Prophet's ignorance.

The literature produced against the Mormons is an evidence for the truth of Joseph Smith's story.

CHAPTER 16

THE VERDICT OF GENEALOGY

Whenever an unusual man appears, people commonly inquire into his ancestry and often seek there the cause of his achievements. Fortunately, the genealogy of Joseph Smith is known in detail back to about 1600.[1]

It is especially important to know the ancestral history of Joseph since some enemies have suggested that he suffered from hereditary weaknesses, which made possible the hoax, as they called it, of the Book of Mormon.

On the direct paternal side Joseph Smith was descended from a Robert Smith, who in 1638, as a boy about fifteen years old, came from England to America. It is very likely that his ancestral home was in Lincolnshire, in or near the town of Willoughby, the home of Captain John Smith of early colonial fame, to whom Robert Smith was probably related.[2] In America, Robert Smith and his descendants lived in Massachusetts, chiefly in or near Topsfield of that state.

On the direct maternal side his genealogy is traced back to John Mack, a Scotchman who in 1669 came to America. The Mack family lived chiefly in and about Lyne, Connecticut.[3]

Joseph Smith's genealogical table reveals an ancestry in which appear numerous highly respected New England family names and personalities, some notable in American history.

Joseph's ancestors took a lively part in the building of the new world. They broke new land, built homes, served in civic capacities, held professional positions, and were generally good, honorable, and often leading citizens. Some acquired substantial properties; others appear to

---

[1]Archibald F. Bennett, "The Ancestry of Joseph Smith the Prophet," *Utah Genealogical and Historical Magazine*, vol. 20, pp. 1, 49
[2]Joseph Fielding Smith, *Life of Joseph F. Smith*, p. 15.
[3]Lucy Mack Smith, *History of the Prophet Joseph*, p. 44.

have had literary gifts; others again were doctors and ministers of the gospel. A number rose to distinction in their pioneer environment.

During the Revolutionary period and before, many of Joseph Smith's ancestors, on both paternal and maternal sides, took courageous and unflinching part in the movements, including army service, that led to the formation of the United States of America. Joseph Smith's great-grandfather, Samuel Smith, took part officially in several activities that led to the break between America and the mother country. He was chairman of the "tea committee" in 1773, when disputes arose with England over taxation. Though of advanced age, he served honorably in the army of the Revolution.

His son, Asael, Joseph Smith's grandfather, who also served honorably in the army of the Revolution, was of strong religious convictions. He looked forward to a more correct and complete Christian worship than was then in existence on earth. He left his views on the subject to his posterity in a published address.[4] Others of Joseph's ancestors had spiritual leanings, hoping for a better way to happiness in this, and salvation in the next world. In this they were not unique, for many looked forward to a religion more compatible with the teachings of Christ.

The ancestors of Joseph Smith were toilers for daily subsistence for themselves and their families. But they were intelligent people, with opinions of their own. They were not visionary people but sturdy lovers of truth and liberty. That is shown, fortunately, by the mass of existing evidence. That some of them had dreams has been held against them. Most people have dreams, and many people discuss their dreams and try to interpret them. That is not uncommon.[5]

Pure honorable blood coursed through Joseph's veins. The family were remarkably free from physical and mental

---

[4] *History of the Church*, vol. 1, p. 9
[5] Lucy Mack Smith, *op. cit.*, pp. 1-44.

diseases. Joseph's ancestry was distinguished for the simple virtues that make a nation great.

The father of Joseph Smith was born at Topsfield, Massachusetts, in 1771; his mother, Lucy Mack, at Gilsum, New Hampshire, in 1776. They were married in 1796. Seven sons and three daughters were born to them.

After a period of financial reverses, they moved in 1815 from New England to the neighborhood of Palmyra, New York State, hoping there to better their circumstances. Their life record up to that date was without blemish. That has been acknowledged even by violent enemies. In Palmyra they sought such employment, aside from their farm labor, as was available. Pomeroy Tucker whose newspaper was printed in the shop in which the Book of Mormon was printed, closely acquainted with members of the family, spoke of them as honest people, busy with "gardening, harvesting, well digging, etc. . . . understood to secure a scanty, but honest living."[6]

They were Bible-reading, religious-minded people, with full respect for the commandments of the Lord. It was a Christian household. Family prayers were always held at home.[7] His mother in her book on her son's life gives a picture of their family life. It was just after Moroni's visit and the first view of the golden plates:

I presume our family presented an aspect as singular as any that lived upon the face of the earth—all seated in a circle, father, mother, sons and daughters, and give the most profound attention to a boy, eighteen years of age, who had never read the Bible through in his life; he seemed much less inclined to the perusal of books than any of the rest of our children, but far more given to meditation and deep study.

However, when the boy announced his First Vision, and especially later, after the publication of the Book of Mormon and the organization of the Church, a storm of persecution broke upon the head of Joseph Smith,

[6]Pomeroy Tucker, *Origin, Rise, and Progress of Mormonism*, p. 12.
[7]William Smith, brother of the Prophet, *Deseret News*, January 20, 1894.
[8]Lucy Mack Smith, *op, cit.*, 1853 edition, p. 84; 1902 edition, p. 84; 1945 edition, p. 82.

which overflowed upon the members of the family. He and they suddenly became, so their enemies would have us believe, a degraded, lazy, shiftless set of people. It is remarkable that in this torrent of charges, no individual has claimed that he himself was injured; it was always some other person. The suddenness of this change is of itself an evidence that the charges were not founded in truth. Gossip and deliberate misrepresentation do not make true history. The frailties of the Smith family, if any, were those of their time and community.

His mother writes:

> Nothing occurred during his [Joseph's] early life, except those trivial circumstances which are common to that state of human existence.[9]

Joseph Smith was a loving, industrious, and obedient boy. In his early boyhood he suffered a leg infection so serious that the doctors thought an amputation of the leg necessary but first made another attempt to cure the malady by scraping the bone. In those days of no anesthetics this was a most painful operation.

Joseph refused to be bound to the bedstead, as was the custom of the day, or to drink the brandy which the doctor felt might help him withstand the pain.

> "No," exclaimed Joseph, "I will not touch one particle of liquor. Neither will I be tied down. I will tell you what I will do. I will have my father sit on the bed and hold me in his arms, and then I will do whatever is necessary to have the bone taken out. . . Mother, I want you to leave the room, for I know you cannot bear to see me suffer so.[10]

The operation, though intensely painful, was successful.

The heroic quality in this story foreshadows the courage that led the boy to seek independently the true Church of Jesus Christ. It reveals also the tender heart, filled with love, manifested in his dealings with all men.

---

[9]*Ibid.*, 1853 edition, p. 73.
[10]*Ibid.*, 1902 edition, pp. 60-63; 1945 edition, p. 57.

Joseph Smith had little formal schooling, for schools were not plentiful in those days. Nevertheless, he learned to read very well and to know the literature available on the frontier, chiefly the Bible. Despite such early limited school training, he later gained much learning in many disciplines such as languages, law, literature, history, etc.

The boy Joseph helped his father on the farm; therefore, he is sometimes spoken of as a plowboy. But in doing such work, he came near to nature and nature's ways, which did him much good in later life.

Joseph's family, who knew him best, believed him to be honest and truthful. Mother Smith tells of "the sweetest union and happiness [that] pervaded our home and [the] tranquility [that] reigned in our midst"[11] when Joseph told of his spiritual experiences.

His brother, William, who lived long after Joseph's death, confirmed Joseph's truthfulness as a boy. He said:

> We all had the most implicit confidence of (in) what he said. He was a truthful boy. Our mother believed him, why should not the children? I suppose if he had told crooked stories about other things we might have doubted his word, but Joseph was a truthful boy. That Father and Mother believed him and suffered persecution for that belief shows he was truthful. No sir, we never doubted his word for one minute.[12]

Most of the near relatives of Joseph Smith, after investigation, accepted Joseph's claims and in course of time became members of the Church. It is difficult to believe that this could occur, if the family were as evil, or if Joseph were as dishonest as reported to be.

Carefully examined, there is no acceptable evidence to support the charges against the Smith family and Joseph Smith as a boy and young man. His life as a boy was normal and worthy of imitation by all lovers of truth. That writers, even in our day, would reproduce silly and untrue charges, suggests that they may have set out to

---

[11]*Ibid.*, 1902 edition, p. 84; 1945 edition, pp. 82-83.
[12]*Deseret News*, January 20, 1894, p. 11.

destroy Mormonism rather than to detail true history. They have used untruth garnered with hate.

In short, Joseph Smith's ancestry, at least for three hundred years, as far as the record goes, was intelligent, honorable, and law-abiding. His immediate family upheld the ideals of their ancestors. His own life showed faith in God, love of truth, courage to think for himself and to face physical pain, and love for his dear ones. These were characteristics of his whole life.

Chapter 17

THE CHURCH FORESHADOWED

Joseph Smith was told in his First Vision that the churches had gone astray and that the true Church of Jesus Christ was about to be restored. How that church was to be organized and what it was to teach and do were not then revealed to him. Later truths were revealed which foreshadowed the structure of the Church in organization and doctrine. These revelations gradually prepared the young man's mind for a more complete understanding of the work he had to do in re-establishing the gospel of Jesus Christ's coming Church. When in 1830 the Church was organized, it was as a completion of truths already taught.

This is well shown in the recorded teachings of Moroni to the young man. When Moroni appeared three years after the First Vision, he showed by quoting freely from the Bible that the time of the promised restoration had long since been prophetically foretold and that it had now arrived.

In quoting from the Bible, Moroni followed the King James English text without change, except when quoting from Malachi 4:5-6. Here he made notable deviations from the text. These are found upon examination to be in the nature of preparatory explanations of the organization and doctrine of the coming Church.

This quotation, preserved as Section Two of the Doctrine and Covenants, reads as follows:

> Behold, I will reveal unto you the Priesthood, by the hand of Elijah the prophet, before the coming of the great and dreadful day of the Lord.
>
> And he shall plant in the hearts of the children the promises made to the fathers, and the hearts of the children shall turn to their fathers.
>
> If it were not so, the whole earth would be utterly wasted at his coming.

The opening words, "I will reveal" carried a pregnant meaning for the young man. It set aside all claims based upon the so-called "inward call." They implied that the Church to be organized must be built upon authority received from God. This would render invalid the churches of Joseph's day, which one after another had originated through the efforts of men who relied upon their own conceptions of the written word. All Protestant churches make no other claim; and the Roman Catholic Church, claiming direct descent of its authority, cannot complete the links of the chain. Instead, authority traceable to God directly was to be the foundation of the Church to be restored. Only when the church is so divinely commissioned are its acts valid. Every officer must make sure that his commission is without flaw if his acts are to be recognized by the Lord.

The following words: "I will reveal the Priesthood," made the first more emphatic. The authority implied in the opening words was that flowing from God himself. In other churches priesthood, the right of men to act for God and in his name, a part of God's own power, had been assumed by men upon their own authority. This was not to be done in restoring the Church of Jesus Christ. On the contrary, its power would rest in a priesthood conferred by God upon men.

How priesthood was to be transmitted appeared in the following words, "I will reveal unto you the Priesthood, by the hand of Elijah." That is, priesthood is received by the laying on of hands by one who has himself received it in that manner. To be valid, the priesthood held by a man must be traceable through the authoritative imposition of hands back to God, the author of the priesthood. That left to the churches of the day, which could not trace their priesthood from man to man to God, only a man-made, invalid priesthood. In short, priesthood authority from God passed on from man to man by actual contact was to be the foundation of the Church which Joseph had been called to restore. Equally pregnant in meaning is the statement that "he [Elijah] shall plant in the hearts of the children the promises made to the fathers." The word "fathers," as used here, unquestionably refers to all the ancestors of man, back to the first father, Adam. The implication is that certain promises had been made to mankind from the earliest man. The mentioned "promises" can only mean those flowing from the priesthood, that is, the gifts of the gospel. The gospel, then, to be taught by the coming Church, is universal, and its ordinances are the same for all. It is not only for the living who may accept it, but also for the "fathers," back to the first day. All who have been sent to earth must have the opportunity to enjoy the blessings of the gospel. The promise to the fathers is that by yielding obedience to gospel ordinances here or hereafter salvation may be won. The door to salvation is never closed. That is the greatest promise made to humanity.

This implies that the earthly ordinances of the gospel must be performed by the living for the dead, who cannot help themselves. All are dependent upon earthly ordinances for legal entry into the Church. The law is the same for the dead as for the living. This work will be done for the dead when, "The hearts of the children shall turn to the fathers." The work will then be done in the spirit of love.

This then would be the duty of the Church: The gospel of the Lord Jesus Christ is for all who dwell or have dwelt upon earth. Those who have not heard it must hear it. Those who have entered the spirit world as well as the living must be taught the gospel. The "other world" is a place of intelligent action, of the exercise of the untrammeled will. All this must be done under the authority of a priesthood descended from God.

It must have stirred Joseph to his very depths as this meaning dawned upon him.

Elijah the prophet had been assigned a certain portion of the work for the salvation of souls. He did appear in the Kirtland Temple on April 3, 1836,[1] and conferred the authority of the priesthood to act on earth for those beyond, who had died while the gospel was not on earth.

All this is to be done "before the coming of the great and dreadful day of the Lord"—the day when Christ shall come—a glorious day for those who have lived righteously. The revelation closes with a warning. This work of universal salvation must be done, the Church must be active in working out the purposes of creation: "If it were not so, the whole earth would be utterly wasted at his coming." Simply: the earth plan is for all men; if all are not given full opportunity to hear and embrace it, the purposes of the Lord for his children will fail.

There is no evidence on record that at this time the Prophet, his associates, or persons anywhere understood the universality of the gospel. Only years after Moroni's visit did this Church receive further information concerning the "promises made to the fathers."

In such vast outlines the work of the coming Church was impressed upon the youth. He began to understand, yet only dimly, the purposes of the Lord in having his Church on earth. After having pondered this message, Joseph could receive more information about his work. The method of divinity is always a series of progressive, unfolding steps. The human mind needs time to absorb new truths. Growth in gospel understanding is noticeable in Joseph's whole career. Moroni's message was followed with more detailed information.

This is the foundation of the temple work of the Church. The spirit of the temples is to knit together the whole human family. This spirit becomes as it were the keystone of the gospel arch. Take it away, and the blocks of the gospel arch fall into a mass of unorganized doctrines.

The greatest, grandest, and most fundamental doctrines of the Church are foreshadowed in the few words that constitute this brief revelation.

Joseph Smith, the boy of little learning, could not

---
[1]*Doctrine and Covenants* 110:13.

have constructed, by his own power, the splendid epitome of faith of the Church of Jesus Christ of Latter-day Saints found in the few simple words of Moroni. Standing as it does, the solitary written monument of the first twenty-four years of the Prophet's life, it becomes one of the most wonderful evidences of the divine inspiration of Joseph Smith.

Four years after the first visit of Moroni, the Book of Mormon plates, the breastplate, and the Urim and Thummim were delivered to Joseph. During the period of translation and the printing of the Book of Mormon, Joseph told his friends of his spiritual experiences. There was in that little group of believers—coming members of the Church to be restored—the spirit of communion between man and God, such as should exist everywhere and at all times. It must have been a happy time for the translator, the scribe, and their friends. Many events and questions required answers.

Joseph made inquiries from the Lord through the Urim and Thummim, which was used in translating the Book of Mormon. These recorded early revelations, numbering about eighteen, cover the period of February, 1829, to March, 1830. Fourteen came during the busy months of translation—months that were filled with intense spiritual experiences. It was a rich preparation for the work of establishing the Church of Jesus Christ. Gospel principles were touched upon in every divine communication. Joseph seemed enveloped in the knowledge and spirit that should pervade the coming restoration of the Church. It was an unparalleled preparation for the work that lay ahead.

Some of these early communications from the Lord were answers to individual requests; others were answers to questions arising in the translation; still others dealt with fundamental doctrine and the organization of the coming Church. They explained that the Father's plan of salvation was under the leadership of Jesus the Christ and pointed out the heavy price he paid in suffering to fill his Father's assignment.[2]   The organized Church was to have a body of men called Apostles, as in former days, to bear witness to the world of the re-establishment of the ancient faith.[3]   Three men were to see the "golden plates" and become witnesses of their reality.[4]   The spirit of revelation which was to guide the Church might be enjoyed by every member as a witness of the truth of the coming restoration.[5]   The ethical structure of the Church was rehearsed, culminating in faith, hope, and charity.[6] Many admonitions were given.   The young Prophet was to seek wisdom, not riches,[7] must not run faster than he had strength,[8] should engage in no contentions,[9] and should always speak the truth in soberness.[10]   How men may realize their good desires is pointed out,[11] and that men may be judged by their desires and wishes.[12]   The value of the human soul is emphasized.[13]   An interesting bit of ancient history appears, involving Jesus and his Apostles Peter and John.[14]   Several of these revelations are answers to requests from individuals to know their duties before the Lord.   Indeed, it was to be a complete restoration of the pure gospel of Jesus Christ as when he, himself, brought it to earth.

This and much else found in the revelations given to the Prophet, before the Church was organized, were as intimations of the truths the Church when organized must bring into action.   Throughout them all runs the doctrine of the supremacy of God, and that eternal blessings and punishments are his blessings and punishments, which are not to be circumscribed by any definition by man.[15]

---

[2]*Doctrine and Covenants,* Section 19.
[3]*Ibid.,* Section 18.
[4]*Ibid.,* Sections 5, 17.
[5]*Ibid.,* Sections 8, 9.
[6]*Ibid.,* Section 4.
[7]*Ibid.,* Section 9.
[8]*Ibid.,* Section 10.
[9]*Ibid.,* Section 18.
[10]*Ibid.,* Section 18.
[11]*Ibid.,* Section 11.
[12]*Ibid.,* Section 18.
[13]*Ibid.,* Section 18.
[14]*Ibid.,* Section 7.
[15]*Ibid.,* Section 19.

They contain doctrine of profound import to humanity far beyond the questions asked.

Running through these revelations are passages of profound meaning hardly to be expected from the mouth of a man unacquainted with the world's learning. They are overflowing with statements and declarations of the greatest importance to mankind. They were necessary in restoring the Church of Jesus Christ. The doctrines that they contain were as foundation stones in the restoration of the gospel of Jesus Christ. They form a remarkable testimony of an "inspiration beyond the natural powers of man."

These revelations are evidences of the method used by Divinity to educate the Prophet for his work. To have given him at one time, inexperienced as he was, the whole content of the gospel would have been beyond the capacity of the young man to comprehend or assimilate. A gradual unfolding of the work was more in harmony with man's nature, whether on earth or beyond. It is the method of natural education. Therefore, the work to be done came to the Prophet as progressive steps, as intimations of the completed plan. Thus the early work of the Prophet may best be understood. In this manner he was prepared for the restoration of the Church itself.

That these revelations were actually submitted by Joseph to his friends on the dates mentioned has never been questioned. Enemies who are seeking refuge by casting doubts upon the correctness of Joseph Smith's own story would do well to review the many verified events of the Church which all point to the improbability of any false date, especially a major one in the simple story of Joseph Smith.[16]

---

[16]Painesville *Telegraph*, March 15 and September 13, 1831.

CHAPTER 18

THE DILEMMA OF AUTHORITY

The translation of the Book of Mormon took a little more than three months. Day by day Joseph Smith dictated, and Oliver Cowdery wrote. For a change and rest they walked to the nearby wood, or to the stately Susquehanna River. Often they were accompanied by interested friends.

Always they discussed the new truths set forth in the Nephite records. They felt the presence and power of God as the meaning of the engravings on the plates was revealed. They were immersed in a spiritual atmosphere of powerful intensity. All this prepared them for the great manifestations to come.

One day, May 15, 1829, Joseph and Oliver found in their work mention of baptism. Then the whole question of this ordinance became a subject of their discussion. Therefore, according to their custom, they went into the woods, and upon their knees asked God to give them light.

Unexpectedly, after the prayer was offered, there appeared before them a heavenly messenger, "in a cloud of light," who declared himself to be John the Baptist, the forerunner of Christ in the Meridian of Time.

He had come, he said, to confer upon them the Aaronic Priesthood, of which he was the head in the days of the Savior. This was to be done so that they might have authority to perform the baptism about which they had prayed. He then ordained them, by the laying on of hands, to the priesthood of Aaron, and told them since they now had the authority to do so, to repair to the neighboring stream and there baptize each other by immersion.

The messenger explained many other things to them. He said that in course of time the Melchizedek or Higher Priesthood would be conferred upon them; that the Church would soon be organized, in which Joseph Smith should be the first and Oliver Cowdery the second elder.[1]

The effect of this experience upon the two young men may be felt in a statement made later by Oliver Cowdery:

> On a sudden, as from the midst of eternity, the voice of the Redeemer spake peace to us, while the veil was parted and the angel of God [John the Baptist] came down clothed with glory and delivered the anxiously looked for message, and the keys of the gospel of repentance. What joy! What wonder! What amazement!
>
> While the world was racked and distracted, while millions were groping as the blind for the wall, and while all men were resting upon uncertainty, as a general mass our eyes beheld—our ears heard. As the blaze of day, yes more, above the glitter of the May sunbeam, which shed its brilliancy over the face of nature!
>
> Then his voice, though mild, pierced to the center, and his words, "I am thy fellow servant" dispelled every fear. We listened! We gazed! We admired! 'Twas the voice from the angel of glory— 'twas a message from the Most High, and as we heard we rejoiced, while his love enkindled upon our souls, and we were rapt in the vision of the Almighty! Where was room for doubt? Nowhere; uncertainty had fled![2]

After the departure of John the Baptist, the young men obeyed his instructions. Joseph Smith baptized Oliver Cowdery first, and Oliver Cowdery then baptized Joseph Smith. Joseph writes:

> Immediately on our coming up out of the water, we experienced great and glorious blessings from our Heavenly Father. No sooner had I baptized Oliver Cowdery, than the Holy Ghost fell upon him, and he stood up and prophesied many things which should shortly come to pass. And again as soon as I had been baptized by him, I also had the spirit of prophecy. When standing up I prophesied concerning the rise of the Church, and many other things connected with the Church, and this generation of the children of men. We were filled with the Holy Ghost, and rejoiced in the God of our salvation.[3]

This experience was brought to the attention of several of their friends. Samuel H. Smith, the Prophet's

---

[1]*History of the Church*, vol. 1, p. 40.
[2]*Messenger and Advocate*, 1834; *History of the Church*, vol. 1, p. 43; Kirkham, *A New Witness for Christ in America*, p. 82.
[3]*History of the Church*, vol. 1 p. 42.

brother, heard Joseph's whole story from the vision in 1820, all that had happened, and the intention of the Lord to restore his gospel and the full authoritative organization of his Church.

Samuel was touched in his heart and requested baptism. He became the first man to be baptized after Joseph Smith and Oliver Cowdery. Then, in succession, a small number of friends who had become convinced by spiritual and material evidence that Joseph Smith was telling the truth entered the waters of baptism.[4]

These baptisms, of course, were not for entrance into the Church, since the Church had not yet been established, but for the remission of sins, following faith and repentance, by which the candidates might begin new lives.

Within a month or so after the glorious visit of John the Baptist, some time between May 15 and July 15, 1829, the two young men were again in the woods praying for further light and understanding. This time, in answer to their prayer, they experienced another glorious event. Three personages appeared, who announced themselves as Peter, James, and John, Apostles of the Lord Jesus Christ, who served with him when the Master was on earth.

They had been sent to confer the Holy Melchizedek Priesthood, of which the Aaronic Priesthood is a part, on the two young men, so that they might have authority to function in the higher spiritual ordinances of the coming Church. These personages then laid their hands upon the heads of the young men, conferred upon them the Melchizedek Priesthood, and ordained them Apostles.[5]

These visitations and ordinations were two major acts in preparation for the organization of the Church. The two young men now had authority to perform under God's direction all necessary work in organizing the Church of Jesus Christ and in carrying forward the work of God

---

[4]*History of the Church*, vol 1, p. 51.
[5]*Ibid.*, vol. 1, pp. 40-41; *Doctrine and Covenants* 20:2-3.

upon earth. Joseph and Oliver began to understand that priesthood means authority and power to perform acts on earth in the name of God; and that priesthood given under God's authority is necessary to build God's kingdom. The meaning of Moroni's variations of the words of Malachi became clear to them.[6]

Little by little during this period of rich spiritual out-pouring all things required for the organization of the Church were provided. Looking back, it is marvelous to note how carefully provision was made for every need, so that the Church might be in possession of full power and authority to carry out the Lord's plan of salvation for his children. It was a continuation of the meticulous care which had been exercised by heaven from the First Vision on the spring day in 1820, in preparation for the restoration of the Church of Jesus Christ.

Joseph and Oliver, who were together every day, knew little about the history of the Christian Church since the days of Jesus. It is doubtful if they had heard of the numerous heated contentions and arguments about authority that had later split apostate Christianity into factions and creeds. Nor did they understand that ecclesiastical history shows with much clearness that the authority of the Christian churches cannot be traced back unbrokenly to the Lord Jesus Christ. The chain had been broken.[7]

It is therefore nothing short of remarkable that these two young men announced that they had received their authority directly from those who received it in ancient days from the Christ himself. It is the more remarkable that in preparation for the organization of the Church, the centuries-old dilemma of Church authority was so correctly solved. Since Joseph and Oliver received their priesthood authority directly from personages who had held the priesthood ages ago, and who had received it directly from Jesus the Christ, there were no broken links

---

[6]*History of the Church*, vol. 1, p. 43.
  [7]James L. Barker, *The Protestors of Christendom*, p. 40; B. H. Roberts, *Outline of Ecclesiastical History*; J. M. Sjodahl, *The Reign of Authority*; James E. Talmage, *The Great Apostasy*; J. Reuben Clark, Jr., *On The Way to Immortality and Eternal Life.*

in the succession for men to quibble about. It would have been so easy for the young men, had they been impostors, to follow the course of other churches, to set up their authority in their own way, and to let it go that way. But that was neither the correct way nor the Lord's way.

Of their own knowledge they probably did not comprehend the full meaning, power, and place of priesthood in the Church. But by the successive visitations here related, they were made to understand that priesthood, which is the power and authority of God, is the foundation of the Church of God. No Church without an authoritative priesthood is acceptable to the Lord, or may function in his name. Further they learned the basic doctrine that priesthood must descend from man to man by ordination, and cannot otherwise be possessed by any man.

The question has been asked, can those who have died reappear to the living, as did John the Baptist, and the Apostles, Peter, James, and John? The question strikes at the foundations of Christianity. Life after death is a basic doctrine of the gospel of Jesus Christ. So is the doctrine of the resurrection, the promise of which is to all the dead.

The Savior himself while on earth took Peter, James, and John to meet Moses and Elijah, long since translated. By the will of God, and under his direction, the dead may reappear on earth. Men who do not believe that such appearances as those recorded by Joseph Smith are possible cannot claim to be Christians.

It should be remembered also that Joseph Smith had an intelligent witness, Oliver Cowdery, to these experiences. He was not alone in bearing witness to the restoration of the priesthood.

The events in Joseph Smith's life never conflicted with the faith and doctrine laid out by the Savior. All this, the revelations, visitations, and ordinations, dovetailing into one another in the organizing of the Church, is another powerful evidence that Joseph Smith was directed by a higher power beyond his natural powers.

CHAPTER 19

THE "CONSTITUTION" OF THE CHURCH

The long-expected Church was to be organized on April 6, 1830. In preparation for this great event there was written, under the spirit of revelation, a simple, brief statement called the "Articles and Covenants" of the Church.[1] It forms a noble platform upon which the Church could be and has been built. This challenging document is often spoken of as the "constitution of the Church."

It is noteworthy that this constitution has remained unaltered since the organization of the Church. Not one word in it has been changed, as finally adopted by the Church. This is the more surprising in consideration of the many changing issues that the Church has had to meet. During this same period most churches have had to change or reinterpret many statements upon which their faith and practices rest. Not so with this statement produced through the inspiration of God by the instrumentality of the unlearned, untraveled, inexperienced youth, Joseph Smith! As need has arisen, new additions have been received, but in every case they are in full harmony with the original, fundamental statement. These "articles and covenants" stand today as another and impressive evidence of the divine nature of Joseph's work.

The revelation, for such it is, falls into four divisions: the authority, doctrine, priesthood, and practice of the Church.

It rehearses first[2] that the Church of our Lord and Savior Jesus Christ is to be organized under the direct authority of God. Joseph Smith, Jr., was called and ordained of God to initiate the work. The authority to perform the later work was left with the Church, for

---

[1]*Doctrine and Covenants*, Section 20.
[2]*Ibid.*, 20:1-16.

Joseph Smith and Oliver Cowdery were both ordained Apostles, so that full authority might flow from them. Further, it reviews the Book of Mormon, declares that its contents were written under inspiration and that the translation is correct.

In this preamble of authority the earlier work of Joseph Smith is briefly surveyed. Despite his youthful "entanglements" in the "vanities of the world" he was found worthy of his high calling. The Book of Mormon which he translated is a witness of the unchanging nature of the Lord, who speaks alike to his children everywhere. The discussion of authority ends with the warning that since Joseph's work has witnesses the rejection of it will turn to human condemnation.

This part of the revelation is a brief but emphatic declaration that the work of Joseph Smith was done under God's authority.

Following this eloquent declaration of authority is a brief but clear statement of the doctrine upon which the faith of the people must rest.[3] It is a concise review of the principles of the gospel and its history throughout the ages—past, present, and future. God created Adam and Eve and gave them the gospel, a plan of salvation. Men, however, transgressed these "holy laws." To raise "fallen" men, God gave his Only Begotten Son who walked on earth a sinless man, and who suffered death, that all who "would believe, repent, and be baptized in his holy name, and endure in faith to the end, should be saved." This salvation was offered to all, those before or after the days of Jesus. All this is done through the loving grace of God for all his children.

This division also ends with a warning: men may "fall from grace, and depart from the living God," unless they pray to God for help and obey his laws and commandments.

The third division[4] sets up the priesthood organiza-

---

[3]*Ibid.*, 20:17-36.
[4]*Ibid.*, 20:38-67.

tion of the Church. Deacons, teachers, priests, and elders are provided to function just as they did in the primitive church. These have different duties in the Church. They are to be ordained by men who have themselves been ordained. However, every ordination must be authorized by the "vote of the Church." The elders should meet in conference "every three months, or from time to time," to dispose of the business of the Church. This division makes possible an orderly government of the Church.

The several ordinances of the Church are last discussed.[5] Those who desire to be baptized must be carefully taught the gospel. Baptism is administered by immersion as a similitude of the burial of Christ and a birth to a new life. He who officiates shall say, "Having been commissioned of Jesus Christ, I baptize you in the name of the Father and of the Son and of the Holy Ghost. Amen." Infants should be brought before the Church to be blessed and given a name. The Church should meet together often. Beautiful prayers are given to be used when the sacrament is administered. A careful record should be kept of all members of the Church and their whereabouts. Certificates of membership may be taken from place to place.

The whole document is simple but comprehensive. In over a century, the Church has not found it necessary to make any changes nor has it felt itself circumscribed by its constitution. When special needs have arisen, additions have been revealed but always as extensions of the basic law of the Church.

Within a few years after its organization, the Church had received practically all necessary supplementary laws and regulations. These also have remained unchanged. There has been no tampering with God's word.

The main additions to the "constitution" were given on February 9, 1831, ten months after the Church was organized.[6] In this revelation, the Mosaic ten command-

---

[5] *Ibid.,* 20:37, 68-84.
[6] *Ibid.,* Section 42.

ments are restated in somewhat different language from the Bible text.

> And now, behold, I speak unto the church. Thou shalt not kill; and he that kills shall not have forgiveness in this world, nor in the world to come.
> And again, I say, thou shalt not kill; but he that killeth shall die.
> Thou shalt not steal; and he that stealeth and will not repent shall be cast out.
> Thou shalt not lie; he that lieth and will not repent shall be cast out.
> Thou shalt love thy wife with all thy heart, and shall cleave unto her and none else.
> And he that looketh upon a woman to lust after her shall deny the faith, and shall not have the Spirit; and if he repents not he shall be cast out.
> Thou shalt not commit adultery; and he that committeth adultery, and repenteth not, shall be cast out.
> But he that has committed adultery and repents with all his heart, and forsaketh it, and doeth it no more, thou shalt forgive.
> But if he doeth it again, he shall not be forgiven, but shall be cast out.
> Thou shalt not speak evil of thy neighbor, nor do him any harm.
> Thou knowest my laws concerning these things are given in my scriptures; he that sinneth and repenteth not shall be cast out.[7]

The laws of punishment and forgiveness are discussed. The offender found guilty by witnesses shall be punished, but the road of mercy that leads to forgiveness is also explained. The protection of the individual from unnecessary publicity is emphasized.

The revelation also sets up the duty of the Church toward the poor, and provides a plan that has been the constant guide of the Church, which has always sought to care for the needy.[8]

The personal requirements of members are expressed in some detail:[9]

[7]*Ibid.*, 42:18-28.
[8]*Ibid.*, 42:30.
[9]*Ibid.*, 42:40-42.

And again, thou shalt not be proud in thy heart; let all thy garments be plain, and their beauty the beauty of the work of thine own hands;

And let all things be done in cleanliness before me.

Thou shalt not be idle; for he that is idle shall not eat the bread nor wear the garments of the laborer.

The healing of the sick through proper care and by faith is enjoined upon the Church.[10]

The Church is to be led by revelation and that which is revealed shall be taught to the people. In that connection missionary work is enjoined upon the Church. Therefore in simple words the process of receiving divine guidance is set forth.[11]

In other revelations which came at frequent intervals other statutes were announced which became additions to the "constitution," for the guidance of the people and the government of the Church. Before the organization of the Church the revelation now known as Section Four in the Doctrine and Covenants set up the whole ethical system of the Church.

Now behold, a marvelous work is about to come forth among the children of men.

Therefore, O ye that embark in the service of God, see that ye serve him with all your heart, might, mind and strength, that ye may stand blameless before God at the last day.

Therefore, if ye have desires to serve God ye are called to the work; For behold the field is white already to harvest; and lo, he that thrusteth in his sickle with his might, the same layeth up in store that he perisheth not, but bringeth salvation to his soul; And faith, hope, charity and love, with an eye single to the glory of God, qualify him for the work. Remember faith, virtue, knowledge, temperance, patience, brotherly kindness, godliness, charity, humility, diligence. Ask and ye shall receive; knock and it shall be opened unto you. Amen.[12]

The Church rests upon a very complete body of statutes which has shown itself capable of meeting the

---

[10]*Ibid.*, 42:43-52
[11]*Ibid.*, 42:56-62, 63-64.
[12]*Ibid.*, 4:1-7.

needs of the Church. Moreover, so may it be repeated, the whole body of Church laws forms a harmonious unit, which does not anywhere contradict itself nor has it been found necessary to alter any part of it.

CHAPTER 20

THE CHURCH IS ORGANIZED

The re-establishment of the true gospel of Jesus Christ was foretold in the First Vision of Joseph Smith in 1820. The promise was reiterated in the later spiritual experiences of the Prophet.[1] At last, ten years after the First Vision, the promised Church was organized. The date set by revelation was April 6, 1830.[2]

These ten years had been a period of preparation, education, and training of Joseph Smith for the prophetic office he was soon to fill. The day of organization had now come! He was glad; yet he stood in fear and trembling before his own inadequacy to assume the responsibility he knew he would have to carry. He was very humble. He had been called of God, but he was only a man. Now, he was to do God's work on earth!

A group of believers in Joseph's message, mostly young persons, had gathered to witness the organization. It was held in the hospitable home of Peter Whitmer, Sr., in Fayette township, Seneca County, New York. The procedure of organization was very simple.

Six of the young men present—the state law required at least six—Oliver Cowdery, Joseph Smith, Jr., Hyrum Smith, Peter Whitmer, Jr., Samuel H. Smith, and David Whitmer were the official organizers. They were all witnesses to the Book of Mormon. They had all been baptized for the remission of their sins. They were young men; the oldest, Hyrum Smith, was about thirty; the youngest, Peter Whitmer, Jr., was twenty and a half years old. Their average age was a little over twenty-three years. Joseph Smith was three months over twenty-four years old.

Though young, they, like Joseph Smith, were earnest

---

[1]*Doctrine and Covenants, Section 20.*
[2]*History of the Church,* vol. 4, p. 536; John Winebrenner, *History of All the Religious Denominations in the United States,* 1849, second edition, pp. 404-410.

seekers after truth. The Church has never been afraid
of youth and young men full of faith. The group voted
unanimously, under the revelations received by Joseph
Smith, first, to organize the Church, and second, that
Joseph Smith and Oliver Cowdery be the first and second
elders, respectively—that is, the presiding officers of the
Church.[3]

That having been done, Joseph and Oliver, who already held the priesthood and now were the heads of
the Church, baptized each other into the Church. Others
who desired membership were baptized on that day.[4]
Among them were, to the great joy of the Prophet, his
father and mother. The newly baptized persons received
the gift of the Holy Ghost by the laying on of hands
and were confirmed members of the Church. Joseph and
Oliver and some others who had joined the newly organized Church were ordained elders in the Church.

The sacrament was administered, using the revealed
sacramental prayer. A revelation was received defining
the duties of the first elder and giving him the titles prophet,
seer, translator, and apostle, and promising that the work
of the Church would not be defeated.[5] It was a day of
great spiritual rejoicing. We can well imagine Joseph's
feelings that evening when he retired. It had been a day
of days for him. The promises, the labors, and the hopes
of a decade had been realized.

Above all Joseph rejoiced in the words of the revelation received that day concerning him:

> For thus saith the Lord God: Him have I inspired to move
> the cause of Zion in mighty power for good, and his diligence I
> know, and his prayers I have heard. Yea, his weeping for Zion
> I have seen, and I will cause that he shall mourn for her no longer;
> for his days of rejoicing have come.[6]

The Church thus organized now had members, priesthood authority, priesthood bearers, and officers. It also

---

[3]*History of the Church*, vol. 1, pp. 75-77.
[4]*Ibid.*, vol. 1, pp. 76-77.
[5]*Doctrine and Covenants*, Section 21.
[6]*Ibid.*, 21:7-8.

had the earlier revelations to Joseph Smith as guides and the precious comprehensive revelation already mentioned, authorizing the organization of the Church, really a "constitution" on which to build the Church.

Joseph Smith and Oliver Cowdery and some others had been baptized before the Church was organized. Now they were baptized again, this time to become members of the Church. Baptism, a sign of obedience, has many meanings, one of which is a requirement for entrance into the Church.

Similarly, Joseph and Oliver had previously received the Aaronic and Melchizedek priesthoods, in their fullness, so far as the Lord's work on earth may require. Now they were each ordained to the office of an elder in the Church of Jesus Christ of Latter-day Saints so that their priesthood could be used within the Church. Whenever the Church of Jesus Christ is on earth, the priesthood held by mortal men must be exercised under Church authority. Failure to understand this principle has caused much confusion.

At first, men received the priesthood as elders in the Church. As the Church grew and its needs multiplied other offices in the priesthood came into existence, each one under definite responsibilities and powers. Thus in the Aaronic Priesthood there are deacons, teachers, priests, and bishops; in the Melchizedek Priesthood, elders, seventies, high priests, patriarchs, and apostles[7] just as the church was organized by Jesus Christ when he was on earth.

However, these are only offices in the priesthood; for example, an elder is a standing minister to the Church; a seventy, a traveling minister; the high priest, a man ready to assist in the administrative concerns of the Church; a patriarch, to pronounce the father's blessings upon the people; and an apostle, to officiate in all the supervisory work of the Church[8] as may be needed.

The men in each office were later organized into quorums of limited size for the more effective personal, social,

---

[7]Ibid., 124:123-145.
[8]John A. Widtsoe, Priesthood and Church Government, pp. 111-131.

economic, and spiritual welfare of the members.[9]   Each
quorum in turn was presided over by officers called for that
purpose.

This more complete organization which came as the
Church grew had been foreshadowed in the early revelations.   It did not force itself upon the Church, but was the
fulfilment of the early promise.

On the day of organization Joseph Smith and Oliver
Cowdery were appointed the first and second elders of the
Church.   A few years later under succeeding revelations,
the presiding authority was vested in a president with two
counselors, assisted by twelve Apostles.   The Apostles
in turn were to be assisted by the First Council of the
Seventy, presiding over the first quorum of seventies.[10]

The lesser division of the priesthood, known as the
Aaronic Priesthood, is to be led by a bishop, one for the
whole Church, and one for each ward.   Each bishop is to
have two counselors.   The whole priesthood is organized
into quorums—twelve deacons, twenty-four teachers, forty-
eight priests, ninety-six elders, seventy seventies, all the
high priests in a stake, twelve apostles, and three presiding
high priests.   Each quorum up to and including the high
priests is presided over by a president and two counselors,
except the priest's quorum which is presided over by the
bishop without counselors, the seventies who have seven
presidents, and the Apostles who have one president.[11]

The formulation of quorums really leads to a series
of brotherly groups, leading to mutual helpfulness in gospel
study, and in economic welfare—really all of life's activities.

Since all righteous or worthy male members not of
the blood of Cain may hold the priesthood, this organization is capable of infinite enlargement by helpers as may
be needed.

In the organization means were provided for the
judicial and economic needs within the Church. The small,

[9]*Doctrine and Covenants*, Section 107.
[10]*Ibid.*, 107:34-38.
[11]Widtsoe, *op. cit.*, chapters 11 and 13.

less important cases and the trials for membership of all who do not hold the Melchizedek Priesthood were to be held and tried by a bishop's court consisting of the bishop of the ward and his two counselors. More difficult cases, especially trials of holders of the Melchizedek Priesthood, were to be referred to the high council, one in each stake consisting of twelve high priests, under the leadership of the stake presidency. There are provisions for appeal from the judgments rendered, even up to the Church Presidency. It is an extremely simple but most effective judiciary system.[12]

The economic organization is equally simple. Each priesthood quorum, a group of brethren, should look after its members, but always in association with the ward bishopric. The bishopric is in fact the chief temporal officer in the Church.

The century and more of experience has shown the successful use of this organization, which follows the organization set up by the Lord Jesus Christ. Everywhere is the evidence that Joseph Smith was nowhere an originator, always a restorer of the multilated gospel of Jesus Christ.

The territorial organization of the Church meets equally well the needs of a large group of people of the same beliefs. As members were won for the Church, they were organized into branches, later as they grew, into wards. Where a number of such wards developed near one another, they were organized into stakes.[13] Territorially, therefore, the Church consists of a series of stakes, each composed of a number of wards (with occasional branches), and missions each made up of a number of branches. The organization permits of continuous expansion.

All this and more was foreshadowed on the day of organization, April 6, 1830.

---

[12]*Ibid.*, pp. 211-237.
[13]*Ibid.*, pp. 189-190.

CHAPTER 21

SOME CHALLENGES OF THE ORGANIZATION

The Church of Jesus Christ, organized on April 6, 1830, broke with many a tradition of the churches then existing.

First, it abolished the practice of a paid, professional priesthood class. Instead, every faithful man might have the priesthood conferred upon him and as needed could be called to use it in the affairs of the Church. The priesthood was in fact conferred upon several of those present on the day of organization. The worthiness to hold this divine power was evidenced by their faith in the work being established. Ever since that day, the priesthood has been conferred upon every worthy man in the Church who has desired it. Thus the traditional "priesthood class" has been eliminated from Church organization.

This set aside the ancient doctrine that religion is mysterious and largely incomprehensible to the ordinary man, a doctrine which had worked religious havoc throughout the years. It was rejected by the actions of the humble men in the Whitmer home on April 6, 1830. Without the book learning of the world universities, they dared to re-establish the Church of Jesus Christ, as they were commissioned by a higher power. They knew the simple, plain doctrine of Christ, and they had authority for their actions. The doctrine and practices of the gospel were easily comprehended.

It was understood that man not only could but also should know for himself the will of the Lord concerning him and his neighbor, and that every member of the Church should be able to explain and defend his beliefs, and that all should take their parts in carrying out the Lord's purposes with respect to man. Man himself, not God, had put mystery into theology and religion.

This struck at the age-old practice that a special class

of persons is needed to act as intermediaries between man and his Maker. If all worthy men can claim and use the priesthood, there is no need of "medicine men" for primitive societies or a ministerial class among the more civilized. "Sky pilots," as the irreverent have called them, paid professional interpreters of religion, were unnecessary in the Church of Jesus Christ. Members of the Church since that great day have performed the work of the Church voluntarily, joyfully, as helpers in the building of God's kingdom on earth. No wonder the churches of that day, especially their clergy, took offense.

Out of this body of priesthood, now great, were drawn, and are drawn the administrative workers of the Church: the First Presidency, the Council of the Twelve Apostles, the Council of the First Quorum of the Seventy; the Presiding Bishopric; the stake and ward officers, and the many others needed, but only for such time as they are needed. The Church has carried on successfully with such a voluntary, unpaid body of officers and teachers.

The government of the Church organized on April 6, 1830, was distinctly a priesthood government, that is, a government by the Lord, for priesthood is an expression of divine power. However, though all nominations are made by existing officers, every important action of the priesthood must be presented to the membership for their sustaining vote. This was a second definite break with most of the church practices of the day. In the words of revelation: "For all things must be done in order, and by common consent in the Church, by the prayer of faith."[1] This is an explicit statement. The government of the Church is under God in the hands of the people.

At the organization of the Church, its officers were sustained by the vote of the membership present on April 6, 1830. All officers of the Church ever since have been so sustained in general, stake, and ward conferences. No officer is exempt.

The people govern the Church. At their option,

_____
[1]*Doctrine and Covenants* 28:13.

officers and practices nominated or proposed by the priest-hood must be approved and sustained, accepted, or re-jected by the Church. It is a democratic government, a government by the people under God's law. However, if a righteous man or an eternal truth be rejected by the people, the Church may be in a state of apostasy.

This places the burden of responsibility of caring for the Church upon each individual member of the Church since there was to be no permanent governing class in the newly restored Church. This was a high and solemn responsibility distinctly new among most religious practices of the day.

All this was in harmony with the cherished Church principle of free agency. There is no domination in the Church. Every person knows the law of the Lord and obeys or disobeys as seems good to him. At his own peril he fails to sustain the Church in its many procedures.

If his disobedience goes too far, he loses membership in the Church. The Church does no more. The sinner is left to the judgment of the Lord. The Church of Jesus Christ is a Church of free people. There is full freedom under God's law in his Church.

While speaking of Church government, one should remember that the nominating power for official posi-tions rests with existing officers, the sustaining power with the people. This distinction, observed from the organiza-tion of the Church, avoids the many puddles of personal ambition. There is no place or opportunity in the Church for political methods. Therefore, positions in the Church cannot successfully be sought.

A third practice shook the traditions of the past. Men and women were included in the proposed type of gov-ernment. That showed how thoroughly the revealed Church of Jesus Christ was out of step with the apostate churches. Men and women have Church suffrage. Men who hold the priesthood may speak for their families only if they are united with the individuals of their families. Otherwise, each individual speaks for himself. Under the democratic organization of the Church everyone exercises his free agency in deciding on all matters presented for the action of the Church. Moreover, women may hold official positions in the organizations of the Church which are auxiliary to the priesthood.

Another notable principle set forth on the day of organization distinguished the Church from others and illustrates the absence of domination in the Church. While Joseph was appointed the first elder of the Church on April 6, 1830, Oliver Cowdery was appointed the second elder. No man should stand alone. He should have those around him from whom he may take counsel. Oliver Cowdery as second elder was to assist the Prophet.

When the Church was further organized to meet the needs of an increasing membership, the rule was set up, under revelation, that every presiding officer in the Church should have two counselors, except as noted for priests and seventies, to assist him. This prevents a one-man rule in any Church organization. It is assumed that while the president has the right of decision he will profit by the counsel of his two associates in the presidency. A president who ignores his counselors betrays a weakness unfitting him for his presidential position.

Many lessons came out of the meeting of April 6, 1830. Those mentioned are significant. The humble, unlearned men of that meeting, despite the general practices of the day, set up (1) a universal unpaid ministry of all the male members of the Church; (2) a government under which new actions of Church officers must be ratified by all the members of the Church; (3) an equal suffrage for men and women; and (4) a leadership in which every presiding officer must have counselors to help him.

Joseph Smith who had been called to the presiding office of the Church could see, though dimly, the heavy duties he would have to perform. He remembered Moroni's words that his name should be known for good and ill the world over.[2] But he was comforted by the revelation

---

[2]*History of the Church*, vol. 1, p. 11.

given on that day[3] in which the Church was told to give heed to "his words and commandments," as if from the Lord's own mouth. That was a promise of continued help from God. Further, the Lord assured the Church that Joseph's well-done work had been accomplished under divine inspiration.

Finally the promise came that "the gates of hell shall not prevail against you; yea, and the Lord God will disperse the powers of darkness from before you, and cause the heavens to shake for your good."[4]

Joseph, undisturbed by the claims of man-made religious philosophies and comforted by the Lord's commendation of his work, knowing that truth had come to the world, slept well that night. But he knew a battle lay ahead.

---

[3]*Doctrine and Covenants* 21:4.
[4]*Ibid.*, 21:6.

CHAPTER 22

SPREADING THE GLAD NEWS

The Church of Jesus Christ was restored, after the ancient pattern, under divine direction on April 6, 1830. It possessed eternal truth and divine authority. Joseph Smith was its first elder, its prophet, seer, and revelator. Great responsibility rested on him. Now, what was to be done? The young Prophet looked heavenward for answer.

There came to him then the words of the ancient Prophet Lehi in the Book of Mormon, the book he had translated: "Adam fell that men might be; and men are, that they might have joy;"[1] the message rang in his ears. So that was his task: to build the Church upon revealed principles of truth in such a manner that men might win joy on earth and salvation in the hereafter.

As he pondered the assignment, he saw as in a panorama the things that contribute to permanent human joy. They are as the centering ribs in a fan. If one is absent, the fan is imperfect. He saw among these factors lying deep in man's earthly and heavenly needs: economic sufficiency, bodily health, social contentment, educational development, joyous family life, emotional satisfactions, and an understandable spiritual program, to hold all else together. All that and more must be provided in a Church that teaches that men are that they might have joy—on earth as in heaven. The Church must deal with the problems of earth as of heaven.

Which one of these human needs was he to sponsor first? Then there came to him the words of the Lord that the work now established was for all the children of men:

The voice of the Lord is unto all men, and there is none to escape; and there is no eye that shall not see; neither ear that shall not hear; neither heart that shall not be penetrated.[2]

---

[1] 2 Nephi 2:25.
[2] *Doctrine and Covenants* 1:2; 6:1; 11:1; 12:1; 14:1.

The meaning of these words came to him as never before. All men are literally children of God, begotten in the pre-existent ages. That moved man to a place of high dignity. He was of the family of gods. For everyone, for each one so to speak, the plan of salvation was formulated, and the Church organized. The joys of the gospel were intended for the welfare of all men. The Church was to be a far flung democracy, under theocratic rule; not a circumscribed man-made aristocracy.

All lovers of truth would have the right to enter it. The message of the Church was world-wide, universal. It must be preached to all men, with eternal natures, the very children of God. This had been repeatedly impressed upon the Prophet and came now, when the work of the Church was to begin, with renewed and double emphasis.

It was clear then that the first duty of the young Church was to spread among all men the glad tidings of the restoration of the gospel. Under this divine mandate, missionary work began soon after the organization of the Church and has been continued with unabated vigor until the present day. Indeed, the members of the restored Church were trembling with the desire to teach to others, to all the world, that which they had found to be true and good.

Samuel H. Smith, the Prophet's brother, with two of the Whitmers, was one of the earliest to carry the gospel message to the world. He was the first man to be baptized after Joseph and Oliver before the Church was organized, one of the witnesses to the Book of Mormon; and one of the six who organized the Church. He was fervent and zealous. After hearing Joseph's story he went into the woods, "wrestled with the Lord," returned and asked for baptism. Henceforth, his activities centered upon the Church.

Very soon after the organization he began proselyting work. Among other places he labored in Canandaigua, not far from Palmyra.

On June 30, 1830, three months after the Church

was organized, he filled his knapsack with copies of the Book of Mormon, and after being set apart, set out for Livonia, a village about twenty-five miles distant. There he was repulsed by the people who would have nothing to do with the "golden Bible." On the way he gave a poor widow, who was kind to him, a copy of the Book of Mormon. In Bloomington, not far from Livonia, he was entertained at the home of J. P. Greene, a Methodist minister. Mr. Greene had to leave on business, but Samuel was impressed to leave a copy with his wife who later became converted. Upon Mr. Greene's return, after reading the book, he also asked for baptism.

Mr. Greene in turn gave the copy to Phineas Young, his wife's brother, who also accepted the gospel. He gave it to another brother, Brigham Young, who after two years' consideration joined the Church and brought his brother Joseph Young into the Church and finally his wife, father and mother and entire family. The book also fell into the hands of Mrs. Roswell (Susanah Gould) Murray, Heber C. Kimball's mother-in-law. Many of the Kimballs were converted.[3]

Thus the efforts of Samuel H. Smith brought a chain of stalwart men and women into the Church. He gave away or sold other copies of the Book of Mormon. It is very likely that it was one of them that fell into the hands of Parley P. Pratt and led to his conversion and indirectly to the conversion of Sidney Rigdon and numerous others.

Samuel H. Smith filled several fruitful missions for the Church, at least three to Livonia in October, 1830. He should be accounted one of the foremost builders in the early years of the Church.

At the September, 1830, conference of the young Church, missionary work really began. Four elders, Oliver Cowdery, Parley P. Pratt, Peter Whitmer, Jr., and Ziba Peterson, were called to go westward into the Indian country to tell the red men that a book about their ancestors

---

[3]Lucy Mack Smith, *History of the Prophet Joseph*, 1853 edition, pp. 151, 157, 159, 166.

had been revealed. They were also in a sense an exploring party, for already the Prophet foresaw the need of a gathering place of the Saints.

These missionaries left in the fall of 1830. On the way they stopped at Kirtland, Ohio, and the neighboring villages. There they preached the newly restored gospel with astonishing results. In Kirtland and neighborhood were hundreds of settlers who were seekers after truth. Alexander Campbell and his flock were there. Some of these, Lyman Wight, Isaac Morley, and Titus Billings, belonged to a group which attempted to have all things in common. There also Parley P. Pratt presented to Sidney Rigdon, his old friend and teacher, a copy of the Book of Mormon.

Before long several persons applied for baptism. Sidney Rigdon, a Campbellite writer and eloquent preacher, entered the waters of baptism. Branches were organized. The field there seemed fertile for the preaching of the restored gospel. The missionaries spent several weeks in the Kirtland territory to expound the gospel to interested listeners.

However, the missionaries had been called to go to the Indian territory. Winter was coming. So about November 1st, they left the congenial Kirtland area and moved westward. On the way they proselyted and left copies of the Book of Mormon here and there.

Then the winter of 1830-31, the severest in the memories of men, descended upon them. The Mississippi River was frozen over, and the usual carriage or riding travel was impossible. But despite the weather, and under great suffering, they walked through snow and over ice for three hundred miles.[4]

At last they reached Independence, Missouri. Since they had disposed of all their copies of the Book of Mormon, Parley P. Pratt was selected to return for a new supply.

Meanwhile, under restrictions set up by the Indian

---

[4]Parley P. Pratt, *Autobiography*, pp. 54-55.

agents, the missionaries had little access to the Indians. But they preached long and loud to the Missouri settlers. To support themselves they did such work as was available. They set up a tailor shop in Independence; some of their patrons became defenders of the Latter-day Saints later when persecution raged.

All in all this mission bore rich fruit.

Some years later missionaries were sent to Canada. A rich harvest was gathered there. Among others was John Taylor who became the third president of the Church.

In 1837, Heber C. Kimball, with others, was sent to England to open the British Mission. Thousands there accepted the message of the restoration, and many of these converts came to America and infused new blood into the struggling Church.

In 1843 Elders Addison Pratt, Benjamin F. Grouard, Noah Rogers, and Knowlton F. Hanks were sent to the South Seas to open the work there. They began their work in Tahiti.[5] Later it was extended to Hawaii and other Pacific Islands.

Two marks distinguished these and all later Latter-day Saint missionaries.

First, they went out, as they do today, at their own expense. They gave and give months or years of missionary service voluntarily to the Cause of the restoration. Some of the early missionaries worked in the summer and preached in the winter. So did Brigham Young, an early convert to the Church, who spent about ten consecutive winters in the mission field. Others found various ways of support while doing missionary work. The service was given in the spirit of loving devotion to the cause of truth.

Second, they were drawn from the whole membership of the Church and had nothing in common with the ministerial profession. Farmers, merchants, tradesmen, and professional men left their vocations to do missionary work. That could be done because every member of the Church

---

[5]Andrew Jenson, *Encyclopedic History of the Church*, p. 804.

was supposed to know the simple truths of the plan of salvation and therefore be able to explain and defend them. Besides, every righteous man engaged in missionary work was given the authority of the priesthood, making him able to perform the ordinances of the Church.

The message of these missionaries was direct and simple.[6] They were instructed to avoid mysteries. This simple method of teaching was the regular method followed. As late as 1844, (March 15) Patriarch Hyrum Smith spoke as follows to the missionaries of the Church:

> I say unto you, you must cease preaching your miraculous things, and let the mysteries alone, until by-and-bye. Preach faith in the Lord Jesus Christ, repentance and baptism for the remission of sins, the laying on of hands for the gift of the Holy Ghost; teaching the necessity of strict obedience unto these principles; reasoning out of scriptures proving them unto the people. Cease your schisms and divisions and your contentions.[7]

They bore testimony to the existence of God and his loving plan of salvation for his children on earth, his spirit children. They declared that God may speak to man and had done so to Joseph Smith, and that he had re-established his Church, which, through man's apostasy from truth, had departed from the earth. They told the story of Joseph Smith and of the restoration of the Church of Jesus Christ, entrance to which might be had through faith, repentance, baptism and obedience to God's laws. Then would follow the great gift of the Holy Ghost.

They presented the Book of Mormon as tangible evidence of the truth of the claims of Joseph Smith. They told simply of their own faith, that the gospel of joy, capable of being used daily to solve life's problems, had been restored, and invited others who loved truth more than anything else to join them. They defended their preaching with the teachings of the Bible with which the Book of Mormon harmonized.

The use of the Bible led, however, to one of the most

---

[6]*History of the Church*, vol. 2, p. 492.
[7]*Times and Seasons*, vol. 5, p. 474.

notable labors of Joseph Smith. The teachings of the Book of Mormon, and the revelations he had received, convinced Joseph that in the Bible were many errors, such as unauthorized additions, incomplete statements, and faulty translations. This seemed to him, a lover and expounder of truth, out of keeping with the sacred nature of the volume.

Therefore, after placing the matter before the Lord, he began the so-called "inspired translation" of the Bible. In June, 1830, less than three months after the Church was organized, there was revealed to him the "Visions of Moses," which gave a more complete account of the events mentioned in the book of Genesis, and set forth many lost doctrines;[8] for example, the meaning of the fall of Adam and Eve, long misunderstood because of the imperfections of existing translations of the Bible, was cleared, and shown to be a necessary act in the development of the Lord's plan of salvation.

Towards the end of the year 1830, with Sidney Rigdon as assistant, he began a somewhat full "explanation and review" of the Old and New Testaments. The work then done is a convincing evidence of Joseph's inspiration.

Thousands of changes were made, all conforming to common sense, and many in full harmony with later modern scholarship. Disputed meanings were made clear, and new doctrines expounded.

Here are some examples: The Bible says about conditions in the days of Noah, "It repented the Lord that he had made man on earth, and it grieved him at his heart."[9] The inspired translation reads, "It repented Noah, and his heart was pained, that the Lord had made man on earth, and it grieved him at his heart." The Bible says[10] that "Melchizedek . . . without father, without mother, without descent, having neither beginning of days, nor end of life; but made like unto the Son of God; abideth a priest continually." The inspired translation clears up this mass

[8]*History of the Church*, vol. 1, p. 98.
[9]Genesis 6:6.
[10]Hebrews 7:3.

of confusion by saying: "For this Melchizedek was ordained a priest after the order of the Son of God, which
order was without father, without mother, without descent,
having neither beginning of days nor end of life. And all
those who are ordained unto this priesthood are made
like unto the Son of God, abiding a priest continually."
Melchizedek, confusedly mentioned in the Bible, was given
intelligent, biographical notice. Other like explanations
abound in this really amazing document.[11]

Joseph Smith may well be accounted one of the
early students who sought to restore the Bible to its original
form and simplicity. All this which came as helps to the
missionaries in the field was opposed by the ministers
whose Bible teaching left the people confused and in a
state of uncertainty.

The early missionaries of the Church, despite all
opposition, made a glorious harvest.

---

[11]*Bible*, Inspired Translation, Genesis 14:26-40, Holy Scriptures.

CHAPTER 23

WHO WERE THE CONVERTS?

It has been a common pastime of enemies of the Church to say flippantly that those who joined the Church were low-grade people, the scum of society. Even some reputable historians have found it easier to accept such statements than to investigate the matter for themselves.

The fact is that the converts to the Church were good representatives of the people who were battling on the pioneer fringe. They were religious-minded people who had a deep love of truth, which they sought to satisfy. They were intelligent, honorable, thinking people, the kind who investigate for themselves and come to personal conclusions. Their sincerity is witnessed by the sacrifices that they unflinchingly made for their beliefs. Their courage to accept truth in the face of contempt and persecution is a lesson for the world.

Such people alone would be attracted, for the Church offered nothing but truth. It invited its members to accept truth and, if need be, to sacrifice and toil. In the words of Brigham Young, another name for the gospel taught by the Church might be "Truth."[1]

The Church had no wealth nor prospects of wealth. Positions in the Church came by call; therefore, no one could with hopes of success set out to win a commanding place in the Church community. To possess its truth could be the only motive for accepting it. Such people, differing in possessions, abilities, and attainments but alike in their love for truth joined the Church then as now. A sampling of the hundreds who joined the Church soon after its organization shows the quality of these converts.

The lives of those who were associated with Joseph Smith in his earliest days and before the organization of the Church are well-known.

---

[1]John A. Widtsoe, *Discourses of Brigham Young*, p. 2; *Journal of Discourses*, vol. 10, p. 251.

The Smith family, both immediately and more remotely connected with the Prophet, were honorable farmers and tradesmen. Even persecutors have failed to find dishonesty among them. So those who in vain have sought occasion against the family have fallen back upon the unproved charge that Joseph and his father were gold diggers and crystal gazers.

Oliver Cowdery, who was associated with Joseph Smith in most of his spiritual experiences, came of good stock, was an educated man, a schoolteacher, later an attorney. His non-Mormon colleagues and the community spoke highly of him.[2]

The Whitmer family, prominent in early Church history, of Pennsylvania Dutch descent,[3] were honorable, successful farmers. All joined the Church. Five of the family testified that on different occasions they saw the Book of Mormon plates. No derogatory word against the Whitmers has been found.

A large harvest followed the visit in Kirtland of the four elders assigned to preach to the Indians. Most of them were well-known in their communities, highly esteemed, and of influence among the people. The converts generally were not idlers, but competent, industrious farmers, tradesmen, or professional workers.

The following are typical examples:

Joseph Knight, Sr., who helped the Prophet before the Church was organized, was a farmer and owner of a gristmill and a carding machine. He was a prosperous, well-respected member of the community.

The converts by Samuel H. Smith and others, almost immediately after the organization of the Church, were good citizens, usually above the average. One of Samuel H. Smith's first converts was John P. Greene, a Methodist minister.

The first organized branch in the Church, at Colesville, New York, was made up of successful farmers with a strong sprinkling of tradesmen. Many of them followed

---

[2] Andrew Jenson, *Biographical Encyclopedia*, vol. 1, p. 246.
[3] *Ibid.*, vol. 1, p. 263.

THE PETER WHITMER FARM, NEW YORK
In his home the Church was organized

THE SUSQUEHANNA RIVER
Where the first baptisms took place

THE THREE WITNESSES TO THE BOOK OF MORMON
David Whitmer, Oliver Cowdery, Martin Harris

the miller's trade and became very useful to the Church when it settled in Missouri and Illinois.

Thomas B. Marsh, who became the president of the first Council of the Twelve, was a successful businessman, interested in a type foundry.

Edward Partridge, the first bishop of the Church, was a successful businessman, trained as a maker of hats.

William W. Phelps, one of the most competent of the early converts, was an editor, writer, and politician. His hymns are favorites among the Latter-day Saints.

The Pratt brothers, Parley P., Orson and William Dickenson, were men of astonishing gifts. Parley P. and Orson Pratt were fervent speakers, lucid philosophers, one a poet, the other a mathematician. They would have risen to eminence anywhere.

Sidney Rigdon, an associate of Alexander Campbell, a printer and an eloquent preacher with a large following, was well-connected, widely known and established.

John Taylor, who became the third president of the Church, was a turner and an intelligent expounder in the Methodist Church.

Horace K. Whitney, another bishop, was a successful merchant of notable talents.

Frederick G. Williams was a practicing physician of good reputation. He had abilities above the average.

Wilford Woodruff, who also became president of the Church, the fourth one, was a miller.

Brigham Young was a prosperous "painter, glazier, and carpenter." He was doing well in his trade when the gospel message reached him.

Naturally, on the frontier, nearly all engaged in some farming and most of the people were farmers. Surprisingly, however, a list of early converts, taken at random, showed that about one-third were farmers, one-third craftsmen, and one-third merchants and professional men. Some college men, scarce in that period, had joined the Church

About five hundred persons converted in the days of Joseph Smith are mentioned by name in the various early publications of the Church. The occupation of these converts is mentioned for only about eighty. Among them were farmers, tradesmen, schoolteachers, businessmen, lawyers, doctors, and preachers. The trades were represented by tailors, shoemakers, cabinet makers, brickmakers, millers, potters, coopers, gunsmiths, blacksmiths, turners, and lumbermen. Statistically, these eighty members with their employments enumerated, are as follows:

Farmers	19
Trades	19
Schoolteachers	11
Businessmen	14
Lawyers	10
Doctors	5
Ministers	2
Total	80

This is but a small and confessedly an inadequate sampling of the many who joined the Church soon after its organization. But a more extended study would show that those who from the beginning helped build the Church were people above the average of the times.

Clearly, the converts to the Church were sane, sober, intelligent persons, representing a high average of the people who were moving the boundary of the nation westward. They were high-grade citizens, far above their neighbors, judging from occupations and stations in the life of those pioneer days.

These converts were so near the foundation events of the Church as to have known intimately Joseph Smith and his family. They were the kind of people who would not associate with unworthy persons or accept falsehoods. Their characters, occupations, and standing in society form a powerful evidence for the honorable life of Joseph Smith and a sufficient answer to careless historians who have belittled the people who became the founders of the

Church. The Church has attracted chiefly honest, intelligent people.

It should be noted also that these people accepted with deep loyalty their leader, Joseph Smith, as a Prophet. They believed that he had had converse with the Lord. They received his revelations as words of God. This was the more remarkable because in human experience it is relatively easy to accept a dead prophet but exceedingly difficult to believe in a living prophet. This allegiance from clearheaded, hardheaded men, such as Brigham Young, for example, is one of the many evidences of the worth of the message of Joseph Smith, and the high character of the Prophet.

A masterful man, Brigham Young, spoke repeatedly of his faith in the truth of the work of Joseph Smith. Constantly he declared that he was proud to be a follower of the Latter-day Prophet.[4] The unity among the majority of Latter-day Saints has always been a chief annoyance to enemies of the restored Church.

---

[4]*Journal of Discourses*, vol. 8, p. 176; vol. 9, p. 366; vol. 10, p. 304.

CHAPTER 24

IN THE INFINITE PAST

Joseph Smith, in common with all intelligent beings, thought much about the nature of the world, and his place in it. He asked the universal questions, Whence did I come? Why am I on earth? Where do I go after death? His mind wandered far and wide in search of answers. He learned early that the happiness promised in the Book of Mormon requires satisfactory answers to these questions. People are not happy when they walk in darkness.

The churches of Joseph's day gave incomplete or unsatisfactory answers to the deep questions of the human heart. The fundamental knowledge of existence had been lost. Corroded by centuries of apostasy, since the days of Jesus the Christ, the religious philosophies of the day had driven men to form their own opinions, or propose their own guesses, concerning the riddle of existence.

Christian philosophy, so-called, as taught in Joseph's day, was narrow, hemmed in by ignorance and superstition. In it, men could not drink freely of truth. True, Jesus the Christ was usually accepted, but the essence of his teachings had been lost in obscurity. Men dealt lightly even with his teachings and attempted to set up their own conceptions of eternal truth. The authority of the priesthood was no longer on earth.

However, with the restoration of the gospel through Joseph Smith, light was thrown into dark places. In the process of restoring the ancient, true gospel, the Lord again revealed truths of existence that had long been lost. Little by little, here and there, in the Book of Mormon and in the revelations to Joseph, these truths appeared. Acceptable answers to the major questions of humanity were given. These answers are simple, coherent, clear-cut, understandable, covering the past, the present, and the future. They formed, in that dark day of apostasy, a new philosophy of existence—the things and nature of existence.

Joseph frankly admitted, of course, that ultimate beginnings are closed to the human minds, yet enough to satisfy the hunger of the human soul may be understood. If all were known, there would be an end to progress.[1] Through inspiration from on high he penetrated more deeply into the nature of existence than any other person over the long centuries. Indeed, his astonishing philosophy of existence is the greatest evidence that he was led by God in his work.

First, he taught that the spiritual and the material worlds are not sharply separated as had long been held, but are only two aspects of the same ultimate reality. There is really but one "world" in the universe. In his own words in the non-technical language of his day:

> There is no such thing as immaterial matter. All spirit is matter, but it is more fine and pure, and can only be discerned by pure eyes; we cannot see it; but when our bodies are purified we shall see that it is all matter.[2]

Analogies supporting this doctrine exist in daily life; for example, the forces of nature are many, such as the electric current, radio and magnetic waves, light and heat. However, all these stem from the same fountain of energy, as shown by the fact that they may be converted one into the other. They are one in essence.

The doctrine of the one world was not wholly new. Some of the world's philosophers had faintly suggested it. Under the title, "Materialism Versus Immaterialism," it had been debated by theologians and philosophers. Some who could not accept the doctrine of the one world made themselves believe that "immaterialism" was possible, which implied in turn that something can be created out of nothing. To this confusing notion, the doctrine of Joseph Smith could give no support. God, angels, spirits, men, and all the things in the universe belong to the same world,

---

[1]*Doctrine and Covenants* 93:28; 1 Nephi 9:6.
[2]*Doctrine and Covenants* 131:7-8.

are organized from existing materials. They differ only in their various forms of organization.

Second, Joseph Smith taught in his philosophy of existence that everything in the universe is eternal, indestructible.[3] In words revealed to him, "the *elements* are eternal,"[4] using the word element beyond the chemical elements. In explanation of this doctrine he said:

> Element had an existence from the time God had. The pure principles of elements are principles which can never be destroyed; they may be organized and reorganized, but not destroyed. They had no beginning, and can have no end.[5]

This had also been a debated idea through the centuries. The majority of uninspired thinkers had come, for example, to accept the doctrine that the Lord could create something out of nothing. They forgot that a thing created may be destroyed; therefore, it is not eternal and everlasting, existing in the past as in the future.

The findings of modern science confirm the fundamental thought of indestructible elements. The chemical elements, for example, may be changed and perhaps reduced to a form of energy, but they cannot be destroyed. The indestructibility of the realities of the universe has long been a basic doctrine of science, set up firmly, however, after the days of Joseph Smith. Without it, science would again become subject to superstition.

This doctrine acted with destructive force upon the teaching that man began his career when he came into this, the material world. If that doctrine of man's origin were true, man could not be classed as one of the major elements of existence. He would not be eternal. Yet most people had leaned upon the false doctrine that God created man and earth out of nothing. It was an easy way to avoid hard thinking. Joseph Smith declared that man lived before he came upon earth, that he really is eternal, that he "was in the beginning with God."[6] This doctrine foreshadowed

---

[3]Orson Pratt, *Absurdities of Immaterialism*, p. 7.
[4]*Doctrine and Covenants*, Section 93.
[5]*The Contributor*, vol. 4, p. 257.
[6]Doctrine and Covenants 93:29.

by some philosophers, Plato, for example, was shocking to a generation brought up to believe that man's birth on earth was his real beginning.[7]

Here, then, are the two fundamentals of existence, according to the restored gospel of Jesus Christ. First, there is but one "world"; second, the elements of the "world," even man, are eternal.

In this one eternal universe, according to Joseph Smith, were matter-energy and personal intelligences. There was apparently nothing more. With these two fundamentals, the whole universe may be explained.

Matter and energy do not exist independently. They always travel together. They can well be spoken of in one hyphenated word, matter-energy. Recent researches indicate that energy confined by powers beyond human understanding becomes matter, and that matter itself may vanish into energy.

The atom bomb depends upon the release of the energy which constitutes matter and makes matter possible. Since that discovery, there has been fear in some minds that the whole world might suddenly blow up in an atomic release of its constituent energy. There is no need of such alarm. The material elements of earth have long held together. The stars in the sky, made of materials like those on earth, appear to be millions and billions of years old. So far only a few substances, and they in a minor degree, in a limited field, have been able to release their energy.

Associated with matter-energy was the implication in Joseph Smith's teachings that the energy in the universe is a form of intelligence; that is, in a manner not fully understood by man, some form of life resides in all matter, though of an order wholly different from the organized intelligence of men or higher living things. Hence, everything in the universe is alive. The differences among rock, plant, beast, and man are due to the amount and organiza-

---

[7]*Encyclopedia Americana*, 1947 edition, vol. 22, pp. 234-236.
[8]*Doctrine and Covenants* 88:25-26.

tion of the life element. Confirming this view, the Prophet in a revelation said:

> The earth . . . shall be sanctified; yea, notwithstanding it shall die, it shall be quickened again, and shall abide the power by which it is quickened.[8]

That implies clearly that the earth is a living organism.

President Brigham Young, who was trained in the gospel by the Prophet, confirmed the teaching that life and intelligence pervade all things, animate and inanimate.

> Are this earth, the air and the water composed of life? . . . We suggest that there is an eternity of organization, and an eternity of intelligence from the highest to the lowest grade, every creature in its order, from the Gods to the animalculae.[9]

We live then in a living universe which in all its component parts is intelligent.

In addition to matter-energy, there are in the universe personal intelligences, having consciousness of varying degrees of advancement. These possess all the attributes of individuals. They have power of action. They can learn. They can act for themselves in their surroundings. Some of them are the men and women of earth.

This is in essence the doctrine of pre-existence. Men lived before they came on earth. Really, if the things of the universe are eternal, this had to be so. If man began life with mortal birth, he is not eternal. Eternal things have neither beginning nor end. In a revelation to Joseph Smith, it is declared that "Ye [men] were in the beginning with God."[10] In one of his sermons he declared that "The spirit of man is not a created being; it existed from eternity, and will exist to eternity."[11] Besides, there is ample proof of this doctrine in theological literature. Jesus the Christ was with God before coming on earth. Why not others?

Pre-existence was an upsetting doctrine to the churches

---

[8]*Ibid.*, 88:25-26.
[9]*The Resurrection*, 1884 edition, p. 3.
[10]*Doctrine and Covenants* 93:29.
[11]Joseph Fielding Smith, *Teachings of the Prophet Joseph Smith*, p. 158.

of Joseph's day, which very often declared that man was made from nothing, in God's love for man before he was created.[12] Yet the history of human thinking shows that pre-existence has been forced on the thinking of many men, notably Plato,[13] as a necessity in explaining the universe.

Personal intelligences and matter-energy would react upon one another under definite, invariable laws. The same conditions would always yield the same results. A straight stick under like conditions would always look bent in a bucket of water. The laws of the universe cannot be changed. To that extent the personal intelligences are limited in their power. They need for their own welfare to learn to know universal laws. The universe is under a reign of law, which every intelligence must respect.

The highest of the universe intelligences is God. He possesses supreme knowledge and power. Indeed we have reason to believe that his knowledge is the sum of the knowledge possessed by all existing personal intelligences and that his power is the sum of the powers of such personal beings.[14] His work with the intelligences inferior to his own constitutes the gospel story.

To summarize: Joseph Smith, under the revelations he received, conceived all things of the universe to be manifestations of one "world." He broke down the barrier between the material and the spiritual. Moreover, the things of the universe are eternal. They are not made from nothing nor are they transient. The universe is eternal, permanent without beginning or end, so far as the human mind can comprehend.

In this universe of one eternal world are matter-energy and personal intelligences. Energy itself may be a form of intelligence, making all matter, to some degree, alive and intelligent. The whole universe is alive. The story of eternity is the inter-action of matter-energy and

---

[12]*Improvement Era*, vol. 1, p. 347, "Doctrine of Presbyterian Church."
[13]S. E. Frost, *The Basic Teachings of the Great Philosophers*, p. 175; See also Plato, *Timeaus*.
[14]*Pearl of Great Price*, Abraham 3:19.

personal intelligences.   The things in the universe are
under the control of law.   To the extent that universal
law is unchangeable, a limitation is placed upon all intelligences, who, as they rise, learn to control or use the law.

The foremost of the hosts of unnumbered intelligences
is God.

Joseph Smith answered well man's first deep question:
Whence did I come?   Considering the humble origin and
lack of school education of Joseph Smith, it is almost
incredible that he could have set up such understandable
fundamentals of existence.   But all that he taught he
received from the Lord.   At no time did he take credit to
himself.

CHAPTER 25

ON THE WAY TO GREATER PROGRESS

The revelations to Joseph Smith indicate that some of the intelligences in the universe became at some time invested with bodies made of spiritual materials. They were born as it were into the spirit world. Then they became known as spirits.[1] This was accomplished through the power of God who therefore became the Father of our spirits. Hence, the life of personal intelligences clothed with spirit bodies is called the first estate of man. From among these spirits came men on earth.

This event, our birth into the spirit world, is but dimly understood. We can conceive, however, that the spirit body became a tool for the exploration of the spiritual world. Thereby, increased power over the spiritual part of the universe was won by the eternal intelligences. An extended education into the things of the spiritual world was made possible by the possession of the spiritual body. Such more intimate contacts and acquaintanceships with a new part of the universe would naturally lead to increased conquest, control, and use—that is mastery—of surrounding spiritual forces. Such added knowledge and power meant progress.

"In the beginning" the intelligences, clothed with spirit-matter, may have made slow progress, but as time went on there came increasing progress. In course of time some of these spirit children reached a stage of development when another forward step towards power over universal elements could be taken.

Here appear two determining laws of progressive existence.

First: It was the love of God for the waiting intelligences that gave them spirit bodies. He wished to help them progress and advance even to his own likeness, by

---

[1]Joseph Fielding Smith, *Teachings of the Prophet Joseph Smith*, p. 158.

learning how to use their innate but slumbering powers. He had learned how, and wished to pass on the joy of development to others. Love of God for other intelligences marked life in the spirit world. Love is the attribute that prompts God to give help to all beings inferior to himself. The purpose of God's love is to lift his children, perhaps through endless ages, toward his own likeness. Such love is the highest manifestation of intelligence. It is a selfless selfishness. Such love has been tendered man from the infinite past. The Lord has no higher purpose. "Behold, this is my work and my glory, to bring to pass the immortality and eternal life of man."[2] Love is the law of laws. Thus, the Lord has always assisted his spirit children as they have striven towards mastery of surrounding forces. He has laid out plans for them by which they might progress.

Second: The love of God is futile and fruitless unless the one who is loved cooperates in love's purpose. The spirits were intelligent. They possessed free agency. They could accept or reject any offering. Their wills were left undisturbed. Since all individualities differ, some of the spirits made better use of the help the Father tendered or followed more carefully the way to progress pointed out by him. The progress made, if any, and the rate of progress, were the result of the operation of the untrammeled will. When man's will follows his own plan alone he may not progress, while under God's plan nothing is impossible. Our personal condition depends from time to time on our acceptance of the divine, eternal plan.

These two laws then—the eternal love of God for his children and man's eternal freedom to choose and act for himself—run through the whole philosophy of Joseph Smith. They are the determining laws for happiness anywhere, under any condition, and of any time. Conformity to God's law is life; opposition to it is death.

The time came when many of the spirits, through God's help and their self-effort, had acquired such mastery over the spiritual world that they were ready for further

---

[2]*Pearl of Great Price*, Moses 1:39.

experience in the world of coarser matter. By such added experience, training the will further for obedience to God's will, added to their experience in the spiritual world, they would be able to command or make use of matter in its various forms, that is, to acquire mastery over all the contents of the universe. Naturally that would require an intimate acquaintanceship with the material world, which could best be obtained by possessing a body built of coarser matter. As the eternal intelligences were given a spirit body with which to explore the spiritual world, so this other body was needed as a tool in the exploration of the material world. Eternal progression requires contact and acquaintanceship with the whole universe.

To accomplish this purpose, the Lord, our Father, perfected a plan for this further progress of his spirit children through education in the material part of the universe. An earth composed of material elements, of earth-matter, was to be organized and fitted for the abode of man. Upon this earth the spirit children of God were to be placed, clothed with material bodies and under definite conditions of life. These bodies, finally purified, were to be retained forever by the spirits as necessary helps in the eternal onward march of intelligences.

In conformity with the free agency bestowed upon all intelligent beings, God called a council of the spirits to hear the plan in detail and to accept or reject it. Freedom always reigns under God's laws. The blessings of God are not forced upon anyone. The further experience on earth must be desired and accepted. The law of free agency reigns in the world of spirits.

Moreover, only those who had so lived as to be worthy of participation in the plan were called into the council. The privilege of coming on earth must not only be desired; it must also be earned. In that great council were set forth the conditions of the plan, the essence of which was that man with the help of the Lord was to work out his own salvation.

Forgetfulness of the previous existence of man was

imposed. Man must walk by faith, and his mind must be centered upon the earth and his life among his fellows. But he would not be left wholly alone. He would be in touch with the Spirit of the Lord by which he would be helped on his earth journey. He would also be helped by a code of laws to be set forth by the Father and delivered to the first man to be transmitted to every human being on earth. Obedience to these would measure the joy of earth life.

Meanwhile, man must battle with the conditions of earth to which his body is subjected. That would foster faith, intelligence, and courage. The evil one would be allowed to range freely upon earth; and man would have to resist temptation. This would discipline the will and turn it into righteous paths. After a short period on earth, man would be separated from the material body, in the experience called death. However, the body would later be restored to him in a purified state.

These conditions seemed hard to meet, but if overcome, would lead to large development of the inmost powers of man. But God never leaves his children alone. The Spirit of God is everywhere present. Those who reach out for help will find it. That was the promise.

In the grand council called to ratify the Father's plan, a great difference arose. The majority, led by the First-Born of the Father, our Elder Brother, Jesus the Christ, was ready to accept the plan with all its conditions. The minority, led by Lucifer, a "son of the morning," feared the isolation and the pains and ills of earth. For them Lucifer proposed that they should be sent to earth, but that provisions should be made by which they would suffer no pain and would not have to make any sacrifices. All of them would be returned with earthly bodies irrespective of their works on earth.

This latter plan seemed so desirable that one-third of those present favored it, in direct opposition to God's plan. Lucifer and his followers were thrown out of the council, and as opponents of God's plan, became the devil and his angels, who strive ever to tempt men to disobey the laws of God.

The story of the great council, appearing throughout the centuries in prose and poem, is but a dim outline picture of the greatest event in the history of pre-existent man.[3] As to the life-giving and death-dealing principles involved, it is clear and decisive. It is nowhere more clearly stated than in the revelations to Joseph Smith.[4]

In the great council under the appointment by the Father, Jesus Christ was placed in charge of the carrying out of the plan. By the help of Adam, another great spirit in the council, Jesus organized the earth. In the Meridian of Time, Jesus came upon earth, and to atone for the act that brought man under the ban of death, he himself suffered death. Through Jesus the leader, all men upon earth call for aid from the Father. In the name of Jesus man approaches the Father.

The plan of salvation is not complex: The eternal spirits are in a process of progression. God's love for his children gives the spirits help. The will of man and his right to choose for himself are eternal. Man rises or descends in accordance with the use of his will. A plan was proposed for continued progress for the spirits. Some rejected it and became the devil and his angels. They who accepted the plan are under the leadership of Jesus. The law of obedience to truth, issuing from the Father, determines their progress. The infinite goal of human progress is the likeness of God, our Father.

Thus, more completely, through Joseph Smith, are answered the questions: Whence did man come? and, Why is he on earth? In the lost centuries the answers were incomplete; the missing parts were added through Joseph Smith.

---

[3]Job 38:4-6.
[4]*Pearl of Great Price*, Moses, chapters 3 and 4.

CHAPTER 26

THE WAY ON EARTH

God's plan, called ordinarily the Plan of Salvation, for man's sojourn on earth had been accepted by the majority of the hosts of heaven. The plan was then carried into effect.

Jesus had been appointed the leader in the divine venture. Under the direction of the Father he set to work, with Adam as his assistant, to create an earth on which the great drama for human salvation could be enacted.

Here Joseph Smith again broke with existing false traditions. It had been taught that God created the earth out of nothing, by the fiat of his word. Instead, Joseph declared that the earth was made from existing materials. That is, the earth was organized rather than created. Latter-day Saints always speak of the "creation" of the earth in that sense.

Through the long periods of creation, not only was the earth formed, but upon it were also placed the plants and animals that beautify the earth today. Jesus and Adam were no doubt often on earth during the periods of creation.[1]

At length the culminating day of creation arrived. Adam and Eve, two of the pre-existent spirits, and helpers in the building of the earth, had been called to be the first to begin the earth journey. They were, through the process of procreation, to be the earth-father and earth-mother of the spirits ready for the earth experience.

Little is known about Adam and Eve. They must, however, have held high places in the celestial company. Adam was the associate of Jesus in organizing the earth. He was chosen to begin the earth work. In a sermon by Joseph Smith, Adam was designated the personage spoken of in sacred scripture as Michael.[2]

---

[1]Joseph F. Smith, *Gospel Doctrine*, 1919 edition, p. 359.
[2]Joseph Fielding Smith, *Teachings of the Prophet Joseph Smith*, p. 168.

Adam and Eve were sent to a place on earth known as the Garden of Eden. This must have been a place dedicated for sacred purposes. In it they received their earth bodies. Out of it they were driven after the so-called "fall."

How the eternal spiritual beings, known to us as Adam and Eve, received their bodies composed of the materials of earth is not known. It is certain, however, that these bodies were made of the "dust of the earth." The many surmises on this subject must be set aside, with our present knowledge, as opinions with little or no background of revealed or discovered certainty. Spiritual beings are not necessarily subject to material laws. It became necessary for Adam and Eve to step down, as it were, to become subject to the conditions of earth, including death. This was in essence the breaking of a law; but the necessary breaking of a lesser law to conform to a higher law: that unborn spirits might come to earth and with their mortal bodies learn the lessons of mortality.

Under the plan mortal men must in time be temporarily separated from their bodies, in the experience called death. Would they, Adam and Eve, eternal spiritual beings, be willing to undergo this experience? They must decide for themselves. The Lord would not command it. They must themselves break some law to bring them under the dominion of death, that a higher law might be observed.

Happily for us, our first parents chose life on earth with its inevitable death. These spiritual beings, now clothed with material bodies, were to initiate the mighty work of creation on earth. They were willing to accept the toils, and often the pains of mortal life, that future life might be increased in power and joy, through the ultimate possession of the earth-won body. That was "the fall" of man.

In sacred literature all this is well set forth:

In that day Adam blessed God, and was filled, and began to

prophesy concerning all the families of the earth; Blessed be the name of God, for because of my transgression my eyes are opened, and in this life I shall have joy, and again in the flesh I shall see God. And Eve, his wife, heard all these things and was glad, saying: Were it not for our transgression we never should have had seed, and never should have known good and evil, and the joy of our redemption, and the eternal life which God giveth unto the obedient.[3]

This was a challenge to centuries of unbelief and incomplete knowledge. Adam and Eve had been looked upon, because of the "fall," to be the meanest among the generations of men, for because of sin they had brought death into the world. In Joseph Smith's philosophy of existence Adam and Eve were raised to a foremost place among the children of men, second only to the Savior. Their act was to be acclaimed. They were the greatest figures of the ages. The so-called "fall" became a necessary, honorable act in carrying out the plan of the Almighty. No wonder the priests of the day hurled anathema against the young prophet. But the new teaching removed the cobwebs of error so that men could discern more clearly the eternal purposes of God, and that they were created in the likeness of God—"male and female created He them."

By the "fall," death of mortal bodies had come into the world. Yet the main purpose of earth-life is to secure a material body for eternal association with the spiritual body. Something was needed to recover the bodies laid down in the grave under the law of earth. A higher law must be brought into action to free men from the consequences of Adam's act. It must be a law of wide extent since all men were to be affected by it. In the plan, Jesus the Christ offered and was chosen to perform the necessary act of redemption. He was to initiate the law of the resurrection. It was required that he take upon himself a mortal body and die as a sacrifice for all men, so that all men might have their bodies, purified, returned to them. This he actually did. In the Meridian of Time, Jesus was born

---

[3]*Pearl of Great Price*, Moses 5:10-11.

upon earth, was crucified, and rose from the grave, as all men will do in the due time of the Lord. It was not an easy task, but one gladly accepted by our Savior.

Such vicarious service is among the commonest of human experiences. One runs an errand for another. The farmer plows and reaps so that the city man may be fed. One man may cut the wires that supply light to a whole city, and one may courageously unite them and restore the light. In uncounted ways, one person may vicariously serve many.

The vicarious service of Jesus the Christ is universal. All men, saints and sinners, will be resurrected. Nevertheless, all must hereafter pay the price of the deeds done in the flesh on earth.

This loving service of Jesus the Christ is commonly spoken of as the Atonement. It is the central event in the plan of salvation. Jesus the Christ is the central figure in the plan. Jesus organized the earth; he is the mediator between God and man; he is the Redeemer of man; he suffered an agony not understandable by man as he hung upon the cross. He died for all,[4] that all may receive their mortal bodies in the resurrection and progress throughout eternity.

At the end of earth time, the heads of the various dispensations will render the accounts of their stewardships to Adam, the first man, who in turn will present them to Jesus the Christ; then he, the First-Born, having accomplished his work, will render a full accounting to God, his Father.[5]

It is because of the recognition of the place and power of Jesus Christ that we pray to the Father in the name of his Son, Jesus Christ.[6]

Such then runs the story of man on earth according to the revelations received by Joseph Smith.

---

[4]Joseph Fielding Smith, *op. cit.*, p. 169.
[5]*Ibid.*, pp. 157-158.
[6]*Doctrine and Covenants* 24:5; 46:31.

CHAPTER 27

THE LAWS OF PROGRESSION

The essence of the plan of salvation was that man was to work out his salvation on earth with the help of God. Men were to develop through self-effort. However, to do this, the waiting spirits received, among others, four important promises.

First, they would not be left alone on earth. The Spirit of God which fills the whole universe would give each one direct communication with the heavenly abode.

Second, the body of truth, upon which progression rests, would be given to the first man, who could communicate it to others for the benefit of all.

Third, authority from God to lay on hands for the reception of the Holy Ghost, and to perform sacred rites, such as baptism and the gift of the Holy Ghost, would be vested in men on earth, who would represent the Lord in such work. This authority would be known as Priesthood. It would be further exercised within the Church.

Fourth, men and women who have complied with the laws of progression would be organized under the name of a church, through which the Lord would officially carry out the principles of the plan of salvation. This organization would operate under the patriarchal or family system directly, or indirectly in the Church when many families are involved. Outside of this organization, or Church, divine authority, priesthood authority could not be properly exercised.

The plan of salvation is a system by which man may progress eternally; that is, it has a definite objective. It must therefore conform to the conditions under which progress is obtainable. Human experience forbids the thought that a settled purpose may be achieved under a hit-or-miss system. A progressive existence is derived from obedience to the laws of progress and can be won in no other way. No candidate for salvation can escape obedience to the laws of progress which form the framework of the plan of salvation.

Faith is the first and fundamental law or principle of progress. It is the highest form of knowledge since it employs in its establishment every power of man. Faith is a certainty of knowledge.

Knowledge tested and tried is the beginning of faith. For that reason "it is impossible for a man to be saved in ignorance."[1] The extent of a person's faith depends in part on the amount of his knowledge. The more knowledge he gathers, the more extensive becomes his field of faith.

The degree of faith possessed by any man depends not upon the extent of his knowledge, but upon the certainty of his knowledge, which leads to the proper use of his knowledge. Thus a man of great knowledge may have weak faith, while one of limited information may have strong faith.[2]

Faith pertains to living beings and therefore is active, growing, ever-increasing. No man has a fulness of faith. Living faith leads its possessor to works corresponding to his knowledge. "Even so faith, if it hath not works, is dead."[3]

Repentance is the second law or principle of the gospel. It is a natural result of faith. A living faith impels its possessor to turn away from evil and toward righteousness. Knowledge which does not so lead men cannot be classed as faith. Repentance, indeed, is active faith.[4]

Repentance has then a twofold aspect. First, the repentant man turns away from the evil revealed by his faith. If he has sinned he sins no more. Secondly, he turns towards that which is good; that is, he performs the duties that the law requires of him. Works are required of the truly repentant man and are the marks of his repentance. Repentance and obedience to law are but as the palm and

[1]*Doctrine and Covenants* 131:6.
[2]*Book of Mormon*, Alma 32:34-41.
[3]James 2:17.
[4]James E. Talmage, *Articles of Faith*, 1925 edition, p. 109.

the back of the hand, parts of the same organ. Wherever we turn within the plan of salvation, the necessity of works becomes evident.

Baptism, the third law and the first ordinance of the gospel, is derived from the two preceding ones. It requires the candidate to enter into agreement with God, to accept the plan and to conform to its requirements. The physical outward sign of this agreement is the ordinance of baptism.

All ordinances of the Church are symbolic. Man lives in a world of symbols. Language itself is but a series of symbols of that which we sense and think. L-O-V-E is but a poor symbol of the most beautiful thing in the world— the greatest of the gifts of God.

Baptism as a symbol is first a physical witness of the faith and repentance of the candidate. Second, it is the signature to a covenant with God to accept and to obey the divine plan of salvation. Third, the mode of baptism, by immersion, is an acceptance of the leadership of Jesus the Christ, for the temporary burial in the water symbolizes the life, death, burial, and resurrection of Jesus the Christ and becomes also a promise of man's resurrection from the grave. Fourth, baptism has a cleansing effect. As water is a cleansing agent, so baptism, with all that has preceded it, will prevent past errors of the candidate from standing in the way of his future progress. He may have to pay the physical price for his errors, but they will not henceforth handicap him in his battle for celestial glory. Fifth, baptism is the authorized mode of entrance into the Church of Jesus Christ.

The gift of the Holy Ghost is the fourth law and the second ordinance of the plan of salvation. It is a confirming of the candidate to be a member of the Church, and the conferring of the gift of the Holy Ghost, a divine power to assist man in his progressive existence as promised him under the plan of salvation. It represents the result of obedience to the three preceding laws. They who have attained faith, practised repentance, and covenanted with the Lord in baptism, are placed by the gift of the Holy

Ghost in official contact with the source of light, understanding, and power. It gives man a claim upon the
assistance needed from the unseen world for his protection
and advancement.[5]

The Holy Spirit and Holy Ghost must not be confused.
The Holy Spirit or the "light of truth"[6] is the spirit that
proceeds from "the presence of God to fill the immensity
of space."[7] It is manifested in all natural phenomena. It
penetrates all men. By its agency, the Lord may communicate with man, and man may receive help from God.
The Holy Ghost, on the other hand, is a Personage, the
third member of the Godhead, to whom has been committed many important phases of the plan of salvation. It
may be that the operations of the Holy Spirit itself are
under the immediate direction of the Holy Ghost.

The gift of the Holy Ghost is a key which may be
used to unlock, whenever needed, the door into spiritual
experiences. It does not necessarily effect an immediate
change in the recipient, but when needed, it is available.
The effects of the gift of the Holy Ghost must be sought
after, must be cultivated. If that be done, it becomes an
open door into a life of beauty and joy.

The gifts proceeding from the Holy Ghost are among
the most precious in the Church. Prophecy, healing, and
speaking in tongues are among these gifts. Every person
who has filled a mission or other positions of responsibility
can testify to the help derived from the spiritual power
given by the Holy Ghost.

After the fundamental principles, faith and repentance, and the initiatory ordinances, baptism and confirmation, have been accepted, real life in the Church begins.
Then follows daily conformity to the several practices of
the Church. The joy of the member may thereafter be
measured directly by his obedient life within the Church;
that is, by his works, and by no other means, will he henceforth find the fulfillment of the promises inherent in the

---

[5]Joseph F. Smith, *Gospel Doctrine*, 1949 edition, p. 59.
[6]*Doctrine and Covenants* 88:6.
[7]*Ibid.*, 88:12.

first principles and ordinances of the Church. Obedience, conformity, works, equivalent in spiritual meaning, become the objectives of all worthy effort.

Obedience within the Church must, however, conform to the underlying spirit of the Church. Obedience or conformity must be intelligent. The meaning of the practices of the Church must be explained to every member, and studied by him in their fullness so that the reason for obedience may be clearly understood. When that is done, it will be found that every regulation of the Church, every practice is for the good of the individual member as well as for the body as a whole. Blind obedience is repugnant to Latter-day Saints; but, necessarily, there may be times when those of less experience rest their judgment temporarily upon the advice of men of wider knowledge and longer experiences. Youth, for example, does well to seek counsel from age. Such obedience soon blossoms into full understanding. Living a righteous law proves best that the law is good for man.

The acceptance of the divine origin of the Church implies the belief that the Church is divinely led and that therefore a member may safely trust that as he grows in experience he will learn to understand the propriety of every Church regulation.

Compulsion is contrary to the gospel spirit. Therefore all obedience or conformity within the Church must be rendered willingly. The rights of men as free agents must never be forgotten. Even when obedience is yielded to a principle not fully understood, it must be done freely, of one's own accord.

Full happiness within the Church demands that men comply with all its laws, regulations, and ordinances. Obedience is incomplete if a person decides to obey one and disobey another gospel requirement. Usually, an attempt to select some practices and ignore others leads to a weakening of the will for righteousness, and soon complete disobedience sets in.

It is true that within the Church are not only fundamental, unchanging laws, but also temporary regulations representing the applications of the unchanging laws to current needs. Full obedience does not distinguish between the two classes of requirements. Conformity to all is the only safe way to happiness.

The principles, ordinances, regulations, and practices of the Church, few in number, meet the various needs of man. In their nature, some are physical, others mental, and yet others spiritual. The physical and mental have, however, spiritual equivalents. Obedience to a physical law, such as the Word of Wisdom, develops spiritual strength and in that manner becomes a spiritual law.

A number of derivative practices have been set up for daily use and remembrance. Essentially these are set forth in the Ten Commandments and the Beatitudes, though many supplementary revelations guide man in his daily walk.

Obedience results in activity, without which progress is impossible. Within the Church, provision is made for every type of proper human activity. The Church itself is in fact managed by its members, and every member may have a share in the labors of maintaining and directing the affairs of the Church. From such activity comes rounded health to him who so participates. Whoever fails to be active in the Church is retrograding, for it is impossible to stand still. Progress cannot be static.

Indeed, the Church only provides the means for salvation. It points the way and offers opportunities. Acceptance or rejection is wholly an individual matter. In the long run then, spiritual success or failure must be won through his activities by each man. The Lord in his mercy assists every man in his righteous efforts but does not transcend the law of free agency.

Faith alone is an insufficient test of obedience. Only by his works, the expression of his faith, may a man be safely judged. He who performs daily the duties placed upon him, however humble they may seem to be, will receive the rewards of obedience.

CHAPTER 28

THE DESTINY OF MAN

Joseph Smith answered more clearly than anyone else since the days of Jesus, the questions, Whence did man come? and, Why is man on earth? With like clarity he answered the third question, Where does man go after death? This question when imperfectly answered has hung throughout the centuries as a pall over the minds of men. Failure to understand man's true destiny has probably been man's greatest sorrow.

The plan of salvation, conceived and proposed by our Heavenly Father, is for all of his children. Our Father will never cease to labor with our stubborn wills, until the last of his children has accepted the requirements of the gospel and has conformed to the plan of salvation. That may lead us into the far eternities, for though "every knee shall bow and every tongue confess that Jesus is the Christ,"[1] yet many will refuse to bend their wills to the requirements of the gospel of Jesus Christ. Such persons must wait for the full blessings of the Lord, until their stubborn wills have learned obedience. However, since progress is eternal, no person has ever reached the end of salvation. Progress need never end. It must be said that such people cannot overtake those who were righteous from the beginning.

During this endless journey, man may rest secure in the eternal love of God. Our Father will help us forever. Never will he forsake us. He will ever seek to convert the sinner to better ways. It is probable that he will not consider his work complete until all of his children are on the road of progression.

The gospel plan is for all who have lived upon earth, who now live upon it, or will live upon it, as well as for those who were present in the grand council in heaven.

---

[1]Romans 14:11.

before the earth was, and accepted the plan of salvation as there proposed. Only those who there accepted the plan could come upon earth to take upon themselves earthly bodies.

The gospel therefore is for the whole human race. Salvation is intended to be universal. If that be so, a question at once arises: if certain ordinances, such as baptism and the gift of the Holy Ghost, are unvarying requisites for full participation in the blessings of the plan, what shall be done about the many inhabitants of earth who have died without receiving these ordinances?

The answer is simple. The dead retain in the spirit world the power to learn, to understand, and to choose. Did not Jesus say that he was going to preach to the "spirits in prison?"[2] The gospel is being taught to them there— those who were righteous and those who have sinned on earth. The ordinances pertaining to the earth, baptism for instance, must be done vicariously for the dead by the living, to become effective when the dead accept the work done for them. This is the work being now performed in the many temples of the Church.

Thus, the door is opened for universal salvation.

Only the ordinances of a strictly earthly character need be done vicariously for the dead; but there is no substitute for them. "Except a man be born of the water and of the Spirit he cannot enter the Kingdom of God."[3] That is the divine statement. Water, however, is an earthly element, and all water baptism must be done on earth.

It is further stated that "whatever ye bind on earth is bound in heaven."[4] Consequently, all sealings for time and eternity done on earth for the dead by proper authority are recognized and accepted as valid in heaven. But they must be accepted by the dead to become effective for them.

In short, all ordinances characteristic of the Church on earth (baptism, marriage, sealings of children to parents in the family relation), may be performed for the dead.

[2] 1 Peter 3:18.
[3] John 3:5; *Doctrine and Covenants* 5:16; Alma 7:14.
[4] *Doctrine and Covenants* 127:7; Matthew 16:19.

Then, when all this is done, the dead may accept or reject the ordinances performed for them.

If men are to be rewarded according to their works, then since the works of men vary, the judgments of God must differ. That leads to the doctrine of graded salvation. Every person will inherit a glory of salvation, which will be the one that he has earned.

> And they who are not sanctified through the law which I have given unto you, even the law of Christ, must inherit another kingdom, even that of a terrestrial kingdom; or that of a telestial kingdom. For he who is not able to abide the law of a celestial kingdom cannot abide a celestial glory. And he who cannot abide the law of a terrestrial kingdom cannot abide a terrestrial glory. And he who cannot abide the law of a telestial kingdom cannot abide a telestial glory; therefore, he is not meet for a kingdom of glory. Therefore, he must abide a kingdom which is not a kingdom of glory.[5]

To be placed higher than a person deserves places him beyond his power to enjoy his surroundings. By slow degrees alone can a man rise to and endure and enjoy higher levels.

Humanity will be saved under this law, according to their works, in three main divisions: celestial (like unto the sun), terrestrial (like unto the moon), telestial (like unto the stars). Within each group there will be many gradations and divisions, according to individual lives.

There can be no talk of hell in such a plan (except for the very few "sons of perdition,")[6] but undoubtedly the regret for lost opportunities will be keen among those in the lower degrees of glory. A religion without a hell seemed impossible to the misled preachers of Joseph's day.

The law of progress continues in full operation for every soul throughout eternity. Every man, however placed, may progress, rise, and advance. Naturally he cannot overtake those on the higher levels, for they have

---

[5]*Ibid.*, 88:21-24.
[6]*Ibid.*, 76:30-38.   See page 233.

won a greater rate of progress, but he may find continued joy in using his powers for steady progress.

Those who die pass first into the spirit world, retaining there all their normal powers, including their free agency. Life there is the spiritual equivalent of life here. The spirit world, itself, is but the spiritual equivalent of earth.[7]

In course of time, the bodies laid down in the grave will be resurrected and reunited with the immortal spirit, the union to continue forever. The body thus brought out of the grave will undergo profound changes, not understood by man, which will fit it for everlasting association with its eternal spirit. While the body will arise as it was laid down, for there can be no life or growth or progressive change in the grave, yet all blemishes and imperfections will be corrected before the unending union of body and spirit takes place.

The resurrection is operative for all who have lived on earth. Jesus died that every soul which has lived upon earth might regain his body. The resurrection is absolutely universal.

The time must come in the eternal hereafter, the day of judgment, when every human being will be judged by the way he carried out on earth his pre-existent agreement with the Lord. He came down on earth with the possibility of winning access to the greatest blessings of God. How far did he approach that goal? How is he now, after earth-life, compared with his pre-existent condition? As effect follows cause, so the answers to such questions will determine the gains of the man from his earth-experience. That is, the judgment measured out will be in accordance with the man's works.

There enters here the vast mercy of God. He is our very Father, in our first, spiritual estate. He loves us with a Father's love. He also knows the conditions under which we have traveled the road on earth. His higher justice,

---

[7]*Book of Mormon*, Alma, chapter 40.

the product of love and mercy with the claims of law, will decide upon the final judgment that we shall receive.

The human race, resurrected and rewarded with a fitting glory, will find their abiding place upon the earth. A process of purification and spiritualizing will have made the earth a fitting home for eternal, resurrected beings.[8]

> For the Lord shall be in their midst, and his glory shall be upon them, and he will be their king and their lawgiver.[9] . . . When he shall deliver up the kingdom, and present it unto the Father, spotless, saying: I have overcome and have trodden the wine-press alone, even the wine-press of the fierceness of the wrath of Almighty God. Then shall he be crowned with the crown of his glory, to sit on the throne of his power to reign forever and ever.[10]

Upon this new earth, we shall continue to use our powers for progress, each in his own sphere, under his own conditions, made by himself throughout the long journey from the dim beginning.

The elements are eternal; man is eternal and imperishable; the plan of progress is never ending; the love of God is everlasting. The gospel of Jesus Christ as restored by Joseph Smith may be called the philosophy of eternalism.

Man is a child of God; and man from the dim beginning has been on the road of progress. The goal of his efforts has been to become more and more like his Father who has helped and guided him from his earliest times.

This approach will continue forever; it cannot end while the will of man strives upward. To become increasingly like his Father in heaven, his God, is the high destiny of man.

So Joseph Smith set forth a philosophy of man's existence, past, present, and future, which answers the many questions of the human heart. That which men had sought to regain throughout the ages, he presented, under the revelations of God, in superbly simple but comprehensive doctrine.

[8]John A. Widtsoe, *Discourses of Brigham Young*, p. 375.
[9]*Doctrine and Covenants* 45:59.
[10]*Ibid.*, 76:107-108.

CHAPTER 29

CHALLENGING FALSE TRADITIONS

In the preceding chapters is given a skeleton outline of the restored plan of salvation, the gospel of Jesus Christ. It is not intended to supply in this book the details of the plan. Yet even in simple outline, it challenges the theologians of the day. It goes further: It gives the lie to many of the cherished beliefs of the day. It is no wonder that the clerical profession hated Joseph and tried to destroy him.

To illustrate the definite break with the Christianity of the day, two doctrines are given, both foreign to the truth of the gospel but taught almost vehemently over centuries by the priests of an apostate Christianity.

The first of these is the doctrine that unbaptized children, should they die, will be sent to hell. The second is that sinners will be sent to hell, there to remain in torture throughout eternity.

The doctrine that unbaptized children who die will not be saved rests upon a misconception of the relation of baptism to man's eternal salvation. It has been made clear that baptism is essential to salvation,[1] but with the provision that the ordinance is valid only if it is understood by the candidate; that is, the person to be baptized must be mature enough to understand the meaning of baptism. Through the centuries, the importance of baptism was held before the people, but the necessity of understanding it was forgotten. At length men provided that baptism should be performed as early as possible in a child's life, perhaps a few weeks after its birth.

Concordantly came the terrible doctrine that unbaptized children would be sent to hell. Throughout the centuries unnumbered mothers with bleeding hearts have wept as they had laid away in the grave their innocent

---

[1] James E. Talmage, *Articles of Faith*, p. 128

children who unfortunately had not been baptized.   True, since Joseph's day, this awful doctrine has been cast out and forgotten by many churches; but in his day, it held full sway in most so-called churches.

Joseph Smith struck hard at such an unnatural and false doctrine.   On January 21, 1836, he records having had a vision in which among other matters, the fate of unbaptized children was made clear.

And I also beheld that all children who die before they arrive at the years of accountability, are saved in the celestial kingdom of heaven.[2]

The vision was but a confirmation of a doctrine set out in a revelation received September, 1830.

Behold, I say unto you that little children are redeemed from the foundation of the world through mine only Begotten; wherefore they cannot sin, for power is not given unto Satan to tempt little children until they begin to become accountable before me; for it is given unto them even as I will, according to mine own pleasure, that great things may be required at the hand of their fathers.[3]

One can well imagine the hate of peddlers of untruth when this favorite doctrine crashed with the simple, logical statement of Joseph.   Well for the world when this unnatural, unholy, unloving doctrine was banished!   But it took courage to stand in such opposition to the Christian world.

In Joseph's day preachers still taught the proverbial hell of everlasting torture.   In the text books of his day, in many nations, were pictures of devils with pitchforks pushing sinners into the flames of hells, there to suffer the agony of being burned, but never consumed.   With one hand the preacher offered a fragment of God's love, and with the other, the torment of an unutterable never-ending hell provided by an angry, unforgiving God.   Under such a cruel doctrine men would be frightened, so it was hoped,

---
[2]*History of the Church,* vol. 2, p. 381
[3]*Doctrine and Covenants* 29:46-48.

into a righteous manner of living. How men could devise
so horrible a future for any one of God's children is a striking evidence of the apostasy from the simple loving gospel
of Jesus Christ.

Naturally the correction of this evil doctrine had to
be made. About a month before the organization of the
Church, a glorious revelation was received by Joseph Smith
which threw into limbo the illogical doctrine of eternal
burnings for sins committed.[4]

In this revelation Jesus Christ affirms that his commission was to carry out the Father's plan for man's salvation. It is explained that the plan includes laws that must
be obeyed. In the final judgment every man will be judged
"according to his works and the deeds which he hath
done."[5] This threw a flood of light on God's treatment of
the sinner. The judgment passed upon any man will be
great or small according to his works and deeds.

Further, the breaking of any law brings punishment
which however may be paid for through repentance. If
repentance does not follow sin, full punishment inevitably
follows. Whatever that punishment may have been under a
higher law, it destroyed completely the unnatural, ungod-
like doctrine of past ages. This has been clearly set forth as
follows:

And surely every man must repent or suffer, for I, God, am
endless. Wherefore, I revoke not the judgments which I shall
pass, but woes shall go forth, weeping, wailing, and gnashing of
teeth, yea, to those who are found on my left hand. Nevertheless,
it is not written that there shall be no end to this torment, but it
is written endless torment. Again, it is written eternal damnation;
wherefore it is more express than other scriptures, that it might
work upon the hearts of the children of men, altogether for my
name's glory. Wherefore, I will explain unto you this mystery,
for it is meet unto you to know even as mine apostles. I speak
unto you that are chosen in this thing, even as one, that you may
enter into my rest. For, behold, the mystery of godliness, how
great it is! For, behold, I am endless, and the punishment which
is given from my hand is endless punishment, for Endless is my

[4]*Ibid.*, 19:1-15.
[5]*Ibid.*, 19:3.

name. Wherefore—Eternal punishment is God's punishment. Endless punishment is God's punishment.[6]

This was a new doctrine in the days of Joseph. It brought enemies to their feet. Eternal punishment, everlasting punishment, all punishment will accord with the mind and will of God. As our works have been, so our reward will be. From that there is no escape.

The implication of this doctrine is that through the ages a sinner may atone for his misdeeds. It was a startling doctrine to hurl at a world traditionated in one of the blackest errors of apostate Christianity.

The whole revelation gives much comfort to all people. Later on the theme was again taken up and enlarged upon. Another revelation, one of the most remarkable in the history of Joseph Smith, was received on February 16, 1832. The Prophet and Sidney Rigdon were engaged in the revision of the Scriptures. They had already learned that the rewards of men varied according to their deeds in the flesh. Then heaven as the place where the departed righteous ones will live must include a variety of divisions. On this point, the scriptures, modern and ancient, were silent.

As the two brethren were considering this question prayerfully, they received a vision which cleared up the unsettled question. This vision, seen by both, and so testified to, of itself is one of the most compelling evidences of the authenticity of the Prophet's divine calling. It now appears in the Doctrine and Covenants as Section 76. It gives the first glimpse of the organization in the heavens.

> Thus saith the Lord concerning all those who know my power, and have been made partakers thereof, and suffered themselves through the power of the devil to be overcome, and to deny the truth and defy my power—
> They are they who are the sons of perdition, of whom I say it had been better for them never to have been born;
> For they are vessels of wrath, doomed to suffer the wrath of God, with the devil and his angels in eternity;

[6]*Ibid.*, 19:4-12.

Having denied the Holy Spirit after having received it and having denied the Only Begotten Son of the Father, having crucified him unto themselves and put him to an open shame.[7]

Very few will be so condemned because very few have the knowledge required. Denial of the truth by those who have not a perfect knowledge does not merit the greatest punishment, to be classed as sons of perdition.

All others, who are not classed as sons of perdition, will be "redeemed in the due time of the Lord"; that is, they will all be saved. The meanest sinner will find some place in the heavenly realm. But somewhere, sometime, he must pay the price for his sins. All this is in line with the love and justice of the Father for his children.

The redeemed will be assigned, according to their works in one of three great classes or gradations of glory, the telestial, the terrestrial, and the celestial. In each of these there may be innumerable sub-classes, for the waywardness of man takes on many aspects, and therefore, demands many different judgments. "Every man shall receive according to his own works, his own dominion, in the mansions which are prepared."[8]

This came as a body blow to the man-made theologians of a world which had taught an hereafter composed only of heaven and hell, that all would be either in heaven or hell.

To the Church came the understanding that in the hereafter, as here, under the law of progression in every assignment there may be progression in the higher glories more rapid than in the lower glories. No glory is hopeless. The love of God for his children overshadows all else.

These two great revelations (Doctrine and Covenants Sections 19 and 76) have completely changed the world's conception of the payment in the hereafter for sins committed on earth and the eternal destiny of man.

The word *hell*, when used in these revelations, refers

---

[7] *Ibid.*, 76:31, 32, 33, 35.
[8] *Ibid.*, 76:111.

to the abode of the devil and his ugly brood. As used in the Bible it has the same connotation.

In the Church of Jesus Christ of Latter-day Saints, there is no hell. All will find a measure of salvation; all must pay for any infringement of the law; but the payment will be as the Lord may decide. There is graded salvation. This may be a more terrible punishment: to feel that because of sin a man is here, when by a correct life, he might be higher. The gospel of Jesus Christ has no hell in the old proverbial sense.

Before these challenges many of the churches have retreated, but without any increasing love for Joseph Smith, and his great revelations from a higher power.

A LATTER-DAY SAINT BUILDING
In Kirtland, Ohio

LATTER-DAY SAINT HOUSE
In Kirtland, Ohio

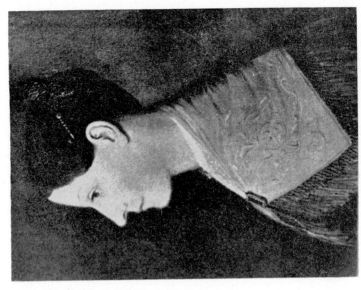

MARY FIELDING SMITH
Widow of Hyrum Smith who crossed the plains
with her family to Utah

EMMA HALE SMITH
Widow of Joseph Smith who remained in
Nauvoo when the Church moved West

Chapter 30

INDIVIDUAL FREEDOM

Joseph Smith accepted the task of applying the principles revealed to him to everyday practices of his people. He recognized clearly that this could not be accomplished unless the Church offered freedom to all individuals. The doctrine of free agency was first in the heavenly council before the earth was; it must remain the foundation of human action on earth.

The right to choose for oneself what one will believe and do is the choicest possession of every intelligent man and woman. The unhindered exercise of this right is freedom. This right of free agency, valued above all else, insures a membership free to think and act for itself and which stands upon its own convictions and conclusions.

Because of this basic law, the Church is diametrically opposed to tyranny or dictatorships of any form or under any name that direct or enslave the minds and actions of men. The Church believes that only through the possession and use of truth can man obtain full freedom. It therefore seeks truth and more truth. Only truth can make men free. "Ye shall know the truth, and the truth shall make you free."[1] And the Lord in these latter days has declared, ". . . Hear my voice and follow me, and you shall be a free people, . . ."[2]

Nevertheless, freedom operates under many conditions or limitations beyond the control of any one person. There are laws of nature, society, and God, which must always be taken into account in the exercise of free agency. Under the right of choice a person may oppose the laws or obey them. It is not possible to abrogate them nor can they be ignored with safety.

A person may choose to jump from the mountain

---
[1]John 8:32.
[2]*Doctrine and Covenants* 38:22.

precipice to the jagged rocks below or seize with naked hands the wires charged with high tension electric power or cast himself into a living fire. The result is certain death. Or he may decide to obey the laws of nature and use them if he can. So he builds a parachute to descend safely from the precipice; with insulated hands he makes the current work for him; and he applies heat to confined water so that he may ride across the continent luxuriously in steam-driven trains. True freedom, in the midst of the multiplicity of natural forces, comes from conformity to law. Thereby, man becomes also the master of nature.

This principle is in equal operation in society. A person among his fellows may think as he pleases; but in his actions he is limited. His inalienable right of free agency does not permit him to interfere with the same right of another individual. Therefore, a sound society sets up rules and regulations by which the right of freedom may be available to all people. To live happily in society these laws must be obeyed. If they are not the best laws, they may be improved; but while they do exist, they must be obeyed. Freedom in society waits only upon those who obey the laws of society.

The Church, essentially an institution for freedom, exists under many laws that govern the right of choice. These are the commandments of God to his children on earth. The best laws enacted by and for society are based upon divine law, such as the Ten Commandments. The great value of the Church to man comes from these laws based upon the will of our Heavenly Father, which may limit the extent of our choice, but which are for our good, if we choose to obey them.

A person must exercise his right of choice when he enters the Church. The new convert is not baptized until he is well acquainted with the doctrine and practice of the Church. After he has been so taught, he asks with open eyes for admission to Church membership. Children are likewise taught the meaning of the ordinance before they are baptized at eight years of age.

This means that the candidate for baptism accepts of his own free will and choice all that the Church has to offer, and all that it requires. He accepts the organization, code of doctrine, and manner of living within the Church. As by the free exercise of his agency he seeks baptism, so by that agency he becomes subject to the order of life within the Church. The requirements of the Church are not in any sense infringements upon his right of choice. He has made his choice. The principles of truth upon which the Church rests must henceforth determine his conduct in life.

In minor matters of Church regulations, when questions arise in his mind, he compares them with the basic truths he accepted in the waters of baptism and judges them accordingly. He soon finds that every so-called Church requirement is for his good and in full harmony with the fundamental doctrines of the Church; for example, obedience to the Word of Wisdom yields health and spiritual power; the payment of tithing makes man master of selfish impulses and a benefactor to others; and attendance at Church service feeds his spiritual nature. Every requirement, if obeyed, lifts man into higher realms of joy; helps him approach the likeness of God.

Political differences show the freedom of action of the Latter-day Saints. Political issues sometimes touch matters which are not of fundamental importance. Whether Jones, Smith or Brown shall be mayor, whether a road shall be built south or north are not often questions of principle. Church members act freely in deciding upon such matters. Likewise, they choose, without interference, from time to time, their political party affiliations, as party platforms change. Should larger political problems arise, such as involve fundamental Church doctrine or practice, they would be solved simply by comparing them with the essential doctrines of the gospel. Latter-day Saint people are free, politically, socially, and spiritually.

Another evidence of the freedom of Latter-day Saints is the manner in which all Church Authorities are sustained, whether general, stake, or ward. It is a law of the Church that all nominations for Church positions, or releases, must be made by the officers of the priesthood; but the men and women thus nominated must be accepted and sustained by the members. Without such confirmation the nominees cannot act, and other choices must be made, as has occasionally happened. Therefore, at the conferences of the Church, or Church divisions, officers are presented for the sustaining vote of the congregations; not only when the names are first proposed, but also at regular, frequent intervals thereafter to insure that the Church continues to be led by worthy men and women.

This is more than an ordinary vote. It is a sustaining vote, which means that we not only accept certain persons as our leaders, but also that we support them with our good will, help, and prayers. Every person may vote freely, for or against a proposed officer and should do so according to his convictions. The voting is not a perfunctory act, but one of great importance.

However, if a member votes against a nominee or officer, it must be for some good reason. If a Church member commits acts unworthy of a Latter-day Saint, charges should be filed against him in the courts of the Church by those who know of his errors; if the charges are substantiated, and no reconciliation is effected, the person may be removed from office.

If the contrary vote is merely a distrust of the person's ability to perform the duties of the office or because of personal dislike, nothing further need be done. The new officer will grow in fitness, if he has the good will, faith, and prayers of the people. Moreover, the history of the Church shows that under the power of the Lord, weak men are made strong, and strong men stronger, to the joy of all. Any personal dislike should, of course, be overcome.

Learning to love our neighbor is a sure path to happiness. Meanwhile, the Latter-day Saints know and trust their leaders so well that they are nearly always willing to accept their nominations and to give those nominated a chance to succeed in the office, which is not for life. The unanimous support of our Church officers is really an indication of the united feeling of the people to carry forward the latter-day work of the Lord.

That the Latter-day Saints are a free people is further emphasized by a treatment given those who fail to keep the promises implied in their baptism. They are not cast out nor held in ill repute. Apostasy and immorality are the usual causes that lead to excommunication. The purpose of the Church is to save souls. They who are weak should be helped into strength, and they who are straying, into the correct path of life.

Those who prate about lack of freedom among Latter-day Saints either do not understand the Church and its organization or are trying to cover up their own weaknesses.

The feeling of the members of the Church is summed up in the words of a vigorous thinker and faithful Latter-day Saint: "If we were not a free people, I would not be a member of the Church."

The Prophet Joseph Smith observed with scrupulous care the right of choice, the free agency, of the people who had come into the Church.

CHAPTER 31

THE EMANCIPATION OF WOMEN

Joseph's first rule in building a Church for man's good was individual freedom. By this rule he touched at once one of the most debated subjects of the years. Was woman as well as man a free agent? Was her freedom the same as that of a man? Were her rights the same as those of the man? In short, were the rights of men and women equal?

Throughout the centuries woman had held, with a few notable exceptions, a place inferior to man. Usually, she was little more than a slave or a plaything. Even when civilization, so-called, dawned upon a part of the earth, woman was not allowed to exercise any functions in government or to own property. She was the property of her father or husband.

Naturally, as human enlightenment became more widespread, voices were raised in defense of woman. In 1792, Mary Wollstonecraft (Godwin) a woman of unusual mental gifts spoke and wrote in behalf of woman's emancipation from her near-slavery. She argued that woman should be educated to establish equality with men.[1] Other voices were raised for woman's right in the ensuing years. The most powerful was John Stuart Mill in *The Subjection of Woman*[2] written nine years after the Prophet's death.

Gradually the grip of tradition loosened, until today in the civilized nations men and women have nearly equal rights. The long clash of the sexes is disappearing.

Joseph Smith brushed the past away. He taught that the Lord loves his daughters as well as he loves his sons, and that woman as well as man is held accountable for her own manner of living. The simple doctrine of free agency demands that woman must receive full freedom of action and must expect personal accountability for her acts. Sub-

---

[1]Mary Wollstonecraft (Godwin), *The Rights of Woman*, 1792, Everyman's Library #825; *The Wrongs of Women*, 1798; Charles Brocden Brown, *Rights of Women*, 1798.
[2]John Stuart Mill, *The Subjection of Woman* (1853), Everyman's Library #825.

stitutes are not acceptable in the heavens for final judgment. By such tokens there must be full equality between man and woman on earth.

The Prophet taught that in the Church there is in fact such equality. The gospel was devised by the Lord for his children, men and women alike. "Male and female created he them." Every person on earth, man or woman, earned the right in the pre-existent life to come here; and must earn the right, by righteous living, to live hereafter where "God and Christ dwell." The privileges and requirements of the gospel are fundamentally alike for men and women.

This doctrine of equal rights is confirmed in the ordinances of the Church, which are alike for man and woman. Faith, repentance, and baptism are the same for all. The rewards, such as the gift of the Holy Ghost and the temple ordinances, are alike for men and women. The gifts and obligations of the gospel are alike for all. The man who holds the priesthood officiates in it, but the blessings of it descend upon the woman, also.

Joseph Smith ever taught such equality. Complaint came to him that women had administered to "the sick by the prayer of faith, the laying on of hands, or the anointing with oil." His answer was, after discussing the matter:

Who are better qualified to administer than our faithful and zealous sisters, whose hearts are full of faith, tenderness, sympathy and compassion. No one.[3] [In his own words;] I . . . gave a lecture on the priesthood, showing how the sisters would come in possession of the privileges, blessings and gifts of the Priesthood, and that the signs should follow them, such as healing the sick, casting out devils, etc., and that they might attain unto these blessings by a virtuous life, and conversation, and diligence in keeping all the commandments.[4]

In the field of revelation she was not forgotten. In July, 1830, Joseph received a revelation calling his wife Emma Smith to compile hymns and to perform other

[3]Joseph Fielding Smith, *Teachings of the Prophet Joseph*, pp. 229, 231.
[4]*History of the Church*, vol. 4, p. 602.

duties for the Church. The revelation further says, "Thou shalt be ordained under his [Oliver Cowdery's] hand to expound scripture and to exhort the Church, according as it shall be given thee by my Spirit."[5] In that revelation other important doctrines are also set forth. These privileges were not for Emma alone but point to opportunities to all women.

This equality of human rights makes individuals of men and women—individuals with the right of free agency, with the power of individual decision, with individual opportunity for everlasting joy, whose own actions throughout the eternities, with the loving aid of the Father, will determine individual achievement. There can be no question in the Church of man's rights versus woman's rights. They have the same and equal rights.

This doctrine has been respected in the history of the Church. Equal suffrage within the Church has always been recognized. Church members, men and women, have always been asked to sustain by vote of the uplifted hand, those nominated to fill the various offices of the Church.[6]

The right of woman to develop her native gifts through education has been held before the Church from its organization. Women have, indeed, been urged to train for the various life pursuits of society.

However, the Church has never ignored, as many political and social theorists have done, the natural differences between men and women. These differences in function should determine the major duties of man and woman. The unit of the Church is the family composed of husband, wife, and children, in heaven as on earth. In family life all should find their greatest joy and also their chief incentive to useful activity. The Church recognizes that whenever this purpose is ignored, the frustrated functions lead to defeat in life. Therefore, the Church has

---

[5]*Doctrine and Covenants* 25:7.
[6]*Doctrine and Covenants* 20:65; 26:2; 107:22; Joseph Fielding Smith, *op. cit.,* 75; Joseph F. Smith, *op., cit.,* 1949 edition pp. 156-157; *Journal of Discourses,* vol. 7, p. 228.

taught man that the family is another evidence of equality, since, in conforming to natural law, greater freedom and power are won by all.

For the woman, this means that she, at least during a large part of her life, devotes herself chiefly to the duties of home; for the man that he devotes himself chiefly to the providing of the means of support for the home. Naturally, this does not prohibit a woman from exercising her special gifts and outside interests for leisure or free time.

In harmony with this view, the Church has always favored a system of education to fit man and woman for their respective spheres of activity—that is, a practical education. The major education for her life's duties as homemaker may be supplemented by training for the development of special activities or endowment.

This recognition of natural function appears in the organization of the Church. By divine fiat, the priesthood is conferred upon the men. This means that organization must prevail in the family, the ultimate unit of the Church. The husband, the priesthood bearer, presides over the family; but the priesthood conferred upon him is intended for the blessing of the whole family. Every member shares in the gift bestowed, but under a proper organization. No man who understands the gospel believes that he is greater than his wife, or more beloved of the Lord, because he holds the priesthood, but rather that he is under the responsibility of speaking and acting for the family in official matters. Husband and wife are sharers equally in all the blessings of the priesthood. However, it should always be remembered that the husband can speak for his family only if he is living righteously and the members of his family are in accord with his views.[7] That is one reason why in the councils of the Church, the solemn assemblies, the priesthood bearers are called to express themselves first, as representing, not only themselves, but also the family units, followed by the vote of the women and of the

---

[7]Joseph F. Smith, *Gospel Doctrine,* 1919 edition, pp. 359-360.

general membership. In ordinary general conferences men and women vote as one body.

This organization is a protection to the woman who, because of her motherhood, is under a great physical and spiritual obligation. Motherhood is an eternal part of priesthood. It is a wise provision that the man, who is the freer to move about both at home and abroad, should be called to the family presidency and be under the responsibility of holding the priesthood. This does not limit equality of rights among men and women. Citizens in a free land are not unequal because some hold office and others do not.

In further evidence of the equality of the claims of men and women is the doctrine that the highest attainable glory in God's Kingdom cannot be won by man or woman alone. Only those who have been sealed as husband and wife can attain exaltation in the Celestial Kingdom: "Neither is the man without the woman, neither the woman without the man, in the Lord."[8]

In 1842 the Prophet began the more complete organization of women. On March 17 the Relief Society was organized, to the members of which he gave several important messages, all implying the same doctrine for the benefit of women.[9]

Growing out of the Relief Society are other organizations for the benefit of women. These have the same general objectives as the priesthood organizations—the fitting of the individual more fully for gospel living. These are presided over by women. The Prophet Joseph Smith said when he established the Relief Society:

I will organize the sisters under the priesthood and after the pattern of the priesthood.[10] [He also said,] This Society is to get instruction through the order which God has established—through the medium of those appointed to lead—and I now turn the key to you in the name of God and this Society shall rejoice and knowl-

------
[8] 1 Corinthians 11:11.
[9] *History of the Church*, vol. 4, pp. 602-607; vol. 5, pp. 19-21, 23-25, 39-41.
[10] *Relief Society Magazine*, vol. 6, p. 129; *A Century of Relief Society*, p. 14.

edge and intelligence shall flow down from this time—this is the beginning of better days to this Society.[11]

The comprehensiveness of woman's place in the Church was well stated by the Prophet: "The Ladies' Relief Society is not only to relieve the poor, but to save souls."[12] This is the magnificent commission to the womanhood of the Church!

The place of woman in the Church is to walk by the side of the man, not before him nor behind him. Upon the doctrine of equality of rights among men and women, Joseph Smith set about to build the Church of God. Woman must know that God lives and earn her testimony of the mission of Jesus, the same as does her father, brother or husband. Indeed, it is she who implants righteousness into the hearts of her sons and daughters who are later to become priests and priestesses unto God. Her work and her power are mighty in the furthering of the gospel plan.

She must know that Jesus is the Christ, "That by him and through him, and of him, the worlds are and were created and the inhabitants thereof are begotten sons and daughters unto God."[13]

---

[11]From *Original Minutes*, April 28, 1842, Unpublished.
[12]*History of the Church*, vol. 5, p. 25.
[13]*Doctrine and Covenants* 76:24.

CHAPTER 32

THE WAY TO ECONOMIC PROSPERITY

The philosophy of existence was greatly enlarged by the time-sweeping, light-giving revelations of Joseph. It was as a new theology, clothing the scrawny bones of the incomplete, often erroneous, teachings of the past. Thousands who took time to learn the new message sought membership in the restored Church.

The foundation of the work in Joseph's charge was spiritual. It was his task to convert spiritual principles into everyday service. In doing this he broke again with a practice long established under the name of religion.

The churches had promised salvation in the hereafter, but had generally avoided responsibility for temporal human welfare. Indeed they taught that it was godlike to suffer, that the flesh must be punished for righteousness. Certain sects exist today who mutilate their bodies and suffer agony thinking that they thus serve God.

Joseph realized, however, that an understanding of man's eternal life, with all its attendant principles of action, would be useful on earth only if the new truths were put into service for human good in man's affairs on earth. He knew that men would not be wholly satisfied with promises of a happy hereafter. The gospel of Jesus Christ must have the power to improve and enrich man's conditions on earth as well as to promise joy hereafter. Today on earth is as important as tomorrow in heaven. Today would measurably determine the nature of tomorrow. Man must realize that righteousness causes far greater joy than does sin.

Joseph Smith was therefore much concerned with the temporal welfare of the thousands of faithful people who were joining the Church. What should be done for their comfort and progress was his constant query. The words of the Book of Mormon ever pointed the way. "Men are that they might have joy."[1] Therefore, the Church he had been instrumental in restoring must make its members joyful. This became his constant objective.

The elements of joy are many. He turned much of his early attention to the satisfaction of the needs of physical life. In the teachings of Joseph Smith lay the doctrine that the Lord intends for his children earthly as well as heavenly joy. The affairs of daily life must be the concern of the Church.

Among man's physical earthly needs, as he watched the people around him, Joseph found that the lack of economic sufficiency and reasonable security seemed almost of first importance. The many difficulties among men most frequently had their origin in economic needs and inequalities. Were all men economically protected, reasonable certain of sufficient food, clothing, and shelter, if they labored, there would be less contention and more happiness among them.

Poverty had ugly consequences. He himself had been reared in poverty. After his parents lost their small fortune, every member of the family had to labor, with scant rewards, for the necessities of life. He remembered well this constant, depressing battle for survival.

He observed, further, that under similar conditions one man grew rich, another barely maintained himself. He learned that men differ in their power to win support from their surroundings or to overcome adverse conditions. Men were not wholly to blame for their failures, when nature had not endowed them with enough economic wisdom to forage for themselves, successfully, amidst the practicalities of the world.

Joseph asked himself if it were not the duty of a brotherhood like the Church to give guidance and help to such people. But could any system be devised by which every man could be assured of economic sufficiency?

Many attempts, cooperative and communistic, had sprouted at this period of American history to achieve

---

[1] 2 Nephi 2:25.

general economic sufficiency but always with indifferent success. One such association was in full action near Kirtland, Ohio, where the headquarters of the Church were established in 1831.[2] Others were also known to the Prophet.

As usual, Joseph went to the Lord for help. Out of the answers to his prayers on the subject was revealed an ideal economic system, commonly known as the "United Order." It rejected the weaknesses of the many similar attempts and introduced new, almost revolutionary methods of operation.

Its objective was to provide every man who is willing to work with the necessities and the comforts of life, thus abolishing poverty from the earth. It was to be a cooperative plan but directly opposed to modern communism, since it recognized man as a free agent, respected the rights of private property, and preserved and encouraged individual initiative.[3] The United Order thus established rests upon four basic principles.[4]

First, the earth is the Lord's. Men are only stewards of their possessions. All that man has should be used therefore in accordance with the Lord's expressed will.

Second, all men are children of God—of a divine family. Therefore, the Lord requires that they must help one another as needs arise, provided that he who will not work shall have no claim upon his brother.

Third, every man must be respected as a free agent. He may enter the order at his pleasure. Once in the order, he must be allowed to use, fully, and as he pleases, any properties placed in his hands. He may leave the order at his pleasure.

Fourth, the government of the order is vested in a central agency, sustained by the members of the order, presided over by the bishop, his counselors, and such help-

---

[2]Joseph A. Geddes, *The United Order Among the Mormons*, p. 19; F. Y. Fox, *Co-operation Among the Mormons*, p. 8, Thesis.
[3]*Doctrine and Covenants*, Sections 78, 82, 85, 92, 104; Joseph A. Geddes, *op., cit.,*; Edward J. Allen, *The Second United Order Among the Mormons*; Wm. J. McNiff, *Heaven on Earth*.
[4]*Doctrine and Covenants*, Sections 78, 82, 85, 92, 104; Albert E. Bowen, *The Church Welfare Plan*.

ers as may be needed. This central agency would have power to adjust the disputes normally arising among strongly individualized human beings.

The operation of the order under these four heads is extremely simple. Those who join the order would place all their possessions, irrevocably, in a common treasury— the rich man, his wealth; the poor man, his penny. Then each member would receive a sufficient portion, called "an inheritance," from the common treasury, to enable him to continue in his trade, business, or profession as he may desire. The farmer would receive land and implements; the tradesman, tools and materials, the merchant, the necessary capital, the professional man, instruments, books, etc. Members who work for others would receive proportionate interests in the enterprises they serve. No one would be without property—all would have an inheritance.

A person's inheritance would be his personal property, to operate permanently and freely for his benefit and that of his family. Should he withdraw from the order, his inheritance would go with him, but he would have no claim upon that which he had placed in the common treasury. At the end of the year, or a set period, the member who had earned more than his business and family needs required would place the surplus in the common treasury. Thus, for example, large fortunes would be administered by the order as a whole rather than by one individual. The member who, despite intelligent diligence, had lost from his operations would have his loss made up by the general treasury for another start, or he might with his consent be placed in some activity better fitting his gifts.

In short, the general treasury would set up every man in his preferred field and would care for and help those unable to profit from their inheritance. The general treasury, holding the surpluses of the members, would also finance the erection of public buildings and make possible all community enterprises decided upon by the order.

This remarkable economic order was tried out in Ohio and Missouri, chiefly in 1832-1834. The Church was then organizing settlements in Missouri. Though practiced only a short time, about two years, it showed possibilities of great success. However, in those pioneer days, under severe persecution from neighbors, and with undisciplined selfishness of certain members, the people could not give the order a fair trial.

To neighbors not of the Church, it seemed a threat against the existing system of living, and opposition ensued. Many members of the Church, trained in the traditions of the past, did not have faith enough to place their all in the common treasury, under the supervision of a committee of their fellow believers. Consequently, the order was suspended temporarily. Yet the United Order remains a part of the revealed word of the Lord to Joseph Smith. When the Lord so speaks, it will be again a venture for Latter-day Saints—but not before!

It will be observed that many of the principles and practices characteristic of the United Order have found their way into much modern legislation for human economic welfare, but usually incomplete and misleading.

It is a startling and faith-promoting fact that Joseph Smith, about twenty-five years of age, without the advantages of travel or school education, could foresee the solution of the foremost economic problems of the years and set up so wise a solution. The difficulties of industrial relations, economic upheavals, and individual enterprises would vanish under the practice of the United Order. As it stands, it is a mighty evidence of the divine inspiration under which Joseph Smith ever moved. It will yet cover the earth.

In the later days of Brigham Young, a part of the United Order was again given a trial. It proved itself immensely successful, but selfishness on the part of some of the people, and conditions of persecution in the land led to its abolishment.

After the suspension of the United Order the ancient law of tithing was substituted in 1838.[5] This asks every

---

[5]*Doctrine and Covenants*, Section 119.

member to pay into the treasury of the Church one-tenth of his income to be used for the support of the poor and the establishment and carrying forward of the various activities and enterprises of the Church.

Though the United Order was suspended, one of its underlying principles, cooperation, has ever been used and respected. In the early harassed days of the Church, under Joseph Smith, the people helped one another as needs arose. After Joseph's martyrdom the westward movement and the conquest of the desert might have been defeated except for the brotherly cooperation of the people.

Cooperation was always used by the Church in the many economic problems that arose in Joseph's day. Joseph never lost sight of the Church as a great brotherhood among men, requiring the practice of cooperation; for example, Kirtland, Ohio, headquarters of the Church, was a promising section of the United States. The first temple of the Church was erected there. Many Latter-day Saints lived there, engaged in farming and industrial and commercial enterprises. The Church planned to establish there an important center for its spiritual and material activities. This was met with hostility and often with persecution by the non-Mormon residents of the section.

To facilitate the work of the people there was founded in 1837, under the laws of the day, an industrial stock company, known as the Kirtland Safety Society Anti-Banking Company in which the common good should be paramount. The management was to be in the hands of the respective pursuits of the members according to their life pursuits: agriculture, mechanical arts, and merchandising.

The articles of incorporation included some farseeing principles which would have been beneficial to the stockholders had the society continued. Paper currency or due bills were issued by the society as it was lawful to do in that day. Throughout the venture ran the practice and spirit of cooperation. It met in a practical way most of the problems, such as labor disputes, which give us concern today.

However, it was a poor time to undertake any financial operation, anywhere and of any kind. There was in Kirtland and over the whole country, a wild orgy of inflation. Wild speculation was evident. Money was spent freely. Land prices rose far beyond the ability of the land to repay. The Latter-day Saints were caught in this whirling excitement.

Then came the financial panic of 1837. Banks by the hundreds failed throughout the country.[6] Financial enterprises of all kinds were wrecked. Under the tornado of destruction the Kirtland Company collapsed before it had really begun to operate fully.

Pathetically the Prophet wrote in his journal, about the fate of the company: ". . . No institution of the kind, established upon just and righteous principles for a blessing not only to the Church, but to the whole nation, would be suffered to continue its operation in such an age of darkness, speculation and wickedness."[7]

Persecution became so strong that the Prophet and Sidney Rigdon, to save their lives, had to flee from Kirtland.

Joseph's enemies have seized upon this occurrence to charge him with dishonesty. In fact, however, the currency issued by the company and all other debts were redeemed whenever presented. Years after the failure, search was made for remaining debtors.

The failure of the society was a part of the country's failure. Recently examined, the Ohio events, culminating in 1837, show no dishonesty on the part of Joseph Smith or most of his people. Mormons and non-Mormons were caught alike in a deluge which they could not control.

Wherever the Prophet operated, he preached honesty and practiced it. He wrote in his journal ". . . it is the

6J. T. Adams, *The Epic of America*, pp. 211-213.
7*History of the Church*, vol. 2, p. 497.

delight of my soul to be honest. O, Lord, that thou knowest right well."[8]

Meanwhile, the record of the past shows clearly that it is a principle of gospel action to help one another in economic as other phases of life. The evidence also is clear that in the solution of the world's economic problems, Joseph Smith proposed plans which give him a foremost place among the leaders in economic thought. Out of ventures he began, now only partially used, have remained such principles as industry, thrift, and cooperation, which have contributed to make of the followers of Joseph Smith a mighty people.

The welfare program of the Church, now in full operation, harks back to the early economic revelations to Joseph Smith and gets its vigor and success from these early teachings.

Some day the world under stern necessity will adopt and practice the economic program known to the Church as the United Order—but in a manner wholly different from Socialism or Communism.

---

[8]*Ibid.*, vol. 2, p. 281.

CHAPTER 33

THE LAW OF PHYSICAL HEALTH

The Church of Jesus Christ that Joseph Smith was instrumental in restoring took root first on the frontier fringe of the expanding nation. Beyond Missouri, in which state the Church founded settlements within a year or two after its organization, lay the practically unknown West, with neither white people, cities, nor farms.

As measured by modern standards, pioneer life was hard and toilsome. Comforts were few, and had to be homemade. Luxuries were fewer still. Under the existing pioneer conditions the physical health of the people was none too good. Many had aches and ills; others died out of season.

In those frontier settlements food was usually plentiful but seldom of the best variety. Meat predominated; grains were usually available; vegetables and fruits were scarce. For stimulation resort was often had to home-brewed alcoholic beverages, though there was little or no drunkenness; to tobacco, mostly for chewing; and to tea and coffee. These substances were commonly and freely used when available. This, of course, did not give permanent relief from the pains of the body, which were due in large part to the lack of correct physiological knowledge.

Joseph Smith, keenly intelligent, observed these conditions. He was a compassionate man. In obedience to the Book of Mormon doctrine he labored to bring joy into the lives of the members who, with various backgrounds of experience, had come from far and near to be with the Church and its Prophet. He set aside the false doctrine that pain and suffering were necessary to worship God properly. How to secure real joy and real prosperity for the members of the Church caused him constant concern.

It was clear to Joseph that sick people could not be

useful or fully happy. Then how could the health of the people be improved? Moreover, the alcohol and tobacco habits did not seem to comport with the sacred nature of the Church or the duties of Latter-day Saints.

According to his practice he went to the Lord for help. The answer was the remarkable revelation known as the Word of Wisdom,[1] received in 1833, when the Church was about three years old.

It is a brief but comprehensive document, a code of health, covering prophetically and in full harmony with later scientific developments the whole field of food and drink—a field which has developed greatly in recent years with the growth of scientific knowledge. Its larger message is that men must look upon their bodies with understanding eyes and then treat them with intelligent care. Nothing should be taken into the body for food or drink which will injure it and only those which help maintain good health.

A statement is made in the introduction that it is "To be sent greeting: not by commandment or constraint, but by revelation and . . . showing forth the order and will of God in the temporal salvation of all saints."[2] There are those who claim that the truths taught therein are to be obeyed by one's option since it was not given by commandment or constraint. But if a law is given by revelation showing the order and will of God should it not be really more binding than a command because it calls for man's understanding cooperation?

The Word of Wisdom falls into four main parts:

First, it warns that "in consequence of evils and designs which do and will exist in the hearts of conspiring men in the last days, I have warned you, and forewarn you, by giving you this Word of Wisdom."[3]

The lust for gold had led throughout the ages to fraud and deceit in every field of merchandising, including foods, drinks, and drugs, vital to health. The vast

---

[1]*Doctrine and Covenants,* Section 89.
[2]*Ibid.,* 89:2.
[3]*Ibid.,* 89:4.

propaganda in America a few years ago for patent medicines is an example. Fraud often went so far as to mix a white, worthless mineral with flour to make the loaf of bread weigh heavier. The story of fraud in foods is almost unbelievable.

Repeatedly, governments have been pitted against the forces of evil in attempting to control the practice of fraud in foods and drugs but most often have failed. Only in 1906, in the United States, did Congress succeed in passing the present pure food and drug act,[4] which has done so much in preserving human health.

Nevertheless, fraud is still attempting to circumvent the law. The advertising pages of the best magazines are flooded with attractive, misleading statements about alcohol, tobacco, tea, coffee, and cola drinks, all injurious to the body. The cigaret vendors have gone so far that the American Medical Association recently warned them to desist.

The warning against "evil and designing men" in the Word of Wisdom is more than justified. It was prophetic of this day.

The second part of the Word of Wisdom deals with things people should not use. Three substances are enumerated: Alcohol, tobacco, and "hot drinks."

It is an elementary, fully demonstrated fact that alcohol in any form, of any dilution, is injurious to the body. Persons who think that they are helped by alcohol in or out of their work, in social or other enjoyments, are simply fooling themselves.

Business is done less efficiently when the blood is charged with alcohol, and a social gathering that depends upon cocktails for exhilaration may be said to be a primitive group which has no place in this day of enlightenment. It is an insult in the light of present day knowledge to tell a person he cannot be socially acceptable unless he is under the influence of liquor. Science, including medical science, has condemned the use of alcohol.

---

[4]John A. and Leah D. Widtsoe, *The Word of Wisdom*, p. 32.

Tobacco, whether smoked, chewed, or snuffed is injurious to the human organism. Nicotine, a constituent of tobacco, is a deadly poison, which is made tolerable only because it is taken into the body so slowly that some is eliminated from the circulation as the process of chewing or smoking or snuffing proceeds. Tobacco like alcohol is habit-begetting and compels repeated use. Science has condemned its use. It is difficult to understand why intelligent people, otherwise sane and canny, will subject themselves to the evils of alcohol and tobacco.

Besides, the world's consumption of alcohol and tobacco represents a tremendous outlay of money that the world needs for other purposes. In the United States alone every year is spent for alcohol and tobacco a sum which if used properly would banish much of the poverty and suffering in our land.

The term "hot drinks" was interpreted in early days by the Prophet and his brother Hyrum to mean tea and coffee, the commonly used beverages of that day.

Caffeine, the temporarily stimulating and permanently habit-begetting substance in tea and coffee, had scarcely been discovered when the revelation on the Word of Wisdom was given. Neither was it understood that this stimulation of the nervous system by caffeine is injurious. Heart and kidneys are also unfavorably affected. Physicians frequently advise people to give up the use of tea and coffee.

The substance caffeine is widely distributed over the earth. It is found in many plants. Various caffeine beverages are used by the peoples of the world under various names such as maté of South America and Yonpon tea. Of late, vast quantities of so-called cola drinks—really cold coffee because they depend on the caffeine they contain for their popularity—have flooded the market. Chocolate and cocoa also contain a poison similar to caffeine and in addition interfere with mineral metabolism in the body. For that reason they are injurious and habit-forming. All caffeine-containing beverages, under whatever name, are alike in their injurious effect on the human body.

It is an evidence of revelation that the Word of Wisdom uses the generic term "hot drinks" rather than to specify the caffeine drinks of the day. There are also a number of drinks containing other drugs which come under the term "hot drinks." Brigham Young declared that the narcotic substances in all these beverages is the cause of their popularity—and he was right.[5] These substances whether served hot or cold stimulate the body unnaturally, hence may be termed "hot drinks."

The third part of the Word of Wisdom deals with the foods that should be eaten for good health. This is really the most important part of the revelation but has been largely overlooked. It is the part also which developing science has since confirmed.

A healthy body has little craving for things that stimulate the body unnaturally. The revelation specifies for health, fruits, vegetables, grains, and the sparing use of meat. It also mentions the best times to use these foods when they are fresh and "in season." This part of the revelation is in full harmony with the findings of the modern, growing science of nutrition.

Meat should be used "sparingly." This and other nations eat meat to excess. Many of the diseases that ravage the land may be traced to the inordinate use of meat by people who believe, to their ultimate sorrow, that meat should be a part of every meal.

It is now known without dispute—it was not known scientifically when the Word of Wisdom was received— that the constituents needed for life are found in all whole plant products—if they are grown on truly fertile soil. One may live happily and well without meat, if other foods are chosen wisely, though the Word of Wisdom does not forbid the use of meat. But for the best health, all menus must be so ordered that the necessary proteins, fats, carbo-

---

[5]John A. Widtsoe, *Discourses of Brigham Young*, p. 184.

hydrates, minerals, and vitamins are present in sufficient quantities. That means especially unrefined, natural foods.

The revelation also has a paragraph setting forth the suitability of various grains for different animals. This has in part received startling scientific confirmation while other parts await the verdict of progressing science.

The science of nutrition has had very rapid growth in the last generation. The fact that the recent scientific findings in this rapidly growing science of nutrition confirm the statements of the Word of Wisdom is another unexpected evidence of the prophetic gift of Joseph Smith.

The fourth and last part of the Word of Wisdom recites great promises to those who obey it:

> They shall receive health in their navel and marrow in their bones, and shall find wisdom and great treasures of knowledge, even hidden treasures; and shall run and not be weary, and shall walk and not faint; and I, the Lord give unto them a promise, that the destroying angel shall pass by them, as the children of Israel, and not slay them.[6]

It is conceded that the Latter-day Saints have not obeyed the Word of Wisdom to the letter. Despite this partial obedience, these promises have been partly realized. A more complete observance of the Word of Wisdom would lead to a fuller realization of the promises made.

An increase in physical health is one of the promises. The health statistics of the Latter-day Saints show the fulfilment of this promise. The Church appears to be among the healthiest of any like group in the civilized world. Among the Latter-day Saints the diseases that plague and destroy mankind are reduced when compared with the world's rate.

The most recent statistics show that compared with the United States and the world generally the Church of Jesus Christ of Latter-day Saints has much higher health statistics. For example, tuberculosis is practically nonexistent; cancer occurs less than one-half as often. The other diseases follow about the same ratio. The respiratory

---
[6]*Doctrine and Covenants* 89:18-21.

diseases are those that approximate the statistics for other nations. All in all the Church statistics suggest a body of people in excellent health and with great powers for doing the work of the day.

The percentages among the Latter-day Saints of some of the diseases mentioned and many others could be greatly reduced or even non-existent if people would banish all devitalized foods. Health of mind and body would greatly increase if only natural foods were eaten and properly prepared. If that were done, heart disease and cancer, the cause of most deaths today, could be greatly reduced. The Lord has given a guide to health if only people would listen and obey his word.

The Word of Wisdom also promises that wisdom and knowledge will come to those who observe it. This has been marvelously fulfilled. Studies by non-Mormons have shown the Latter-day Saints to stand foremost among similar groups in education, and in achievement in the affairs of men.[7]

Note the prophetic elements in the revelation known as the Word of Wisdom. It predicts the growth in the world of fraud and warns against it; it foretells the evils of caffeine beverages before the physiologic action of caffeine was known; it prescribes a nutritional code of living in full harmony with the science which was born long after 1833; and it predicts results from obedience to the code, which have been verified.

The remarkable thing about this document is that it is presented in the name of the Lord. This removes it from the field of fads. It becomes a law for all who seek health. It also confirms the claim that Joseph Smith was a modern Prophet of God.

The spirit of this great document is that mankind should avoid all things injurious to the body and use only the foods and drinks that are nutritionally sound. It does not present lists of permitted or prohibited articles. That

---

[7]*Improvement Era*, July, 1947, p. 445.

should not be expected of the Church in this day of universal enlightenment. Every person may inform himself which of the multitude of food and beverage offerings are harmful and should be avoided and which are good and may be safely used.

The Word of Wisdom is best kept by those who are masters of their appetites. This gives the revelation a high spiritual value. Self-mastery is an objective of Latter-day Saints.

The Word of Wisdom shows the importance of the human body, aside from the question of physical well-being. It is the earthly home of an immortal spirit. In its celestialized condition it will be the eternal possession of that spirit in its unending progress. It is sacred, should so be held. It is the duty and should be the joy of all to give care to the body, to observe the Lord's law of health, in full, as given in this wonderful revelation.

The Word of Wisdom as it stands is another convincing evidence of the prophetic power and divine inspiration of Joseph Smith.

CHAPTER 34

LOOKING TOWARD A HAPPY SOCIETY

During the brief life of Joseph Smith, the Church did its work under much persecution, mainly in and near Kirtland, Ohio, later in the State of Missouri, and finally in and near Nauvoo, Illinois. There was little opportunity in any of these places for long-continued operations by the people.

In 1831, soon after the organization, headquarters of the Church were established in Kirtland, Ohio. The Saints settled in the village and in the neighboring territory. Church headquarters remained in Kirtland until 1838.

The first stake of Zion, with its various organizations and officers, was organized in Kirtland. It was there the Church, in its poverty, built its first temple, easily the finest structure in the neighborhood. Many of the fundamental revelations of the Church were received during this period. In Kirtland also the Saints undertook their first social, educational, and economic ventures. This was a foundation-laying period in the history of the Church.

The Prophet felt the need of having the people begin the great work of establishing the kingdom of God in some place less settled than the Ohio country. There were big things to be done by the Church. Freedom and opportunity were needed. Of course he did not plan to withdraw his people from other people or places. He was practical-minded. Neighbors could be converted to the faith. To be in the world, but not of it, was a motto of the people. In short, he looked for a place where his people could best begin to build Zion according to God's revealed word.

He looked westward, near the extreme western borders of the United States, in Missouri. Soon after the organization of the Church in September, 1830, he sent a missionary party to the Indian lands of the West. Under the leadership of Oliver Cowdery, second elder of the Church, they were to preach to the Indians and tell them of the new book about their forefathers. This they did until the official Indian agents, fearing religious excitement among the Indians, asked the missionaries to withdraw.

The small missionary company then spent the winter of 1830-31 in Independence, Missouri. This city, village it was then, with the surrounding country, the whole state, in fact, was on the western populated boundary of the United States. The country was sparsely settled in the midst of abundant fertile, vacant land. The Missouri country appeared to be a place where industry and frugality could build the Church of Jesus Christ in peace and acceptably to the Lord. It seemed to be the place desired.

After inquiring from the Lord,[1] it was decided to establish Church settlements in the Missouri country, which became in the minds of the Saints, "the land of Zion." There cities and temples would be built. There the law of the Lord could and would be kept. The Prophet arrived there in July, 1831. On the 3rd of August he dedicated a spot "A little west of Independence"[2] for the site of the central temple of the Church. Thousands of Saints then moved to Missouri, broke land, raised crops, built towns, and saw amidst pioneer hardships the promise of prosperity, spiritually and temporally.

Soon, however, jealousies and antagonisms by surrounding peoples developed against the Saints. The older settlers could not live the clean teachings of the Latter-day Saints. Besides, they feared that the newcomers would take possession of the state and rule it. Slave-owning, to which the Saints were opposed, also became a live issue. Animosities broke out. Unspeakable persecutions began, and at last in 1838 the Church as a whole left Missouri, literally expelled or driven out after untold tragedies of mobbing, burning of homes and even murder. It was Missouri's loss.

---

[1]*Doctrine and Covenants*, Section 57.
[2]*History of the Church*, vol. 1, p. 199.

The story is one of the ugliest in American history. This unhappy and indefensible chapter of unprincipled persecution was only in full keeping with the prophetic warning Joseph Smith had received.[3] He who bears a truth which is contrary to tradition is seldom well-received.

During the Missouri period, on June 25, 1833, Joseph Smith prepared a plan for an ideal city, the central city, the city of Zion, to be built at or near Independence but as a model for other cities the world over. The rough sketch is in the L. D. S. Historian's Office in Salt Lake City, Utah. It is an intriguing contribution to city planning, and the social welfare of humanity, as worthy of consideration today as then.[4]

Joseph Smith was aware of the social needs of people. He did not favor isolated living on farms. For social happiness people must live in groups, not apart. The members of the Church should live in compact communities, devised to meet the social needs of all people. To support this view, and to show its practical accomplishments, he prepared a plat with accompanying explanations of the "city of Zion."

The city proper was to be a mile square. It should provide accommodations for fifteen to twenty thousand persons. If the population overflowed the set limits, another similar city should be laid out. If necessary, the world might be covered with such small cities. Throughout the years since then it has become more and more evident that a large city seldom provides a fully natural, wholesome life. In the large cities also there are more opportunities for crime and indecent living.

It is a common saying that from the farms and small villages comes refreshing blood for the city. It is a common practice for those who can afford it to have country homes or participate in enjoyments simulating an uncrowded, unhurried life. Joseph's ideal city is therefore of special interest in our day when the difficulties

---

[3]*Journal of Discourses,* vol. 15, p. 358; *Doctrine and Covenants* 90: 34-37.
[4]*History of the Church,* vol. 1, p. 357.

and disadvantages of the large city have been demonstrated.

The blocks of the city were to cover ten acres. A home or building lot was to cover one-half acre, with a frontage of sixty-six feet, and a depth of three hundred and thirty feet. There should be but one house on a lot, and it should be built of brick or stone. The houses would be set back twenty-five feet from the street. The front yard of each lot was to be planted to flowers and shrubs; the back yard was to be a garden with fruit bushes and trees for the food support of the family.

The provision of a home garden has become of increasing interest since Joseph Smith's day, especially to those understanding the need of fresh food "in the season thereof." The machine age has gradually overtaken us. Relief from the monotony of machines is becoming more and more necessary. The home garden, for flowers and food, has appealed to many keen students of human welfare, such as Henry Ford,[5] as a solution of the problem.

The conditions of the present large city deprive people of their needed contact with nature and increase monotony until the people seek recreation of doubtful value in serving the needs of body and mind. A farm-factory or farm-city arrangement, by which the worker could, during a good part of the year, spend time daily in the open, under the sky, in contact with the soil, would furnish change, increase health, and contribute materially to the family food supply and its health. It would also divert attention from the many less desirable recreations of the day. It was a very simple, natural solution of a living problem especially needed today.

In the crowded European cities where the need has been felt as everywhere, the areas of small household gardens are in the suburbs, the only available space. In the United States a large number of experiments have been tried which recognize the unnatural, fulltime fac-

---

[5]Ford and Crowther, *My Life Work*, pp. 188-191.

tory life, such as the "little landers," "three acres and liberty," etc. Henry Ford actually undertook to make provision for a factory-farm life by making home gardens available.[6]

There were to be no barns and stables in the city proper. A special area on the south of the city, but adjoining it, would be set aside for such purposes. The consequent health advantages are apparent. All other activities, factories, etc., would also be just outside the square mile of the city.

Enough land should be under cultivation outside of the city, but near it, to supply the people with food. The time lost by the farmer in going back and forth between home and farm would be compensated for by the advantages of the ideal city life. Since the city was to be small, distances to the farm and back would not be great.

The streets were to be eight rods, or one hundred and thirty-two feet wide, much wider than was common in those days. These wide streets laid out at right angles clearly foreshadowed prophetically the need of parking space in our automobile age.

The public buildings, temples, churches, schools, etc., were to be grouped in the center of the city where they could be reached easily in the small city. No one would have to go more than half a mile from home to reach a public institution.

Several of the public buildings indicated on the plat are called temples. They were to be used in the work of the Church. Each office in the priesthood would have its own temple in which its special work could be performed.

There were also to be twenty-four community centers, in which no doubt were intended rooms for meetings, recreation, and probably schools. Twenty-four such community houses would mean that the city population would be divided into sizable groups of six to eight hundred souls. This corresponds well with the numbers found

---

[6]Bolton Hall, *Three Acres and Liberty.*

to be best in effective ward organization. It seems also that places were set aside for commercial establishments.

All in all, the principles applied in this layout of the ideal city correspond largely with the best thinking of the present day. In principle, it may be used successfully in the world today and may aid in the reorganization of cities that have grown up Topsy-like.

Many a disadvantage, now recognized, would have been avoided in the cities founded in the world since his day had Joseph's plan for an ideal city been kept in mind. Unfortunately, the Missouri and later persecutions prevented the building of the planned city. Principles of the plan survive in the cities the Saints built in the far west.

Let us repeat, Joseph Smith was conscious of the social needs of people. It was not enough that they were healthy in body or well-to-do economically. To be happy, they must be brought together under attractive conditions. So instead of the isolated farm, or the overgrown city, he proposed an ideal city conforming to the natural needs of man.

It is astonishing that this suggestion for city building came from an unlettered young man about twenty-six years of age, untrained in the world's way. But it was characteristic of Joseph Smith. Wherever he went, he blazed new paths. With fearlessness, in every quarter, he tried to improve existing conditions. He always brought light into dark places. He was daring and defended himself with the possession of truth.

He was not only a planner of buildings and cities, he was also a builder. From the beginning of his career he erected houses where the people could live or assemble to study or to hear God's word. That he could do this under constant persecution and much travel is a wonder.

In 1833, though the infant Church was exceedingly poor, preparations were made to build a temple in Kirtland, Ohio, then the headquarters of the Church. The Lord had so commanded. Four years later, on March

27, 1836, the building, notable for the time and place, was dedicated. It is still a see-worthy structure, and must have been a monument to the Church in early pioneer days. Architecturally, and in the quality of the work of the builders, it has won much admiration.

Another temple, the most notable building of Joseph's time was built in Nauvoo, Illinois, also after years of persecution and poverty of the Saints. The Prophet did not live to see it dedicated; but it stood until destroyed by vandalism, storm and fire, an evidence of the greatness of the vision of Joseph Smith in planning and achievement. He selected sites for several other temples, which of course were not used when the people were driven into the western deserts.

October 21, 1841, the cornerstone of the "Nauvoo House" was laid. However, this was never completed during the lifetime of the Prophet. August 31, 1843,[7] he moved into the "mansion house" in Nauvoo, a private dwelling, in which traveling guests could be entertained. He knew that our Father in heaven, the Being with whom he communed, has an interest in the minute details of human life. We are always in his mind and may appeal to him about any need, however simple it may seem.

Whatever the Prophet touched was changed for the better. Despite the persecutions and hardships of his life, he would not follow the traditional patterns of the past if they could be improved upon to meet existing needs. The events of his life unite to bear testimony that of himself he could not have accomplished the gigantic work of his life.

He had help from higher powers!

---

[7]*Doctrine and Covenants* 124:22-24.

CHAPTER 35

A BASIS FOR POLITICAL GOVERNMENT

Joseph Smith understood that a form of earthly government is necessary when people dwell together. He learned early in his life that the kind of government and the administration of it determine largely the happiness of a people.

His own political philosophy set up the government of God as the ideal which all earthly governments should attempt to imitate. He looked forward to the coming of Jesus as the earth's ruler when the nations would unite in building the kingdom of God, that is, would use the laws of God for their guidance. Then the battle against evil would be won; happiness would be man's portion. Until that time man-made governments would properly be in the world.

Joseph Smith was an idealist who desired to better all human practices; but he was a practical idealist. He and the Church he had been instrumental in restoring were but a handful in a large and growing country. The best that they could do would be to be good citizens in the land, take an active part in its affairs, and by their teachings and example help to better existing conditions. He understood that the coming kingdom of God would not come by revolution but by the gradual change in the hearts of men. He foresaw that it might take a long time. Meanwhile he and his people must help perfect governments as they now exist, by planting in them the principles of the gospel, slowly at first, victoriously at last, always patiently, but with no lack of faith in the outcome, certain that they were preparing for Christ's coming.

During his life he had frequent contacts with the law and with politics which helped him understand the political needs of the people and the law of his day and

214 JOSEPH SMITH — SEEKER AFTER TRUTH

the land in which he lived. These have been summarized briefly as follows:

1. He stood before law courts, for various reasons, from March, 1826, until the end of his days: justices' courts, county, municipal, and district courts of the American states, and the Federal District Courts.

2. He secured copyrights, deeds, and other rights and privileges, including bankruptcy, from government.

3. He organized the Church in conformance with the laws of the State of New York, and eventually modified its internal control by the device of the trustee-in-trust under the laws of Illinois.

4. He organized a frontier military expedition, Zion's Camp. He later re-shaped the military institution into the Far West, Missouri, militia (which was unsatisfactory), and eventually into the independent Nauvoo Legion.

5. He managed various lobbies before the Missouri and Illinois legislatures, before the U. S. Congress, and himself spent the winter of 1839-40 in Washington, D.C., as special pleader.

6. He "concocted" the Nauvoo Charter and contrived several additional political schemes within the framework of the American system such as requesting Congressional authority to enlist one hundred thousand men, not to be constituted a member of the Army, to police the Rocky Mountains and bring Texas, the western Mexican and British claimed Oregon territories into the American Union.

7. He was mayor of the largest city in Illinois and simultaneously chief justice of the most unique municipal court ever seen in America, and Lieutenant-General of the most unique body of troops. He was mayor, chief justice, general and religious leader, all rolled into one.

8. He ran for President of the United States and organized a campaign throughout the United States.

9. These, and many other things, could be cited. Many of them defy explanation. They seem fantastic today. But our concern with history, Joseph Smith's or any other,

is not merely for what happened in the past, but in what history suggests by way of principle for the present and the future.[1]

His practical political philosophy began by declaring that every form of government should rest upon a foundation of righteousness, that is, upon the laws of the Lord. That would be a test of the quality of any government. That having been done, he set up a few simple principles to be observed by makers of governmental systems. In his many political utterances he showed himself, "acquainted with the fundamental problems of governmental practice—and of the difficulties incumbent on (present) political life."[2]

First: He said that an acceptable government must be instituted and operated for the safety, protection, and general welfare of society—for all the people. If it allows a man or group of men special unearned privileges it is evil. It must be fair and just to all.

Second: A good government must secure for every citizen the free exercise of conscience. Matters of belief or religious practice should not be interfered with, unless they oppose laws formulated for the common good. There should be no mingling of religious influence with civil governments. The two can help each other without trespassing upon each other's fields.

Joseph Smith's philosophy of government, whether heavenly or earthly, really began with freedom for every individual man. Governments must respect man's free agency. All must have the right to accept or reject any offering. There must be no coercion, no tyranny. Full liberty must reign. Any attempt to curtail individual freedom is of the devil.

Only two limitations were placed politically upon the free agent: He must not interfere with the rights of others, and he must obey the laws of the majority. Government "should guarantee to all parties, sects and de-

---

[1] G. Homer Durham, "Joseph Smith and the Political World of 1950." Published in the *Logan Herald Journal,* December 15, 1950. Talk given at the Utah State Agricultural College.

[2] G. Homer Durham, *Joseph Smith, Prophet-Statesman,* 1944 edition, p. 21.

nominations, and classes of religion, equal, coherent and indefeasible rights."[3] Moreover, those who enforce the law should not depart from these principles.

The laws of the land should conform to the government of God. In Joseph's own words:

> The government of God has always tended to promote peace, unity, harmony, strength and happiness; while that of man has been productive of confusion, disorder, weakness and misery.[4]

He insisted that all men should labor to the end that God's government be established.

Third: Citizens of any country are bound to obey and uphold the laws of the land in which they reside. Latter-day Saints should be the best citizens wherever they live. If not satisfied, they should move elsewhere or with lawful means seek to correct existing conditions.

Fourth: Officers of the government should execute the laws of the land honestly, in fairness and justice to all. Weak and strong should be treated alike. Joseph Smith was painfully aware of possible abuses by officers of the government. He had observed, in his own troubled career, the frequent miscarriage of justice flowing from the improper exercise of authority. He spoke of his own experiences when he called on the President of the United States to ask for constitutional redress for the suffering of his people. The answer was, "Your cause is just, but I can do nothing for you."[5]

All this and more pertaining to political government is set forth in a document published in 1835, as Section 134 of the Doctrine and Covenants, with confirmatory statements in various revelations to the Prophet.

In eloquent words he stated the political motto of the Church in a rhapsody on the government of the United States:

> Peace and good order in society. Love of God and good will to men. All good and wholesome laws, virtue and truth above all

---

[3]*History of the Church*, vol. 3, pp. 303-305.
[4]*Times and Seasons*, vol. 3, p. 855.
[5]*Journal History*, March 21, 1850 edition, p. 4.

things, and aristarchy live forever! But woe to tyrants, mobs, aristocracy, anarchy and toryism, and all those who invent or seek out unrighteous and vexatious law suits, under the pretext and color of law, or office, either religious or political. Exalt the standard of Democracy! Down with that of priestcraft, and let all the people say Amen! that the blood of our fathers may not cry from the ground against us. Sacred is the memory of that blood which bought for us our liberty.[6]

The Prophet held that the American government most nearly approached his political ideals. The Constitution of the United States, he was told by the Lord, was formulated by "wise men" who were raised up for "this very purpose, and who redeemed the land by the shedding of blood."[7] In discussing the effect of the Constitution on human lives, he said, that

. . . the Constitution of the United States is a glorious standard; it is founded in the wisdom of God.
It is a heavenly banner; it is . . . like the cooling shades and refreshing waters of a great rock in a thirsty and weary land. It is like a great tree under whose branches men from every clime can be shielded from the burning rays of the sun.[8]

Yet he recognized the human weakness in it which should gradually be modified.[9]

His views on political government for the protection of its citizens are well expressed in the charter of the city of Nauvoo, of which he wrote "is of my own plan and device." He adds, "I concocted it for the salvation of the Church, and on principles so broad, that every man might dwell secure under its protective influence, without distinction of sect or party."[10]

In 1844, a few months before his martyrdom, Joseph Smith became a candidate for the Presidency of the United States. He felt he should do this in defense, under the Constitution, of the religious and civil rights of his people.

As part of his political campaign he prepared and

---

[6]*History of the Church*, vol. 3, p. 9.
[7]*Doctrine and Covenants* 101:76-80.
[8]*History of the Church*, vol. 3, p. 304.
[9]*Ibid.*, vol. 6, pp. 56-59,
[10]*Ibid.*, vol. 4, p. 249.

circulated a document (February 7, 1844) known as "Views of the Powers and Policy and the Government of the United States."[11]

This is a remarkable document. It summarizes Joseph's political views as applied to life in America at that time. It is good reading for the politicians of today.

First among his major declarations is the doctrine that popular government should "study the convenience of the people more than the comfort of the cabinet." This is a body blow against prevailing political selfishness and office-seeking. He held further that since the central government has means to foresee many of the needs of the country it should plan how to satisfy them.

He urged that the government should foster agriculture and the industrial arts. To do this he thought that a "judicious tariff" would be justified.

In international matters the objective should always be peace, openly stated. There is no place for secret agreements. He also laid down the doctrine that "To be prepared for war is one of the most effectual means of preserving peace."[12]

He warned against personal selfishness in practical politics and suggested that political promises should not be made to win votes nor should they be believed.

He believed that a smaller Congress would make it a more workable body. He said wisely, "Curtail the officers of government in pay, numbers and power."[13]

He urged prison reform upon the nation and recommended remedial, corrective measures instead of the traditional methods of confinement and capital punishment. He said, "Let penitentiaries be turned into seminaries of learning." He would abolish entirely the practice of that day to imprison persons for debt.

His solution of the slavery question then imminent was most statesmanlike. He proposed that the government should purchase the slaves from their owners then set the

---

[11]*Ibid.*, vol. 6, pp. 197-209; see especially, G. Homer Durham, *Joseph Smith, Prophet-Statesman*, Chapter 30.
[12]*History of the Church*, vol. 6, p. 199.
[13]*Ibid.*, vol. 6, pp. 204-205.

slaves free. Had this been done, the bloody Civil War would have been avoided, and the feeling between the North and the South would have been mitigated.

He spoke out against waste in government. Waste is never defensible. Public business should be conducted economically. In the field of economics he recommended a decentralized but national bank system, the profits of which should be applied towards national and states revenues.

To the President of the United States he would give power to suppress mobs in behalf of civil liberties in internal affairs. That has a direct bearing on present-day problems as it did upon the needs of the young Church in Joseph's day.

Finally, looking again towards the coming kingdom of God, which shall cover the earth, he recommended the annexation of Oregon, Canada, Texas, and Mexico. He said, "Let the Union spread from the east to the west sea."

This campaign document is an intelligent, comprehensive, forward-looking statement of policies, worthy of a trained statesman. Many of the Prophet's recommendations have been adopted in the progressive passage of the years. All of them are reasonable and sound.

However, Joseph Smith distinguished sharply between political and religious matters. He said:

> It is our duty to concentrate all our influence to make popular that which is sound and good, and unpopular that which is unsound. 'Tis right politically for a man who has influence to use it—in relation to politics, I will speak as a man; but in relation to religion, I will speak in authority.[14]

The political utterances and practices of Joseph Smith point to him as a statesman[15]—one from whom the statesmen of the day could win help. Looking back to his day, one cannot help marveling at the breadth of his vision and how sanely he dealt with the problems of the day.

---

[14]*History of the Church,* vol. 5, p 286.
[15]For a fuller study of this subject read, G. Homer Durham, *op., cit.*

When he touched a matter, whatever its nature, Joseph Smith overtopped the crowd. He has not yet been recognized as he should have been, as a prophet-statesman. Everywhere he is revealed as one who did work beyond the ordinary powers of man. He was led by God.

CHAPTER 36

OPENING THE KINGDOM OF THE MIND

Joseph Smith was building, under God's direction, a Church for human joy. He understood that such joy requires more than temporal satisfaction. Economic security and social advantages, political protection, important as they are, do not of themselves provide full joy. Things of the mind and spirit, eternal truths, must be added. He was an intense lover of truth. He would have all men know the fierce joy of possessing and using truth—all truth in every division of human activity.

Joseph himself had had little school training. He recognized his deficiency and sought to make up for it by later study. One might, of course, ask if this was necessary. He was a prophet of God. He was in communion with divine sources. Could he not go there for any needed information? That is an erroneous conception of revelation and education.

The children of men are expected to use their own powers in all their affairs. The gathering of knowledge is no exception. Only when man has gone as far as he can, and more knowledge is required, does the Lord come with direct help. The restoration of the gospel demanded help beyond the powers of man. Such help was given in translating. But it was expected of Joseph that he would exert himself to find knowledge through the use of his natural senses.

The Lord set up for his people the importance of learning. They were told that "The glory of God is intelligence, or in other words light and truth."[1] Light and truth were the key words of Joseph's educational search. The people understood that intelligence was a compound of knowledge and use of knowledge under the plan of salvation.

---

[1] *Doctrine and Covenants* 93:36; 88:78-80.

The Lord also said to them, "Seek ye out of the best books words of wisdom; seek learning even by study and also by faith."[2] So Joseph reached out for more knowledge, more training, to use in his divine work.

A tremendous value, new to the people of Joseph's day, was given to education: "If a person gains more knowledge and intelligence in this life through his diligence and obedience than another, he will have so much the advantage in the world to come."[3] "Whatever principle of intelligence we attain to in this life, it will rise with us in the resurrection."[4] He fortified this doctrine by declaring that, "It is impossible for a man to be saved in ignorance."[5] Education in its spiritual and secular sense had never before been lifted to such a height.

One of the first demands for secular knowledge came from the field of languages. To understand the views of the various translators of the Bible he needed to know some of the languages of the original Bible manuscripts and of the languages into which the Bible had been translated. Therefore he became a student, somewhat proficient, of ancient and modern languages.

He did not depend entirely on self-education. He employed, for example, Professor Joshua Seixas, a capable Hebrew scholar, to teach Hebrew to himself and other members of the Church.[6] He dipped into Greek and Latin. He continued these studies throughout his life. As late as a year or two before his death, he was studying German.

He did the same in the field of law. The persecutions heaped upon the Church brought him into frequent contact with the law and government of the country. He felt the need of a better understanding of the law and legal processes. He undertook, therefore, in the chaotic Missouri days, the study of law. He, with Sidney Rigdon, employed Generals Doniphan and Atchison to teach them law.[7] In fact, Joseph Smith acquired a good knowledge of the law,

---

[2]*Ibid.*, 88:118.
[3]*Ibid.*, 130:19.
[4]*Ibid.*, 130:18
[5]*Ibid.*, 131:6.
[6]*History of the Church*, vol. 2, p. 368.
[7]*Ibid.*, vol. 3, p. 69.

which helped him much in defending himself and his people.

His active mind led him into other fields: history, literature, and many other subjects. By the time of his death, his assiduous seeking for knowledge had made Joseph Smith, in worldly terms, a well-educated man. This is the more remarkable when the constantly unsettled conditions of his life are considered.

The study of his works reveals a mind of high quality and of good secular education and superior spiritual knowledge.

Scarcely had the Church been organized before he began to provide for common schools for children.[8] At that time public schools were few on the frontier. In June, 1831, a year after the organization of the Church, Oliver Cowdery and W. W. Phelps were appointed a committee to select and write books for the schools.[9]

A year later appeared the first number of the *Evening and Morning Star,* the first periodical published by the Church.[10] The Church has always believed in the efficacy of the printed word. Therefore, wherever the Church went or was driven in those days, a periodical was founded for the benefit of the Church. In this first issue of its first periodical the Church is urged to lose no time but to get common schools organized and under way. The importance of this is pointed out, for "Children soon become men and women. Yes, they are they who must follow us."[11]

Parents and guardians were warned that though they may have to wait for the erection of schoolhouses, the education of children need not be delayed. The youth of Zion should be taught by their elders, parents or others, at home and everywhere. The Church has always placed home training as of equal or greater importance with training in schools.

The famous words of Moses concerning the laws of the Lord are quoted:

---

[8]*Ibid.,* vol. 1, p. 276.
[9]*Doctrine and Covenants* 55:4.
[10]*History of the Church,* vol. 1, p. 276.
[11]*Ibid.,* vol. 1, p. 277.

Thou shalt teach them diligently unto thy children, and shalt talk of them when thou sittest in thy house, and when thou walkest by the way, and when thou liest down, and when thou risest up.[12]

There was an eagerness in the Church for education.

Many of the older men who had come into the Church had a meager school education, though some were far above the average of the day. All were bearers of the glad tidings of the restoration of the gospel. They should possess every available help in their work. The Prophet threw aside the old myth that older people cannot learn.

He organized by December, 1832, a school for adults, which he called the School of the Prophets.[13] By that act, the Church virtually became the forerunner of adult education which, in the last few years, has swept over the world.

The imagination is stirred by the picture of the mature, bearded, hard working members of the Church, going to the schoolroom, after the day's labor, to study the elements of education, and often venturing into the higher fields—languages and history, mathematics and science— to prepare themselves more fully for the task of preaching the restored gospel to the world.

The School of the Prophets was given careful instructions as to what should be done.[14] The program of study was all that any university might devise.

Teach ye diligently and my grace shall attend you; that you may be instructed more perfectly in theory, in principle, in doctrine, in the law of the gospel, in all things that pertain unto the kingdom of God, that are expedient for you to understand; of things both in heaven and in the earth, and under the earth; things which have been, things which are, things which must shortly come to pass; things which are at home, things which are abroad; the wars and the perplexities of the nations, and the judgments which are on the land, and a knowledge also of countries and kingdoms.[15]

When traveling, men might be found at resting periods with their textbooks on the wagon tongue, while the mother

----

[12]Deuteronomy 6:7.
[13]*Doctrine and Covenants* 88:127.
[14]*Ibid.*, 88:136-141; 90:7-13; 95:10-17; 97:5-6.
[15]*Ibid.*, 88:78-79.

taught the children in the tent. Copies of the textbooks used by the School of the Prophets are extant. They were among the best of that day. No fear, only love of learning seemed to characterize the schools of the Saints.

In the prayer offered at the dedication of the temple in Kirtland, Ohio, in 1836, Joseph Smith asked that all who should worship in the house may be "taught words of wisdom out of the best books, and that they may seek learning even by study and also by faith."[16] Education was held a sacred duty of the Latter-day Saints. The upper or attic story of the Kirtland Temple was divided into several classrooms for the use of the Saints.

When the Prophet laid out the plan for the ideal city of Zion, ample provision was made for schools. The need of mental development was never forgotten.

When, after a decade of persecution, the Church members hoped, in 1839, that they had a permanent abiding place in Nauvoo, Illinois, their thoughts turned without delay to education. In the charter of the city, provision was made for a university, "an institution of learning," in which could be taught the "arts, sciences and learned professions."[17]

This was one of the first, if not the first, city university to be supported by the taxes of the people. It was organized according to the best practice of the day.

Sometime later the supervision of the common schools in Nauvoo was transferred to the university. Thus all the school activities of the city were placed under one head.[18] This vexed question of the present day was settled satisfactorily in Nauvoo. Authority was centralized.

The development of education under Joseph Smith is notable. He lifted learning to eternal heights. He insisted on the foremost necessity of schools; he pointed out the value of home training combined with school training; he set up education for adults at a time when only young

16Ibid., 109:14.
17History of the Church, vol. 4, p. 301.
18Ibid.. vol. 4, p. 303.

people were thought able to learn; he entered the field of higher education and declared that higher education was so necessary that it should be supported by taxation; he unified all educational activities in a district under one head.

The desire for light and truth, imbedded in the very structure of the restored Church of Jesus Christ, became the driving force in the labors of Joseph Smith. Light and truth were the keys with which he attempted to unlock the door to the kingdom of the mind. In the gospel that he was called to restore, there was no place, no room, for darkness, error, or confusion.

It must be said also that despite the hardships endured by the early Church, the mobbings, drivings, and expulsions, the love of the things of the spirit never left the people. They were kept alive by the love of truth inherent in the gospel.

The Kirtland Temple was built in the deep poverty of the Saints. Yet the workmanship is a thing of beauty. The Nauvoo Temple, now destroyed, also shows the reaching out for beauty. The surviving homes of the Saints of Joseph's day show the same strong desire for beauty. Things of the spirit were fostered by Joseph Smith.

In poetry and writing generally this desire was likewise expressed. Men and women were led to write beautiful thoughts. The hymns of that day were sung with joy and are used today. The Church touched the creative arts in home construction, decoration, even in painting.

These pioneer people, rich beyond their fellows in the knowledge of eternal truth, lived amidst their daily toil largely in the domain of the mind.

The present foremost educational standing of Latter-day Saints may be traced back to the impetus given by Joseph Smith.[19] The educational desires of Joseph's day have been carried over to this day and have increased with the added years.

---

[19]John A. Widtsoe and Richard L. Evans "The Educational Level of the Latter-day Saints," *Improvement Era*, vol. 50, p. 444.

Yet, he was an unlettered young man, twenty-five years of age, when the foundations for this work were laid!

It is simple enough. Whoever makes light and truth the issues of the day, though he is poor in worldly goods and persecuted by the evil minded, will live joyfully in the splendors of the mind.

CHAPTER 37

THE CLEAN FAMILY UNIT

It is nothing short of miraculous that the enemies of Joseph Smith, who have resorted to almost every untruth about him, have seldom charged him with sex immorality. Forty-seven times he was obliged to defend himself in courts of law against trivial charges which were not sustained by evidence.[1] In not one of these was he accused of unseemly relations with women. No woman's name was ever linked, sinfully, with his. He was so clean morally that even those who hated him and his doctrine most did not venture to accuse him of moral wrong.

True, the doctrine of plural marriage announced a few years before his death—though revealed to him about 1831—was declared by enemies to be only a subterfuge for licentiousness. But plural wives were held in honor: there was an infinity of distance between polygamous relations in which all wives were held equal with good homes and education for the children, and the submerged, lawless sex associations of the day.

Likewise, the Church as a whole met no charges of immorality. Life was not polished on the frontier, in speech, manners, or practices. Moral looseness was too often condoned. Though in the midst of such pioneer conditions, sometimes lawless, the Church clung to the commandments of God. The evidence declares that strict chastity and morality for men and women alike ruled within the Church.

Joseph was building a Church for human joy. He was thoroughly aware that to accomplish his purpose morality must be observed. Immorality corrupts and ultimately destroys man's power to lift himself into higher realms of joy. Cleanliness, which is allied to truth, must be the foundation of man's eternal journey toward the

---

[1] *Journal of Discourses,* vol. 8, p. 16.

likeness of God. The voice of truth cannot be heard in an atmosphere of moral sin. Men and women must keep themselves clean to win God's favor, and to live lives of joy. Morality was always taught by the Prophet. Note the extract from his journal in 1843:

> I was present with several of the Twelve, and gave an address tending to do away with every evil, and exhorting them to practice virtue and holiness before the Lord; told them that the Church had not received any permission for me to commit fornication, adultery, or any corrupt action; but my every word and action have been to the contrary. If a man commit adultery, he cannot receive the celestial kingdom of God. Even if he is saved in any kingdom, it cannot be the celestial kingdom. . . . I condemned such actions *in toto,* and warned the people present against committing such evils; for it will surely bring a curse upon any person who commits such deeds.[2]

From the organization of the Church strict morality was required of Church members. The ancient law was restated. To quote:

> . . . thou shalt love thy wife with all thy heart, and shall cleave unto her, and none else. And he that looketh upon a woman to lust after her shall deny the faith, and shall not have the spirit; and if he repents not he shall be cast out. Thou shalt not commit adultery; and he that committeth adultery and repenteth not shall be cast out.[3]

This command led to action. Those found in moral sin were brought before Church tribunals and tried for their Church membership. One of the most notable of such actions was the excommunication, in the early days of the Church, of Philastus Hurlburt. His excommunication for adultery and the refusal of the Church to restore him to membership, after another sin, made him a bitter enemy of the Church and led him to write the scurrilous book called, *Mormonism Unvailed,* which has been used over the century as the basis of anti-Mormon literature. But in obeying the Lord's commands, the Prophet did not count the cost.

[2]*History of the Church,* vol. 6, p. 81.
[3]*Doctrine and Covenants* 42:22-24; 42:75-80; 59:6; 63:14-16; 66:10; 132:41-44.

On the other hand, the Church was taught to hold lawful marriage in high esteem. In the early days of the Church there was a society in America which forbade marriage. The members of that cult approached Church members with their propaganda. This brought explicit words from the Lord through the Prophet:

> Whoso forbiddeth to marry is not ordained of God, for marriage is ordained of God unto man. Wherefore it is lawful that he should have one wife, and they twain shall be one flesh, and all this that the earth might answer the end of its creation, and that it might be filled with the measure of man, according to his creation before the world was made.[4]

It was always understood that the family is the unit of the Church. As individuals are, so the family is and will be, and as families and family life are, so the Church is and will be. Frequently, also, family ideals determine the behavior of members of families. This was recognized, and the family was therefore given constant attention by the Prophet. The place and purpose of the family form an interesting chapter in the history of the Latter-day Saints.

Family loyalty, founded in love, was emphasized in all of Joseph's teachings. Unless members of a family are loyal to one another, the value of the family vanishes. And that loyalty must be carried into the actual support and care of unfortunate members of the family. He himself displayed in his life and in his journal an inimitable family loyalty. He voiced his emotion of love for the loved ones so that they might know how he felt. Love expressed in word and action is a cementing power in family life. Inarticulate love means little. His words were overflowing with love for his wife. His tenderness included every member of his family and his many friends.

Soon after the Church was organized he broke out in blessings upon his family and fellow workers.[5]

Joseph Smith also emphasized the obligations and

---

[4]Ibid., 49:15-17.
[5]History of the Church, vol. 1, pp. 465-467.

responsibilities of family life. Members of a family must care for one another. Each member must preserve in his way the integrity and the welfare of the family to which he belongs. Parents are under obligations to support their children until they come of age, to provide education for them, and to teach them light and truth; that is, to train them in the gospel.[6] Parents who failed to do so were sternly chastised[7] and brought under condemnation.

Even Sidney Rigdon and Frederick G. Williams, Joseph's counselors in the First Presidency, and others, were at one time severely rebuked for not setting their houses in order. They were warned that carelessness in family life would give evil forces power over them. There must be felt among the members of a family a mutual responsibility. They must help one another in every righteous activity throughout life, otherwise the family is not acceptable to the Lord.

Family unity is the bulwark of strength and the protection from evil within the Church. Besides every individual member of such a family partakes of the spirit of his family to help him throughout life. These principles apply also to the Church as a whole. The Church with its philosophy and practice is best understood when viewed as a great family. Family obligations rest upon the Church. These were necessary family practices in the young Church and are so today.

In addition to all this, Joseph restated prophetically a lost doctrine which raised marriage and the family to inconceivable heights of unending joy. He taught from the Lord's revealed words that happy family associations may be continued eternally in the life after death. In the hereafter as on earth, the family unit may be preserved, and family relations continued.[8]

In the eternal future, after life on earth, the family retains its prominent place among the hosts of heaven.

[6]*Doctrine and Covenants* 55:4; 68:25-28; 31; 83:4.
[7]*Ibid.*
[8]*Doctrine and Covenants* 132:46; Joseph Fielding Smith, *The Way to Perfection,* 6th edition, 1946, p. 253.

The statement through the ages that men and women are wedded only until death parts them need not be true for the righteous. This was of course almost a necessary conclusion from the doctrine of the pre-existence of man. There may be no end of marriage and family relations if they are consummated under the power and authority of the priesthood. Then they may endure forever. In the glorious words of the revelation pertaining to eternal marriage:

> [It is a] new and everlasting covenant. . . . All covenants [and] contracts . . . that are not made and entered into and sealed by the Holy Spirit of promise . . . are of no efficacy . . . in and after the resurrection . . . [but] if a man marry a wife by my word, which is my law, and by the new and everlasting covenant, and it is sealed unto them by the Holy Spirit of promise . . . whatsoever my servant hath put upon them in time and through all eternity . . . shall be of full force when they are out of the world . . . therefore they shall be from everlasting to everlasting because they continue.[9]

This doctrine gave a new value to marriage and family relationships. It placed marriage among the eternal things, attainable to all who prepare themselves for it. The two on earth, husband and wife, with their children may continue eternally to build and to extend the everlasting, universal kingdom of God. This goal, under the powerful impetus of love, tempers and shapes the problems of daily life on earth. The family with its associations is given an infinite value and raised to new dignity.

Such sealings for eternity must be performed under the authority of the priesthood. The restored doctrine was stated in noble words:

> All covenants . . . that are not made and entered into and sealed by the Holy Spirit of Promise of him who is anointed, both for time and for all eternity . . . are of no efficacy, virtue or force in and after the resurrection from the dead; for all contracts that are not made unto this end have an end when men are dead.[10]

The practice of plural marriage is not an integral part of eternal marriage. It is an adjunct thereto, to be

---

[9]*Doctrine and Covenants* 132:19-20.
[10]*Ibid.*, 132:7.

practised only under direct commandment of the Lord. It came to the Church by revelation and commandment from the Lord to Joseph Smith shortly before his death. He himself practised it as the wives who survived him have testified, in addition to the testimony of those to whom he taught the principle. Yet only about two or three per cent of the male population ever practised it. The restrictions placed upon the practice were severe, and it demanded great personal sacrifices. It was admittedly an honorable relationship, which did not in any way violate the high marriage and family ideals of the Church.

In 1890, under revelation from the Lord to the then Prophet, Wilford Woodruff, the practice of plural marriage was suspended. Unfortunately it was not understood and since the time of Joseph Smith, has been the basis of a library of untruthful, unholy, indecent books about the Latter-day Saints.

The conception and vision of endless family life as husband, wife, and children were tremendous additions to the means provided by the restored gospel to win daily joy. It makes every day a part of eternity. This new light which makes love and its fruits eternal, which the teachers of the dark centuries had failed to understand, is another evidence of the divine inspiration and prophetic power of the Prophet of the restoration, Joseph Smith.

CHAPTER 38

PLURAL MARRIAGE

Moral purity is required of all Latter-day Saints. Men must be as clean as women, and both must be free from any violation of the moral law. That is the requirement of all marriages performed under the authority of the restored gospel in the Church of Jesus Christ of Latter-day Saints.

The Church solemnizes two kinds of marriages: first, those that unite husband and wife for the duration of mortal life; second, those that continue the family relationship after death, in the hereafter. The latter are known as eternal or celestial sealings or marriages.

Faithful members of the Church hope to enjoy celestial marriage. They wish to be wedded for time and eternity, that is, to continue their wedded associations forever. To be able to do this is one of the happiest privileges of Church membership. Such marriages, properly called sealings, must be performed in the temples, whenever they exist.

Several approaches to eternal marriage may be made. Two living persons may be sealed to each other for time and eternity. A living man may be sealed for eternity to a dead woman or a living woman to a dead man. Two dead persons may be sealed to each other for eternity. It is also possible, though the Church does not now permit it, to seal two living persons for eternity only, with no association on earth.

Further, under a divine command to the Prophet Joseph Smith, it was possible for one man to be sealed to more than one woman for time and for eternity.[1] This sealing of husbands and wives is one of the important rituals of temple service. It is an earth ordinance since there is no marriage or giving in marriage in heaven.

---

[1] *Doctrine and Covenants* 132:61-62.

The remarkable and soul-stirring doctrine of eternal or celestial marriage came as the result of a question presented to the Lord, as to how the early patriarch, Abraham, was justified in having more than one wife. In the revealed answer came also the principle of plural marriage among the Latter-day Saints. By another divine command to Wilford Woodruff, a successor to Joseph Smith, this order of marriage was withdrawn in 1890. Since that time the Church has not sanctioned plural marriages. Anyone who enters into it now is married unlawfully by persons who have no authority, and is excommunicated from the Church.

Nevertheless, almost the first question asked by strangers to the Church is about the practice of plural marriage in the early days of the Church. The young people of the Church likewise ask why the Lord authorized his Church to practise a principle obnoxious to many in the world.

In the absence of the revealed answer to the question, it may be suggested that the philosophy of the Church implies an answer.

Those who live faithfully to the Lord's commandments may receive the sealing blessings of the gospel. They are then wedded for time and for all eternity. They and their children are then the ones who in the eternal ages will constitute eternal families, and will increase in the eternal years toward the very likeness of God. It becomes therefore a priceless privilege to be born into such a family, sealed for eternal existence in the holy temples of God. The waiting spirits destined to come on earth, and understanding the vast meaning of the gospel, perhaps asked, perhaps pleaded to come through such a worthy lineage, even if the man, the coming father, had to assume the responsibility of a plural household. Perhaps in that manner came the practice on earth of plural marriage. Moreover, the practice is Biblical. It is in line with the fundamental gospel doctrine of eternal progression, and provides for the use of man's free agency. Thus the practice of plural marriage takes its place with the spiritual gifts of the gospel.

Looked upon in this light it becomes a glorious privilege of begetting bodies for the waiting spirits.

It is granted that this or any other explanation carries along with it many unanswerable questions. Certainly, however, plural marriage did not come because of economic or social reasons as some have suggested.

The principle and the practice came to the Prophet through revelation from the Lord. Its practice was always permissive. Plural wives could be taken only under severe restrictions and upon the recommendation of bishops, stake presidents, General Authorities, and finally by the President of the Church. The man who entered plural marriage must be fitted in every way for this holy privilege.

The divine purpose of plural marriage, since the Lord has not explained it, is but dimly understood by man.

That Joseph Smith actually was the person who introduced plural marriage into the Church and that he practised it himself are amply proved by existing facts.

The revelation known as Section 132 in the Doctrine and Covenants, which contains the doctrine of celestial marriage and also the permission to practice plural marriage, was dictated to his scribe, William Clayton, by Joseph Smith on July 12, 1843, a year before the martyrdom of the Prophet. It had been received by the Prophet some years before and taught to many, but was not reduced to writing until 1843.[2]

The evidence seems clear that the revelation on plural marriage was received by the Prophet as early as 1831. A sermon delivered by Joseph F. Smith, then a counselor in the First Presidency, later the President of the Church, was reported as follows:

Here the speaker said, perhaps for the first time in public, that the women who entered into plural marriage with the Prophet

---

[2]*History of the Church*, vol. 5, p. 501; Andrew Jenson, *Historical Record*, pp. 224-226.

Joseph Smith were shown to him and named to him as early as 1831, and some of them were given in marriage to him as early as that date, although it was not then prudent, under the circumstances, to make these facts public. And when the Lord showed those women to Joseph some of them were not even acquainted with the Church much less him. God knew their hearts, as is proved by the fact that they have been true and faithful through all the trying vicissitudes through which they have passed, and that too in the face of a frowning world; they have endured it all, and are today examples of womanhood and purity.[3]

It seems that Fannie Alger was one of Joseph's first plural wives. She lived many years after the Prophet's death and never denied her relationship to him.[4] There were other noble, pure women who gave like testimonies.

William Clayton lived as an honorable citizen of the highest character. On December 4, 1879, thirty-six years after the revelation was written he died. He never wavered in his simple declaration that the revelation as now found in the Doctrine and Covenants was dictated to him, sentence by sentence, by the Prophet. He adds that "after the whole was written, Joseph asked me to read it through, slowly and carefully, which I did, and he pronounced it correct."[5]

On the day the revelation was written, or the day after, Joseph C. Kingsbury was asked to make a copy of it. This copy was carefully compared with the original by Bishop Newel K. Whitney and preserved by him. Elder Kingsbury, of unblemished character and reputation, lived fifty-five years after this event (he died October 5, 1898), and always bore solemn testimony to the written origin of the revelation in 1843 through the lips of the Prophet. In further corroboration of the claim that the revelation came from the lips of the Prophet are the statements of numerous men and women, then living, who either saw the revelation or heard it read. In fact, the document was read to the high council and presidency of the stake of Nauvoo[6] on August 12, 1843, a month after it had been

[3]*Journal History*, February 17, 1882; *Deseret News*, February 17, 1882.
[4]Andrew Jenson, *Historical Record*, pp. 233, 942.
[5]*Ibid.*, pp. 225-226.
[6]*Ibid.*, p. 227.

reduced to written form on July 12, 1843.[7] Many of the council members testified that the revelation was read at that time.[8]

In 1886, President Smith of the Reorganized Church attempted to secure from Leonard Soby, estranged from the Church, but a member in 1843 of the Nauvoo high council, a statement to the effect that the revelation was not read at the said high council meeting. This Soby refused to do, but volunteered to testify that the revelation was actually read at that meeting in his hearing.[9]

A number of men, who in their lives proved themselves honest, have testified that they actually performed the ceremonies that united Joseph Smith to plural wives. Among these were Joseph B. Noble, Hyrum Smith, James Adams, Newel K. Whitney, Willard Richards, and others.[10] Several of these men lived long after the Prophet's death and always declared that they officiated in marrying the Prophet to a plural wife, giving place, date, and the witnesses present.

Many of the women who were thus sealed to Joseph Smith lived long after his death. They declared that they lived with the Prophet as his wives.[11] These women were of unblemished character, gentle and lovely in their lives, who understood this to be a righteous principle as revealed to their Prophet-husband. They always spoke with loving respect of their martyr-husband and they substantiated in detail the statements of those who performed the ceremonies.

Many of the elders in Nauvoo entered into plural marriage under the authority of Joseph Smith while he was living, as certified to by the men and their wives. Among these were William Clayton, Orson Hyde, Hyrum Smith, John Smith, Erastus Snow, Lyman Wight, James J. Strang, Gladden Bishop, William Smith, Heber C. Kimball, and

[7]George Q. Cannon, Life of Joseph Smith, p. 412.
[8]George Q. Cannon op., cit., p. 413; Andrew Jenson, Historical Record, p. 227.
[9]Journal History, January 6, 1886, p. 4; Deseret Evening News, January 6, 1886.
[10]Andrew Jenson, op., cit., pp. 221-233.
[11]Ibid., pp. 233, 240.

Brigham Young.[12] These men and their wives who survived the Prophet made affidavits of their marriages in Joseph's day in answer to the charge by enemies of the Church that plural marriage was not instituted nor practised, neither authorized by the Prophet. These men and women who assisted in the sealings or were sealed to plural wives, were good citizens, so well-known over such long periods of time that their concordant declarations cannot be gainsaid.

The Nauvoo Temple records, which are in the possession of the Church, likewise furnish evidence that Joseph Smith practised plural marriage. Before the completion of the temple, sealings were usually performed in dedicated rooms in the home of the Prophet. When the temple was dedicated in 1846 for such ceremonies, the plural marriages of Joseph were given temple sanction, and where the original marriages were for time only, they were often later performed as sealings made to continue through eternity.[13]

This was done within a year and a half of the assassination of the Prophet. Later, many more received plural wives in the Nauvoo Temple. It is utterly improbable, if not impossible, that such a new doctrine could have been conceived and carried out immediately by the men who succeeded the Prophet. There would have been a serious resentment among those who entered the temple if the teachings of the Prophet had been violated. Such criticism would have overflowed to the outside.

After the death of the Prophet, women applied for the privilege of being sealed to him for eternity. They felt no doubt that in the eternal ages they would share the companionship of the Prophet. They wanted to share eternity with the man whom they revered as one chosen of God to open the last dispensation of the gospel on earth. To these requests, assent was often given. Such action by women who lived in the days of the Prophet implies a

---

[12]There can be no question about the matter since the written records are so extensive as to places, dates, and witnesses. See the records in the Historian's Office, L.D.S. Church Office Building, Salt Lake City, Utah, also the Nauvoo Temple Records.
[13]See Nauvoo Temple Records.

belief in plural marriage. These women, who were not in any sense earthly wives of the Prophet, have been counted by uninformed or antagonistic writers as wives of the Prophet.[14]

Women no longer living, whether in Joseph's day or later, have also been sealed to the Prophet for eternity. The request for such unions has usually come from relatives or friends who would have their loved ones share eternity with the Prophet rather than with anyone else. Unscrupulous and unreliable writers have even added such marriages to the list of Joseph's wives.

Another kind of celestial marriage seems to have been practised in the early days of plural marriage. It has not been practised since Nauvoo days, for it is under Church prohibition. Zealous women, some of them married as well as unmarried, loving the cause of the restored gospel, considered their condition in the hereafter and asked that they might be sealed to the Prophet for eternity. They were not to be his wives on earth, in mortality, but only after death, in the eternities. Such marriages led to much misunderstanding by those not of the Church and unfamiliar with its doctrines and practices. To them marriage meant only association on earth. Therefore any ceremony uniting a married woman, for example, to Joseph Smith for eternity seemed adulterous to such people. Yet in any day, in our day, there may be women who prefer to spend eternity with another than their husband on earth.

Such cases, if any, and they must have been few in number, gave enemies of the Church occasion to fan the flaming hatred against the Latter-day Saints. The full truth was not told. Enemies made the most of untruth. They found it difficult to believe that the Church rests on truth and virtue.

The existing literature dealing with plural marriage in Nauvoo in the day of Joseph Smith is voluminous. Many affidavits on the subject are in the Church Historian's Office in Salt Lake City. Many of the books and news-

---

[14]*Nauvoo Temple Records.*

paper and magazine articles on the subject are found there also.[15]

A clinching proof that the Prophet had taught plural marriage is found in his journal under date of October 5, 1843. He writes:

Gave instructions to try those persons who were preaching, teaching, or practicing, the doctrine of plurality of wives; for, according to the law, I hold the keys of this power in the last days; for there is never but one on earth at a time on whom the power and its keys are conferred; and I have constantly said no man shall have but one wife at a time, unless the Lord directs otherwise.[16]

The careful study of all available information leads to but one conclusion. Joseph Smith received the revelation in question and practised plural marriage. This issue is not one of doctrine but of history. No honest student can declare the host of witnesses, hundreds of them, from Nauvoo days, Mormon and non-Mormon of various residence, pursuit, and temperament to have united in lying about the matter. The evidence is confirmed by those who place the introduction of plural marriage on others, for they seek feeble, unworthy shelter in the statement that Joseph Smith did practise plural marriage but later repented of it.[17] That is throwing dust in the eyes of seekers after truth.

The case is clear. Authentic history says that plural marriage originated with Joseph Smith, the Prophet. So it did. The apparent denials by Church leaders in early Nauvoo days that the Church practised plural marriage were correct. At that time, the Church members as a whole had not heard the revelation nor had they been given an opportunity to accept it. But many of the leaders knew of it and were polygamists under Joseph's authority.

The chaotic conditions of the years immediately following the Prophet's death delayed the formal presenta-

[15]For a fairly condensed but complete discussion consult Andrew Jenson, *op. cit.*, pp. 219-236; Joseph Fielding Smith, *Blood Atonement and the Origin of Plural Marriage*, pp. 67-94; *Women's Exponent*, volumes 13 and 14; *Deseret News*, especially in 1886.
[16]*History of the Church*, vol. 6, p. 46.
[17]*Saints' Herald*, vol. 1, pp. 9, 26, 27.

tion of the revelation to the whole Church. That explains the statement of 1838 in answer to a question whether the Mormons believed in having more than one wife. The principle of plural marriage had not at that time been presented to the Church.[18] Soon after the Church was established in the Great Salt Lake region, at the conference in 1852, the doctrine of celestial and plural marriage was accepted by the Church as a whole. During the intervening years, however, it was taught and practised.

[18] *Elders' Journal*, vol. 1, p. 3.

THE KIRTLAND TEMPLE
Kirtland, Ohio

ADAM ONDI AHMAN, MISSOURI

LIBERTY JAIL, MISSOURI
Where Joseph Smith was incarcerated and where he received
several revelations

CHAPTER 39

THE BASIS OF SPIRITUALITY

The objective of the gospel of Jesus Christ as restored through Joseph Smith is to help men approach daily the likeness of God. This high objective is the life-giving element of every principle and ordinance of the gospel.

The plan of salvation roots in God's love for his children. Therefore, the activities of men must lead them to love their fellow men as well as their Father in Heaven. To the extent that this is accomplished the ultimate purpose of God's plan for his children is achieved.

Moreover, as man surmounts the difficulties of life and grows in support of this plan to save all, he increases in spiritual power. That is indeed the meaning of spirituality. No man can claim access to the spiritual life who lives only for himself, who excludes others in his strivings for happiness.

The organization of the Church and the contents of the gospel make provisions by which men may be helped to establish in thought and action the spirit of brotherhood, the real basis of spirituality.

First, through instruction in meetings and by published materials the plan of salvation is taught and explained. Then the various activities are so ordered by the Church that brotherhood shines through them all. One cannot well be active in the Church and escape the obligations of brotherhood placed upon every person.

Nowhere is this more forcefully and peremptorily placed upon the membership of the Church than in the work done in the temples of the Church. In these temples all ordinances of the Church, from baptism to the higher sealing ordinances, are performed. It is not sufficient, however, that each member receive these blessings of the temples. Being ordinances of the earth they must also be done for the dead, for those who had no opportunity to secure these blessings for themselves, but who in the spirit world may accept the gospel. For them, helpless as to earth ordinances, help must come from the living.

This only confirms the doctrine of universal salvation. The great plan of the Father was for all the children of God who assembled in the Grand Council and accepted the plan. The opportunity of salvation must be given to all. This was plainly taught to Joseph by the Prophet Moroni. In fact, the words then uttered stand as the first written revelation to the young Prophet:

> Behold, I will reveal unto you the Priesthood, by the hand of Elijah the Prophet, before the coming of the great and dreadful day of the Lord. And he shall plant in the hearts of the children the promises made to the fathers, and the hearts of the children shall turn to their fathers. If it were not so, the whole earth would be utterly wasted at his coming.[1]

The consummation of God's plan rests on the willingness of the living to labor for the dead, "else the earth would be utterly wasted."

It must not be overlooked that this entails even a higher brotherhood than that which may exist among the living. The dead are usually merely names to us. Yet they stand for members of the human family of the past, entitled to every privilege of the gospel. It is a searching requirement to ask the living to accept brotherhood with those who have gone before. Yet only as we yield to that demand made upon us will the Lord's earth-purposes be brought to an acceptable end.

The doctrine of this higher brotherhood binding upon Joseph Smith and his people makes of them a temple building organization. In Kirtland, Ohio, a temple was constructed under great hardships but with great faith. It was dedicated on March 27, 1836. In this temple, a part of the temple endowment was given. In 1841 the foundation for the Nauvoo Temple was laid. Diligently, with much

---

[1]*Doctrine and Covenants*, Section 2.

sacrifice, it was built. It was completed after Joseph's death, dedicated first by Joseph Young, a member of the First Council of the Seventy, on April 30, 1846,[2] and later by Elders Orson Hyde and Wilford Woodruff, of the Council of the Twelve, on May 1, 1846.[3]

Joseph Smith seemed to sense his early demise. On May 4, 1842,[4] the upper rooms in his store were dedicated for the purpose, and he gave to an invited group of his followers the order and ritual of the temple endowment.[5] Later, others, including some women, received these blessings. Therefore, when the Nauvoo Temple was dedicated, after the Prophet's death, the proper use of temples for the living and the dead was understood by the people.

The temples furnish superb opportunities for spiritual growth. The living after having received their own temple endowments may go again and again to receive the endowments for their dead relatives. Thus the spirit of brotherhood may continue to live in human lives. Experience has shown also that for all who have some leisure time, notably older people, temples furnish marvelous opportunities for continual spiritual exercise.

Merely from the human point of view the temples and temple worship of Joseph's day are evidences of the deep wisdom of the Prophet's labors.

It was inevitable that those who have sought to destroy the truth of the Prophet Joseph Smith's message would misinterpret the temple endowment. They have declared that outrageous immoral actions took place within temple walls.[6] Furthermore they have set up the theory that Joseph Smith merely adopted the temple conception and ritual from rituals of fraternal, secret organizations.[7] The temple endowment is far more comprehensive than the ritual of the said fraternal, secret organization. The charge that the temple endowment is so derived is not confirmed by the evidence at hand.

[2]Nels B. Lundwall, *Temples of the Most High*, p. 51.
[3]*Ibid.*
[4]Joseph Fielding Smith, *Essentials In Church History*, p. 318.
[5]*History of the Church*, vol. 5, pp. 1-2.
[6]J. W. Buel, *Metropolitan Life Unveiled*, pp. 367-373.
[7]S. H. Goodwin, *Mormonism and Masonry*, 1925, p. 32.

First, almost from the organization of the Church, Joseph promised the people a higher endowment, a continuation of that received in baptism. It was to be a gift bestowed upon those who had attained a greater maturity in gospel life.

To this end the Kirtland Temple was hurried to completion in 1836, though amidst much toil and sacrifice. Then at the dedication some ordinances were given preparatory to the fuller endowment to come. There was nothing new about temple work when it came in its greater completeness. It was expected.

Second, on January 19, 1841, when Joseph Smith had not yet belonged to a fraternal organization, he recorded a revelation which explains in general outline the temple ritual. It says:

> For there is not a place found on earth that He may come to and restore again that which was lost unto you, or which he hath taken away, even the fulness of the priesthood . . . .
> Therefore, verily I say unto you, that your anointings, and your washings, and your baptisms for the dead, and your solemn assemblies, and your memorials for your sacrifices by the sons of Levi, and for your oracles in your most holy places wherein you receive conversations, and your statutes and judgments, for the beginning of the revelations and foundation of Zion, and for the glory, honor, and endowment of all her municipals, are ordained by the ordinance of my holy house, which my people are always commanded to build unto my holy name . . .
> For I deign to reveal unto the Church things which have been kept hid from before the foundation of the world, things that pertain to the Dispensation of The Fulness of Times.
> And I will show unto my servant Joseph all things pertaining to this house, and the priesthood thereof, and the place whereon it shall be built.[8]

From the pulpit the Prophet announced thenceforth the building of the temple and the work to be done therein for the living and the dead.

On May 4, 1842, he administered the temple endow-

---

[8] *Doctrine and Covenants* 124:39-42.

ment in rooms in the upper story of his brick store, improvised for the purpose.[9] All the while, before and after, he gave instructions concerning the temple to be built and the endowment therein to be given.

Third, many of the men who joined the Church were brethren in fraternal circles, such as the Prophet's brother Hyrum Smith, Heber C. Kimball, Newel K. Whitney, George Miller, Austin Cowles, John Smith, Elijah Fordham, and others. Nowhere can a word be found from these many men indicating that they placed temple work in a class with the ritual of the fraternal orders to which they belonged. Had there been such, some of these men would have mentioned it, for not all remained true to the Church.

Fourth, that there are similarities in the services of the temple and some secret organizations may be true. These similarities, however, do not deal with basic matters but rather with the mechanism of the ritual. Moreover, they are not peculiar to any fraternity. They are used and have been used by people throughout the centuries. They belong to the common heritage of mankind. Joseph Smith had the right to employ such commonly used methods and symbols without being charged with plagiarizing from any particular group. The Prophet taught baptism by immersion, but none so far has held that he purloined that type of baptism from the Baptists. Immersion comes down the ages from the days of Jesus Christ and before and is unquestionably the mode of his own baptism. The beginnings of such practices are lost in the mists of antiquity.

The temple ritual as revealed to Joseph Smith and communicated by him to his brethren is essentially symbolic. Its ordinances are not only ancient but also represent profound truths. They may be widely used by others than Latter-day Saints, but not in their fullness nor comprehensive meaning.

Fifth, women as well as men receive the temple ritual. Only a man and a woman together can receive the highest

---

[9]*History of the Church*, vol. 5, p. 1.

blessings of the temple. In the man-made fraternal orders, men only are admitted to membership. Yet the Lord has said that "neither is the man without the woman nor the woman without the man in the Lord." Man and wife should be one in the journey through life. Usually, perhaps always, men only receive the rituals of the many man-made secret societies. The women form auxiliary organizations.

Sixth, there is a great difference between the objectives of temple work and those of the many secret organizations, though they no doubt have high ideals of living.

In the temple endowment the final ideal is that by obedience to God's law man may be privileged to associate with him throughout eternity. The endowment also offers the promise of eternal growth, of endless blessings. This is not the objective of a man-made secret society.

Seventh, finally it may be said that the temple endowment is not secret. All members of the Church who meet the requirements for entrance to the temple may enjoy it. Since it is sacred, it is not bandied about the streets or in gossiping parlors.

It is, in outline, the story of man's eternal journey; instructions to make the endless journey increasing and progressive; covenants that we will so live as to make the life journey an upward one; a warning that sometime we shall be called upon to show whether we have kept our covenants; and a pointing out of the great reward that comes to the faithful and the righteous.

Every member of another organization if also a member of the restored Church of Jesus Christ will know whether this is like his fraternity ritual.

Members of secret societies have joined the Church of Jesus Christ of Latter-day Saints. Many have been faithful and have abandoned their man-made fraternal orders. As they have come to the temple of the Lord, they have said, in the words of one former member, "Secret societies have nothing to teach the Latter-day Saints."

Carefully and intelligently studied, the proposition that the Mormon endowment was built upon secret fraternal rituals cannot be accepted by any thoughtful person.

Joseph Smith received the temple endowment and its ritual, as all else that he promulgated, by revelation from God.

CHAPTER 40

PRESERVING TRUTH

The restoration of the gospel of the Lord Jesus Christ was a major event in the history of mankind. This was understood by Joseph Smith. He knew that the loss of the original accounts of the labors of Jesus the Christ had caused much confusion and error. Therefore, he took steps to prevent the loss of the true story of his commissioned work. He kept a careful record of the several experiences that finally led to the organization of the Church. On the day of the organization of the Church, a historian was appointed to keep a record of the coming historical events of the Church.[1] He himself also continued to keep a record of the things that transpired. These records were to be kept in full and published in full for the world to read. Joseph was sincere or he would have permitted some events to be hidden and only major concerns of the Church to come before the public. There was no undercover planning in his work—there was nothing to hide.

Records so accumulated were presented in great detail in printed form in periodicals and books, and widely circulated. The use of the modern printing press ensured the continued existence of the correct history of the Church. This had not been possible in the early days before the use of movable type.

The literary labors of Joseph Smith, intended for permanent use, fall into six main parts, each containing revelations received by the Prophet.

1. The correction of King James translation of the Bible.
2. The Book of Mormon.
3. The Doctrine and Covenants.
4. The Pearl of Great Price.
5. The History of the Church.
6. Miscellaneous.

---

[1] *Doctrine and Covenants, Section 21.*

Joseph Smith accepted the Bible as far as it was translated correctly but felt that many errors which should be corrected had crept into the work of the copyist and translators. During the first year of the Church and almost to the end of his life, he endeavored through inspiration from on high to correct those many departures from the original text. This was not fully completed when he died, but his manuscript exists in the original and in copies, and has been published by the Reorganized Church of Jesus Christ of Latter Day Saints. It is a remarkable evidence of the prophetic power of Joseph Smith.[2] Hundreds of changes make clear many a disputed text. It is interesting to note that in so many instances his inspired corrections correspond to the text of modern translators. In every case his version makes the Bible statement much more understandable.

The Book of Mormon, the translation of which came by revelation, has been published in large editions. It would not be possible to change any part of it without being discovered.[3] It has been thus preserved for all time.

The Doctrine and Covenants is a compilation of the revelations received by Joseph Smith to individuals and for the guidance of the Church. From the first years of the work the Prophet kept every scrap of paper pertaining to the progress of the work. In fact this care of things that must have seemed trivial is one of the evidences of the sincerity of the man. For example, when John and Peter Whitmer asked for help, he received for each of them a revelation, substantially the same:

Hearken, my servant Peter, and listen to the words of Jesus Christ your Lord and your Redeemer. For behold, I speak unto you with sharpness and with power, for mine arm is over all the earth. And I will tell you that which no man knoweth save me and thee alone—For many times you have desired of me to know that which would be of the most worth unto you. Behold, blessed are you for this thing, and for speaking my words which I have given unto

---

[2]Joseph Fielding Smith, *Teachings of the Prophet Joseph Smith*, p. 10; Joseph Fielding Smith, *Essentials in Church History*, pp. 138-140.
[3]The first edition containing several printer's and grammatical errors was corrected in 1833 by the Prophet himself, with no change in any doctrine or history in the book.

you according to my commandments. And now, behold, I say unto you, that the thing which will be of the most worth unto you will be to declare repentance unto this people, that you may bring souls unto me, that you may rest with them in the kingdom of my Father. Amen.[4]

This simple revelation is directed to the individual and at first sight has no permanent value for the Church. Yet as a revelation from God it was preserved and published. An insincere man could have eliminated this and other similar revelations as of little consequence. Not so with Joseph. The Lord had spoken. The words were part of the building of the kingdom of God, and the same advice would be useful to many men then and now.

The revelations to the Prophet Joseph Smith were cherished by the people as words from the Lord. They were usually read in private or public assemblies. Longhand copies were made and circulated among the members of the Church. The monthly Latter-day Saint magazine *Morning and Evening Star*, which appeared in 1834, printed the revelations as space permitted.

Meanwhile, with publication in mind, the Prophet began as early as July, 1830, under God's command,[5] to copy and arrange the revelations thus far received. This compilation, to be known as the Book of Commandments, was completed in 1831, and the printing undertaken in Independence, Missouri, which had been designated as the city of the center stake of Zion.[6]

Enemies of the Church, however, destroyed on July 20, 1833, the printing plant, including the printed sheets for three thousand copies of the Book of Commandments. A few friends had secured copies, perhaps fewer than twenty, as the sheets came off the press,[7] but they are incomplete, ending with the word Ephraim, Section 64, Verse 36.

[4]*Doctrine and Covenants*, Section 16.
[5]Hyrum M. Smith, and Janne M. Sjodahl, *Doctrine and Covenants Commentary*, p. 14; *Doctrine and Covenants* 6:26-27; 9:1-2; 35:20.
[6]*History of the Church*, vol. 1, pp. 221-222, 234, 236; *Doctrine and Covenants*, Sections 69, 70.
[7]*History of the Church*, vol. 1, pp. 390, 411, 412.

Nothing daunted, after this outrage, the Saints who wanted the precious words of the Lord made arrangements to have the book printed in Kirtland, Ohio. Other revelations had been received to be included, and so the book of Doctrine and Covenants proved to be larger than the original Book of Commandments. At a solemn assembly, August 17, 1835, the book, under the title the Book of Doctrine and Covenants was presented to the people and accepted by them. Since that time, in later editions, the later revelations to Joseph have been added.

The book as it now stands, with verse divisions by Orson Pratt in 1876, with footnotes added in 1879, contains one hundred and thirty-three revelations to the Prophet, three of which are excerpts from letters written from Liberty Jail.[8] It also contains one revelation to Brigham Young, with a statement of the Church's views on civil government, and another on the martyrdom of Joseph and Hyrum Smith. The section on marriage found in the original edition has been omitted, as Section 132 has superseded it.

The Church needed steady guidance in the beginning. Consequently, before 1830, seventeen revelations were received, covering thirty-four pages. From 1830 to 1836, during the period of organization, there were received one hundred and five revelations covering three hundred and thirty-six pages. From 1836 to 1843, the twenty-five revelations received cover seventy-two pages.

The revelations in the Doctrine and Covenants deal with a variety of subjects, many of them profound in their nature. They were given occasionally, as need arose. They were all answers to questions and prayers for guidance but unique in that the answers usually go far beyond the extent of the question. The sections are generally concise and short. The average length of each revelation varies from six and one-half pages to one third of a page. Most of them are about three pages in length. The book is fascinating in its power to awaken thought. It remains a constant serviceable guide. It sweeps the horizon of thought

---

[8]*Doctrine and Covenants,* Sections 121, 122, 123.

on life here and hereafter. This requires that the book be read carefully and intensively.

The book itself is a witness for the truth of the Prophet's claims. The explanations of old doctrines and presentation of new ones are convincing evidences of their divine origin. Enemies of the Church have rather carefully avoided the discussion of this book. They have been afraid of it.

The Pearl of Great Price contains the Book of Moses as revealed to the Prophet in 1830 shortly after the organization of the Church. This book came as a part of the revision or inspired translation of the Bible. Since the Church has not yet attempted to publish Joseph's Bible revision in full, the Book of Moses, not complete, has been published separately. This publication was made in the days of Joseph Smith.[9] The Book of Moses amplifies many of the brief accounts given in the Bible rendition of Genesis. It includes doctrines of the utmost importance in forming a correct philosophy of life.

The Book of Abraham came out of the translation of some Egyptian papyri from the catacombs of Egypt which fell into the hands of the Prophet. It gives a more lucid account of Abraham's early life and his doctrine than is found in other sacred scripture. It also contains a wealth of doctrinal information not to be found elsewhere. The account of the creation of the earth there found is perhaps the most challenging subject in the book. The Book of Abraham was also published in the days of the Prophet.[10]

Seven years after the Prophet's martyrdom the Book of Moses and the Book of Abraham were made part of a compilation known as the Pearl of Great Price.[11] This compilation was made by Franklin D. Richards.

It also includes a revision of chapter twenty-four of the Gospel of Matthew. The changes made are revealing to all students of sacred history.

The Pearl of Great Price further contains extracts from the early history of the Prophet, recounting especially the

---

[9]*Evening and Morning Star*, vol. 1, p. 44.
[10]*Times and Seasons*, vol. 3, pp. 703-719.
[11]*Pearl of Great Price*, first edition, published seven years after the death of the Prophet.

events connected with the First Vision and the visitation of Moroni.

The compilation closes with the Articles of Faith of the Church. These articles originally formed a part of a letter to Mr. John Wentworth, newspaper editor of Chicago.[12] They are now used by the Church at home and abroad and are held to be the best brief cardinal statement of the faith of the Latter-day Saints. Not only were these articles written by Joseph Smith but also published in his day with his approval.[13]

The first edition of The Pearl of Great Price was published in 1851 in Liverpool, England, by Elder Franklin D. Richards. He felt as many others that the precious revelations to Joseph Smith, all of them, should be available to the public.

There are those who have questioned the value of the revelations in the Pearl of Great Price, chiefly because they were not issued as a separate pamphlet by the Prophet himself. The fact is that they were published, though not in compiled form, in the days of the Prophet. All who know the events of the Prophet's life before his martyrdom will understand how difficult it was in those days to do many things that would have been done in more normal times. The Prophet did see and authorize the contents of the papers now published in the Pearl of Great Price.

The *History of the Church* is another of the literary efforts of the Prophet Joseph Smith. On May 2, 1838,[14] in the Far West Settlement in Missouri,[15] he began the writing of the history of his people, from a mass of manuscripts in his possession. This work was continued for some time, at least more than a year, to bring it up to date, for on Tuesday, June 1, 1839, in Commerce, later Nauvoo, he says, "I commenced dictating my history for my clerk James Mulholland to write."[16] This history is an account, almost day by day, of his own doings and those of the Church.

---

[12]*History of the Church*, vol. 4, p. 535.
[13]*Ibid; History of Denominations in the United States*, pp. 344-439.
[14]*History of the Church*, vol. 1, p. 2; vol. 1, pp. 18-19.
[15]*Ibid.*, vol. 3, p. 26; *Pearl of Great Price*, Joseph Smith 1:60.
[16]*History of the Church*, vol. 3, p. 375

The personalities who helped build the early Church appear before the reader.

It should be noted that the writing of this history was undertaken soon after the troubles in Kirtland, Ohio, and amidst growing persecutions in Missouri. A man looking for his own welfare would not have chosen such a time and place for such a labor. He was a prodigious worker and a man of natural literary leanings.

Fortunately, also, when in this history he notes that he gave an address somewhere, very often an abstract of what he said, made by others, also appears. These abstracts give added value to the history, since none others exist.[17]

In those days, on the frontier, shorthand writers were not available. In fact there were few anywhere. Therefore, when Joseph was to make an address, several of his friends would take longhand notes and later compare them. Thus the reports of the sermons of Joseph Smith came into existence and are very accurate.

Most of these reports have been extracted from the history and published in a volume edited by Elder Joseph Fielding Smith, *Teachings of the Prophet Joseph Smith.*

The *History of the Church* and the utterances therein contain, if read properly, a continued evidence that Joseph Smith told the truth about the coming forth of the restoration. It is a precious production that will be counted as a blessing throughout the years.

There are also some scattered, miscellaneous products of the Prophet's pen which have not yet been assembled in printed form. A few of his revelations may have been overlooked. Editorials written by him as editor of *Elders' Journal* and *Times and Seasons* and other such writings have not been touched by the compilers. Some of these, however, seem to be of much value and may someday be reprinted.

This brief survey shows that Joseph Smith left behind a considerable output of written matter. Considering the harrowing, restless conditions of his life, this is remarkable. Throughout all his writings runs the simple spirit of truth.

---

[17]*Ibid.,* vol. 1, pp. 39-41

They show him to be indeed a seeker after truth. There is in them no attempt to "cover up" any act of his life. The story of each event is told as it happened. Mormon history and doctrine have been carefully preserved in the published records of the Church—and all has been published. Such was the counsel of Joseph Smith. The Church need not go astray. The preservation of Church records forms ample protection.

Chapter 41

HOW REVELATIONS WERE RECEIVED

There was little self-assumption in Joseph Smith. He did not attempt to display his own powers nor to depend upon them. When questions arose in his work, and among his fellow workers, he followed the method of the First Vision. He appealed to the Lord, and received the required help.

As far as known, every revelation came as an answer to a prayer to God for help. His life was led by revelation. The Church which he was instrumental in organizing rests upon continuous revelation. In the words of the prophet of old, the Lord "slumbers not nor sleeps."[1] This gives revelation first place in the life work of Joseph Smith.

It is significant that no revelation appears to have been volunteered by the Lord. The First Vision came in answer to prayer; all later ones followed the same pattern. The revelations may therefore be viewed as answers to questions that arose from time to time to meet the issues of the day.

The answers frequently went beyond the question. A simple question was often answered with a wealth of new knowledge. God cares less for the completeness of a question than for the need and humble attitude of mind and heart of the questioner.

While Joseph Smith asked questions because of conditions that confronted him, it must be conceded that at times the Lord inspired him to ask questions. Joseph Smith was commissioned by the Lord to do a great work. Naturally, the Lord often moved upon him as needs arose. But he always asked questions. He was never content with ignorance. He was always the seeker after truth.

However, revelation following questions did not mean that the individuality of the man was eliminated. From

---

[1]Psalms 121:4.

the beginning, the man himself was a party to the process of revelation. The manner of the question and the use of the revealed answer always involved the personality of the man. His fitness to commune with the unseen world and how soon, how emphatically, how courageously, how persistently the revelation was requested and used were parts of the nature of the man himself.

Revelation did not always come to Joseph Smith in the same manner. In fact, the exact manner in which most of the revelations were given is only partly known. But the manner in which some were given may be clearly understood.

The first revelation, the so-called First Vision, was received by the boy Joseph directly from God the Father and God the Son. They spoke to him as man to man. A week following the dedication of the Kirtland Temple, the Savior appeared in that sacred building and spake in person to Joseph Smith and Oliver Cowdery.[2] When the revelation teaching that the degree of human salvation varies with our works was given, Joseph Smith and Sidney Rigdon had direct visual and oral communication with the Lord.[3]

On several other occasions communications came from heavenly beings delegated to perform certain tasks. Moroni, an ancient American Prophet, conversed several times with Joseph concerning the plates of the Book of Mormon, Joseph's work in translating them, and the restoration of the Church of Jesus Christ.[4] Later John the Baptist, and after him the Apostles, Peter, James, and John, personally conferred upon Joseph Smith and his companion Oliver Cowdery, respectively, the Aaronic[5] and Melchizedek Priesthood.[6] On one occasion, Joseph Smith was seeking wine for the sacrament. A heavenly messenger met him by the way, and explained that water could be used instead of wine.[7] Such direct messages from the Lord or from delegated

---

[2]*Doctrine and Covenants,* Section 110.
[3]*Ibid.,* Section 76; *History of the Church,* vol. 1, p. 245.
[4]*History of the Church,* vol. 1, p. 12.
[5]*Ibid.,* vol. 1, p. 39; *Doctrine and Covenants,* Section 13.
[6]*History of the Church,* vol. 1, pp. 39-40.
[7]*Doctrine and Covenants,* Section 27.

personages were not many. Most of his revelations were obtained otherwise.

Before Joseph received the Urim and Thummim he had a stone, obtained during the digging of a well for Clark Chase. This stone through the blessing of the Lord, became a seer stone which was used frequently by him in his spiritual work.[8]

The use of the seer stone explains in part the charge against Joseph Smith that he was a "peep stone gazer." All his activities were well-known and performed above board. The use of the seer stone and the Urim and Thummim was well-known to the people of his time and neighborhood.[9]

The use of stones in sacred work has been frequent; for example, the ball known as the Liahona,[10] the rod of Aaron,[11] and the twelve stones used by Lehi.[12] The brother of Jared used sixteen small stones which gave light in the barges.[13] Aids to human senses are always recognized in ecclesiastical history.[14]

Along with the plates of the Book of Mormon were the Urim and Thummim, "two stones in silver bows," used by Joseph Smith as helps in the translation of the inscription on the plates. When the young man was in a suitable spiritual and mental condition, these instruments made the meaning of the inscriptions clear to the translator's mind.

The Urim and Thummim were also used by him at the beginning of his work to receive revelations from the Lord. Several of the early revelations begin with the statement, "I inquired of the Lord through the Urim and Thummim, and received the following," or words to that effect.[15]

---

[8]Edward Stevenson, *Reminiscences of the Prophet Joseph*, p. 30; *Millennial Star*, vol. 24, p. 119; vol. 40, p. 49; George Q. Cannon, *Life of Joseph Smith*, p. 56.
[9]George Q. Cannon, *Life of Joseph Smith*, p. 56; B. H. Roberts, *Comprehensive History of the Church*, vol. 1, p. 129; Edward Stevenson, *Reminiscences of the Prophet Joseph*, pp. 10-19; David Whitmer, *Address to the World*, p. 32; B. H. Roberts, *New Witness for God*, vol. 2, p. 113 (Y.M.M.I.A. Manuals); B. H. Roberts, *Comprehensive History of the Church*, vol. 6, p. 230; B. H. Roberts, *Defense of the Faith and the Saints*, vol. 1, pp. 255-311.
[10]1 Nephi 16:28; Mosiah 1:16.
[11]Exodus 4:20; Numbers 17:6-9.
[12]1 Nephi 2:7.
[13]Ether 3:1; 6:2.
[14]Arch S. Reynolds, *The Urim and Thummim*, and *How Did Joseph Smith Translate?*
[15]*Doctrine and Covenants*, Sections 3, 6, 11, 14, 17.

The available evidence indicates that the use of these sacred instruments required intense mental and spiritual effort. They were not merely a kind of magnifying glasses. Revelation did not come easily, even with the Urim and Thummim. The price of self-effort had to be paid for them. It seems likely that these helps enabled him to concentrate sufficiently to hear and understand messages from the unseen world.

After the translation of the Book of Mormon, Joseph Smith seldom referred to the Urim and Thummim in the revelations that came to him. Indeed he may not any longer have had them in his possession. Instead he seems to have developed the necessary spiritual and mental power or concentration within himself to communicate with the unseen world, without external help, under the influence of the higher priesthood which he had received.

Thus he often says that revelations were received "By the spirit of prophecy and revelation"[16] or "The Holy Ghost was poured out upon us to a very great degree, some prophesied, whilst we all praised the Lord, and rejoiced exceedingly. Whilst yet together, I received the following commandment."[17] In this manner most of his revelations were received.

Some of the revelations were received in the presence of others. Elder Parley P. Pratt has left the record of one such event:

After we had joined in prayer in his translating room he dictated in our presence the following revelation.[18] Each sentence was uttered slowly and very distinctly, and with a pause between each sufficiently long for it to be recorded by an ordinary writer in longhand.

This was the manner in which all his written revelations were dictated and written. There was never any hesitation, reviewing or reading back in order to keep the run of the subject; neither did any of the communications undergo revisions, interliniugs, or corrections.

As he dictated them, so they stood, so far as I have witnessed;

---
[16]*Doctrine and Covenants,* preface to Section 20.
[17]*History of the Church,* vol. 1, p. 78.
[18]*Ibid.,* vol. 1, p. 170.

and I was present to witness the dictation of several communications of several pages each.[19]

Remember that this was the procedure also in the translation of the Book of Mormon.

This method of direct inspiration or revelation was the one commonly used. That Joseph Smith could so obtain the deep truths of the gospel was due, first to his divine call, then to his pure love of the work.

His earlier spiritual experiences had developed within him a power of intense concentration. Those who were present when such revelations were received have commented upon the physical change in the man, his pallor as if the blood had drained out of his face, and his complete absorption in communicating with the unseen world.[20]

Except in revelations copied from spoken words of celestial messengers, the language of the revelations is almost wholly the language of Joseph Smith, made forceful and eloquent by the exaltation of inspiration. God gives the ideas; the Prophet expresses them as best he can.

In the preface of the book containing the revelations, the Lord says:

Behold, I am God and have spoken it, these commandments are of me, and were given unto my servants in their weakness, after the manner of their language, that they might come to understanding.[21]

That is a good lesson for all teachers.

This procedure seemed simple to the onlooker. Oliver Cowdery, Joseph's scribe and close companion who shared with him several heavenly manifestations, desired the gift of translation and communication with the unseen world. He was given permission to try it. He failed completely. Thereupon the Lord through Joseph Smith said to Oliver:

Behold, you have not understood; you have supposed that I would give it unto you, when you took no thought save it was to

---

[19]Parley P. Pratt, *Autobiography of Parley P. Pratt*, 1938 edition p. 62; 1874 edition, p. 66.
   [20]Preston Nibley, *Exodus to Greatness*, p. 2; John A. Widtsoe, *Discourses of Brigham Young*, p. 142; *Journal of Discourses*, vol. 9, p. 89.
   [21]*Doctrine and Covenants* 1:24; *History of the Church*, vol. 1, p. 222.

ask me. But, behold, I say unto you, that you must study it out in your mind; then you ask me if it be right, and if it is right I will cause that your bosom shall burn within you; therefore you shall feel that it is right.

But if it be not right, you shall have no such feelings, but you shall have a stupor of thought that shall cause you to forget the thing which is wrong; therefore you cannot write that which is sacred save it be given you from me.[22]

This is a major key to revelation—a universal key—which was always followed by Joseph Smith and by those who have followed him in the leadership of the Church. It is a method that may be followed by all men who desire communication with a higher power. But it requires, as in the case of Joseph Smith, an unwavering love of truth, a pure mind and heart with a consuming desire to know what to do, and an intense concentration upon the subject.

As far as is known, the revelations to Joseph Smith came (1) through words spoken directly by the Lord, (2) through messages spoken by heavenly messengers delegated to visit him, (3) through the help of the Urim and and Thummim and similar helps, (4) and, most frequently, through inspiration after intense desire and earnest prayer.

While we may not know fully how Joseph Smith received revelations, we can test their contents by any proper method for their verity. They have withstood assaults of doubters through the years. The contents of the revelations certify to their divine origin.

It should be added that revelation is not confined to one man or set of men. Every child of God has the need for revelation to fit his personal needs and may claim it. All members of the Church are entitled to communications with the unseen world. Such manifestations depend, however, upon the need of the individual, recognized by the Lord, and also upon the worthiness of the seeker to receive such a blessing.

Impressions from the unseen world come with varying degrees of emphasis, depending usually upon the fitness of

---

[22]*Doctrine and Covenants* 9:7-9.

the recipient to sense the message. Men must labor to become sensitive to such messages.

All individual manifestations are for the comfort and direct help of the individual and should be kept sacred and not noised abroad. Those who seek such help should not expect such messages as came through Joseph Smith. He received revelations not only for himself but also for the Church he was commissioned to restore.

Official communications for the Church or its divisions come only through officials of the Church. The President of the Church receives revelations for the whole Church; none others may do so. Communications for stakes and wards come only through the properly appointed heads of these units of the Church and must be in harmony with the voice of the President of the Church.

All communications from the Lord, inspirations and impressions, are in reality varying degrees of revelation. They are all phases of the Lord's communication with his children on earth. An official divine communication for the Church is usually called a revelation. A personal communication is commonly spoken of as an inspiration. But they all come from the same sacred source to men of worthy lives.

The revelations to Joseph Smith form a body of truth convincing to all honest readers of Joseph's close communion with heaven. The contents of the revelations form the best proof of their divine origin.

It may be said here that much time has been wasted in the attempt to learn just how Joseph translated the Book of Mormon plates. David Whitmer held that the English version appeared above the characters until it was copied. Numerous other explanations have been offered. These are all wrong. The exact mechanism is not known. Joseph Smith the translator merely says that they were translated by "the gift and power of God."[23] That is enough.

---

[23]B. H. Roberts, *Comprehensive History of the Church*, vol. 1, p. 138.

CHAPTER 42

THE USE OF THE URIM AND THUMMIM

The sacred instrument known as the Urim and Thummim, "two stones in silver bows," accompanied the Book of Mormon plates and was used by Joseph Smith in the translation of the Book of Mormon. For some time it was used also in securing revelations from the Lord. The use of this instrument is an evidence of the truth of the Prophet's story of his spiritual experiences leading to the work entrusted to him.

The Urim and Thummim is mentioned in the Bible in connection with priestly functions. It was to be used in making the will of the Lord clear and comprehensible to the priest. Aaron was instructed to wear the Urim and Thummim "upon the heart," when he went to secure "judgment" from the Lord; and his successors were instructed to use the Urim and Thummim when they asked "counsel" from the Lord. Clearly, the Urim and Thummim was used in early days in official communications with the Lord. Beyond that, little is known of it.[1]

The use of physical aids to help man in sacred work is age-old. Enoch,[2] Noah,[3] Abraham,[4] Moses,[5] Aaron,[6] and the later prophets used such means in their work.

Such helps are mentioned also in the Book of Mormon. Mosiah speaks of the possession of the Urim and Thummim by the Jaredites.[7] The brother of Jared molded sixteen small stones, which after being touched by God, became luminous and gave light on the voyage across the ocean.[8] Lehi on the way to the ocean found the Liahona which was used to guide them in traveling over the ocean.[9]

---

[1]Exodus 28:30; Leviticus 8:8; Numbers 27:21; Deuteronomy 33.8, I Samuel 28:6; Ezra 2:63; Nehemiah 7:65; Arch H. Reynolds, *The Urim and Thummim.*
[2]Moses 6:35-36.
[3]Orson Pratt, *Sacred Records*, pp. 414-415.
[4]Abraham 1:16.
[5]Deuteronomy 33:7-8.
[6]Numbers 27:20.
[7]Mosiah 28:13.
[8]Ether 3:1.
[9]1 Nephi 16:10.

Such helps were not confined to translation as in the case of Joseph Smith, but also for giving light and setting the course of travel.

How such aids to human senses operate is not known. Divine power, using the forces of the universe, set them in motion for those who are authorized to employ them in their work. It seems probable that they demand an intense concentration upon the theme in mind, which brings about the communion with divine forces, necessary to do the required work, such as translation of unknown languages. The instrument itself is valueless unless used by an authorized person.

Naturally, such aids and instruments have had many imitators. There are spurious peep stones and crystal globes everywhere, which usually mislead the people.

In modern times the Urim and Thummim reappeared. The Prophet Joseph Smith records an explanation made by the ancient American Prophet Moroni.

He said that there was a book deposited, written on gold plates . . . also, that there were two stones in silver bows—and these stones fastened to a breastplate, constituted what is called the Urim and Thummim—deposited with the plates; and the possession and use of these stones were what constituted "Seers" in ancient or former times, and that God had prepared them for the purpose of translating the book.[10]

When the actual work of translation began, the Urim and Thummim was found to be indispensable. In various places the statement is made that the translation was made "by means of the Urim and Thummim."[11] On one occasion, when the Prophet, through the defection of Martin Harris, lost a part of the manuscript translation, the Urim and Thummim was taken from him, and the power of translation ceased. Upon the return of the sacred instrument, the work was resumed.[12] It must be concluded that the stones were essential to the work of translation.

Though the Urim and Thummim was necessary, it

---

[10]*History of the Church*, vol. 1, p. 12.
[11]*Doctrine and Covenants* 10:1.
[12]*History of the Church*, vol. 1, p. 23.

need not be concluded that it relieved the person who used it of effort on his part. On the contrary, the Prophet was required to place himself in the proper spiritual and mental attitude before the Urim and Thummim became of any real help. It required great concentration of desire and thought, even with the Urim and Thummim, to secure the sought-for results in translation or revelation. At the best, this instrument served as an aid to the Prophet's natural senses. Some people have suggested that all the Prophet had to do in the work of translation was to look into the stones and then to dictate what the Urim and Thummim revealed. This as has been said is incorrect.[13]

Some use was made also of the seer stone and occasional mention was made of it. This was a stone found while the Prophet assisted in digging a well for Clark Chase. By divine power this stone was made serviceable to Joseph Smith in the early part of his ministry.[14] There is no evidence that this stone was used in Joseph's sacred work.

Speaking of those early days the Prophet usually says, "I inquired of the Lord through the Urim and Thummim, and obtained the following."[15] The "stones in silver bows" seemed, therefore, to have possessed the general power of making spiritual manifestations understandable to him.

The Prophet did not always receive revelations by the aid of the Urim and Thummim. As he grew in spiritual power, he learned to bring his mind into such harmony with divine forces that it became, as it were, itself a Urim and Thummim to him; and God's will was revealed without the intervention of external aids; that is, truth may become known without outside help when one is in harmony or in full tune with the requirements of the subject in hand.

Similarly, such changes may be accomplished in science; for example, if a piece of soft iron is wrapped with a wire carrying an electric current, the iron becomes a mag-

[13]B. H. Roberts, *Comprehensive History of the Church*, vol. 1, pp. 129, 133.
[14]George Q. Cannon, *Life of Joseph Smith*, p. 56; B. H. Roberts, *Comprehensive History of the Church*, vol. 6, p. 230, vol. 1, p. 129; Edward Stevenson, *Reminiscences of the Prophet Joseph*, pp. 10-19; David Whitmer, *Address to the World*, p. 32; B. H. Roberts, *New Witness for God*, vol. 2, p. 113 (Y.M.M.I.A. Manuals)
[15]*History of the Church*, vol 1, pp. 33, 36, 45, 49, 63.

net and remains so while the current flows through the wire. In some such manner, through appeal to heavenly forces by prayer, men may become cognizant of spiritual conditions wholly beyond the ordinary senses of man. It is an ancient law applied by all faithful men and women and by the prophets of all times.

To win such a change in the spiritual field requires a complete surrender to the task. Prayer becomes the power corresponding to the electric current around the iron. That is one of the virtues of prayer; by its use multitudes have communed with heavenly truths. That is how thousands have won a testimony of the truth of Joseph Smith's claims. Men living correctly and seeking truth may be so changed that they may receive help from the great unseen world.

The possession of the Urim and Thummim by Joseph Smith with its purpose and use becomes a strong evidence of the truth of Joseph Smith's message. It is a commonplace of science that the senses of man are so poor as to make them inadequate, unless aids are provided, to discover more than a small fraction of universal truth.

Indeed, with unaided senses, man stands helpless before the many phenomena of nature. Eyes and ears of themselves discover only a small part of that which may be seen and heard with seeing and hearing helps. It is an elementary fact that aids to the senses of man, when found, open up larger and new vistas of knowledge. Every aid to a human sense becomes in fact a door to a new field of scientific exploration.

The history of science is largely the story of the accumulation of aids to man's senses. A great lens in a telescope has now been made which will enable the human eye to see light of the intensity of a small candle forty thousand miles away! The microscope and electron, enable the eye to pierce the world otherwise beyond man's vision. By the use of a glass prism ordinary sunlight is broken into the seven prismatic colors and the science of spectography is made possible. Upon the thermometer the doctor rests many of his judgments as to human illness or health. By the sensitiveness of silver chloride to the light at the upper end of the spectrum the art of photography came into being. Uranium glass changes the invisible rays at the violet end of the spectrum into light rays. A magnetic needle makes known the presence in a wire of low tension electric current. The magnetic currents over the earth are indicated by the compass. By X-rays the bones of the body are made visible. The tube in the radio enables man to hear sounds produced hundreds, sometimes thousands, of miles away. Such examples might be multiplied! Without aids to human senses, our knowledge would be small indeed.

Astronomy, chemistry, physics, biology, and the other sciences would be elementary, fragmentary, incipient, dried up, misleading disciplines of the mind were it not for the discovered aids to the senses of man.

There is also another class of instruments which enables man's senses to recognize forces which do not act directly upon the consciousness of man. If a musical note is produced by a violin near a piano, the piano string, if tuned correctly, will give out the same note. Through this law of sympathetic vibrations, it is possible to make a piano give out any note within its acoustical range, without the piano keys being touched by anyone. If a radio receiving apparatus is tuned properly, it may select from the tumult of distant sounds the message from the station desired. Such aids to our senses do not depend upon the nature of the materials involved but upon the degree to which they are brought into sympathy with the force to be recognized. It was Joseph Smith's task in his spiritual labors to bring himself into harmony with spiritual forces. Then he could hear, see, perceive, and understand.

In short, it is by aids to the senses that man has conquered much of the unknown. It is by such aids that science has progressed and built its bulwarks. An aid to the senses when discovered invariably opens a new and vast field of knowledge. It is the same with spiritual affairs. They are experienced by mortal men, when aids such as prayer or faith are used in the search.

Joseph Smith's career and teachings show that there is no real demarcation between the material and spiritual worlds. We live really in one world. It is not surprising therefore to find in the events of Joseph's life a recognition of the principle that by the use of proper instruments the world beyond man's five senses may be brought within man's understanding. In Joseph's day modern science was in its swaddling clothes, and he was not familiar with the little that was known. He was guided by a higher power. His use of the Urim and Thummim is but another unanswerable evidence of the consistency of his work.

Joseph Smith was but a humble, inexperienced lad. He was assigned a tremendous task. His need of help, such as the Urim and Thummim, until by mighty prayer and effort his body and spirit became spiritually "tuned," seems logical and scientific. Besides, if an iron rod, surrounded by a coil of wire carrying an electric current becomes a magnet, it is not so difficult to understand that a man surrounded by spiritual power may become so changed as to know things ordinarily beyond human power.

Every Christian knows the power of prayer. After communing with the Lord, a person arises not only comforted in his feelings, but also with a clearer vision of the solution of the problems of the day. Prayer is but a variation of the principle of placing oneself in harmony with outside, unseen forces.

It should be noted also that the Prophet does not enter into any argument to prove the necessity of the use of the Urim and Thummim. His simple, frank mention of them argues strongly for his veracity. An impostor would probably have attempted an explanation of the "seer stones," the Urim and Thummim.

The Urim and Thummim was an aid to Joseph's spiritual senses. How it operated is not known. For that matter, the methods of operation of most physical aids to man's senses are not understood. Science accepts the facts and uses the instruments. Joseph's claim to the need of such aids, as is made by every worker in pursuit of new knowledge, becomes an evidence for the truth of his life's labor.

The frank admission, without apology, of his possession of the Urim and Thummim, as a help in his work of translation is in line with all the events of his life. His experiences were of the kind often called supernatural. He offered neither explanation nor apology for them. He said that they came through the gift and power of God. That was enough.

The fact that the events of his life transcend the expected knowledge of a young man without school or special training, astonishes us, then convinces us that Joseph Smith told the truth.

It is so with the Urim and Thummim. In a day when many of the well-known sciences of today were yet to be born, he set up very simply in his declared use of helps in translation, a very fundamental condition found necessary in all science, in every department of knowledge. It is but one of the many marvelous events in Joseph Smith's career, but it is really convincing of his inspiration.

Joseph Smith's own story is really the best defense of its truth.

CHAPTER 43

WHEN AND WHERE OF REVELATIONS

Nearly all the revelations to the Prophet, one hundred and thirty-two of them, have been gathered in the volume known as the Doctrine and Covenants. When and where the revelations were given is summarized in the attached tables, together with some information concerning their length.

It will be observed that they are not long, from one to six pages, averaging about 3.3 pages or from nineteen hundred to two thousand words. That made them not only easy to copy but as easy to remember as they came one by one, at suitable intervals.

The revelations were answers to Joseph's requests for help. As the Church grew and moved about, new problems constantly arose. Consequently, the revelations were received at various places and times. Therefore, they are practically a record of the movements of the Prophet during his short ministry.

The first thirty-nine revelations were received in and about the region where the Book of Mormon was translated and the Church was organized, in the states of New York and Pennsylvania.

When Given

Year	Number of Revelations	Number of Pages	Length of Revelations Pages
1823	1	2	1.0
1828	1	2	2.0
1829	15	34	2.3
1830	19	42	2.2
1831	37	108	2.9
1832	16	62	3.9
1833	13	38	3.0

1834	5	24	4.8
1835	2	12	6.0
1836	3	12	4.0
1837	1	4	4.0
1838	8	9	1.1
1839	3	9	3.0
1841	3	20	6.6
1842	6	10	1.7
1843	4	16	4.0

The journeyings of the Prophet are roughly shown by the places where the revelations were given.

Number of
Revelations

Harmony, Pennsylvania 15
Manchester, New York 4
Fayette, New York 19
Perrysburg, New York 1
Hiram, Ohio 15
Kirtland, Ohio 46
Orange, Ohio 1
Amherst, Ohio 1
Thompson, Ohio 1
Independence, Missouri 6
Fishing River, Missouri 1
McIlawin's Bend, Missouri 1
Bank of Missouri River, Missouri 1
Far West, Missouri 6
Spring Hill, Missouri 1
Liberty Jail, Missouri 3
Nauvoo, Illinois 8
Ramus, Illinois 1
Salem, Massachusetts 1

The Church moved in 1831 to Ohio, in Kirtland and its neighborhood. There it prospered greatly. There also were found many of the men who became the leaders of the young organization. There also were received, among others, the revelations for the building of the United Order, for an effective missionary organization, and for the doctrinal guidance of the people. The answers that came then in response to Joseph's request are contained in sixty-three revelations.

Meanwhile, the Church was moving westward into Missouri, where the headquarters of the Church were to be established. There problems of settlement were many, and persecutions raged. It was a time of much excitement. Nineteen revelations were received during the Missouri period.

Then in 1838 and 1839, the persecuted people fled from Missouri and settled in Illinois where they built the city of Nauvoo and other settlements. By this time the organizational and doctrinal needs of the Church had been partly supplied by revelation, so that only about thirteen revelations were there received. But these were of profound importance.

The whole restless history of the Church is really sketched by the succession of phases in which the Prophet received his revelations. It was a natural and normal procedure.

The revelations were generally answers to questions concerning the immediate needs of the people. The answers however were not only replies to the questions but also gave much additional information, usually of a doctrinal character.

That seemed to be the way of the Lord; always to give more than was asked for. The Lord expects men to turn to him for help. Then he gives abundantly to the inquiring mind. It was a lesson to the young Prophet and to us all.

Among the one hundred and thirty-two revelations to the Prophet, recorded in the Doctrine and Covenants, fewer than half a dozen deal purely with organization or doctrine. Thus it comes about that to secure a complete statement of the organization, priesthood, or doctrine of the Church, one must search through the revealed literature of the Church. Grains of unexpected wisdom are found here and there, which gathered and brought together under one heading make a full statement of the subject considered.

There are some notable exceptions, as for example Section 107 dealing entirely with priesthood and Section 132 dealing wholly with marriage, and there are others dealing almost wholly with one subject, but in the main several subjects are touched upon in each revelation.

It is notable also that the revelations move from subjects of somewhat common discussion to others that were new to the Church. In that respect the revelations become an excellent illustration of the more logical educational method of moving from the better to the lesser known.

It is also notable that the fulness of doctrine came gradually to the Prophet and his people. Critics have urged that the Lord should have given all needed information at once, in a systematic, orderly manner, and then both he and the people would have been done with the matter. This would have been strictly unpedagogical. It is nowhere used. The Lord gave in this gradual approach to full truth a method that should always be respected.

The revelations came as needed. That is the answer to all questions about the when and where of the revelations.

CHAPTER 44

REVELATION AS PROPHECY

Joseph Smith was a revelator. That which had been lost through the dark centuries of apostasy he restored in simplicity through revelations from God. The mysteries of the ages were blown away and replaced by plain understandable truth. People in dark places walked in new light under his revelations. For example, the doctrine of the pre-existence of man was revealed to him. That changed the whole tenor of gospel teachings. The doctrine of eternal damnation had hung over imperfect humanity as a keen-edged sword. To Joseph came the revelation that the true meaning of eternal punishment is God's punishment which is always just but also merciful. Salvation had been defined to be a sudden change after death, placing the departed in God's kingdom or in hell. Joseph learned that all mankind will be saved but that the degree of salvation will depend measurably on their works. He lifted loving hearts into joy by the doctrine that family relationships may continue in the hereafter.

He was a great revelator who brought together the gospel shattered by centuries of apostasy. The people who learned the complete truth were filled with gladness. So with Brigham Young who said:

I never saw anyone, until I met Joseph Smith, who could tell me anything about the character, personality and dwelling-place of God, or anything satisfactory about angels, or the relationship of man to his Maker. Yet I was as diligent as any man need to be to try and find out these things.[1]

When I first heard him preach, he brought heaven and earth together; and all the priests of the day could not tell me anything correct about heaven, hell, God, angels or devils; they were as blind as Egyptian darkness. When I saw Joseph Smith, he took heaven, figuratively speaking, and brought it down to earth; and he took

---

[1]*Journal of Discourses*, vol. 16, p. 46.

the earth, brought it up, and opened up, in plainness and simplicity, the things of God; and that is the beauty of his mission.[2]

I feel like shouting Hallelujah, all the time, when I think that I ever knew Joseph Smith, the Prophet whom the Lord raised up and ordained, and to whom he gave keys and power to build up the kingdom of God on earth and sustain it.[3]

His ideas have traveled far and wide. Frequently a copy of his teachings is found in a teacher's or preacher's or politician's desk. This is not surprising, for he taught only the gospel of Jesus Christ which had been only partially understood.

He was a notable foreteller of future events. The prophetic element was nearly always present in whatever he said. He seemed to be immersed in the spirit of prophecy and looked into the future with a vision given to few men.

In the revelations given to him, printed in the Doctrine and Covenants, are found nearly eleven hundred statements that may be classed as prophecies of the future. Nearly seven hundred of these are of a spiritual nature, as, for example, "And it shall come to pass that he that asketh in Spirit shall receive in Spirit."[4] The remaining four hundred deal more directly with things of earth.

The prophecies or predictions of Joseph Smith concerning future events are unique in one respect. They are offered as direct revelations from the Lord. That sets them apart from the mass of human prophecies or guesses made throughout the centuries.

Before the Church was organized, Joseph Smith foretold many things that have come to pass. While yet an obscure lad, off the highways of the world, he declared that the results of his labors would be known as a great and marvelous work;[5] that missionaries would be sent over the earth;[6] and that people from the four corners of the earth would accept his message and join the Church he was

---

[2]*Ibid.*, vol. 5, p. 332.
[3]*Ibid.*, vol. 3, p. 51.
[4]*Doctrine and Covenants* 46:28.
[5]*Ibid.*, 4:1; 6:1; 11:1; 12:1; 14:1; 35:1.
[6]*Ibid.*, 1:4; 35:13.

to restore.[7] These predictions and others like them have been literally fulfilled.

Practically every encyclopedia in any language has an article on Joseph Smith. Innumerable books, pamphlets, and articles have been written about him. Upwards of a hundred thousand missionaries have traveled the world over to preach the gospel to the earth's inhabitants. People have joined the Church he was instrumental in establishing from almost every land and clime. There has been a literal fulfilment of the prophecies made by Joseph Smith while he was an unknown youth.

While translating the Book of Mormon, he predicted that three witnesses would see the golden plates and testify of their experience.[8] This seemed a daring thing to do. Men find it difficult to foretell what others will do, especially in so unusual a matter as the Book of Mormon plates. However, David Whitmer, Oliver Cowdery, and Martin Harris did see the plates in a miraculous manner, and their testimony has been printed in the hundreds of thousands of copies of the Book of Mormon circulated in many languages the world over. The witnesses clung to their testimony to the end of their lives. It was a literal fulfilment of a prophecy that could easily have failed. It marked Joseph Smith as possessing true prophetic power.

Judge Stephen A. Douglas, prominent in American history, was well-acquainted with the Latter-day Saints. On one occasion in 1843, after a long and friendly conference, Joseph Smith prophesied that Stephen A. Douglas would some day aspire to the presidency of the United States but warned Judge Douglas that if he ever "turned his hand against the Latter-day Saints, he would feel the weight of the hand of Almighty God upon him."[9] More than fifteen years later, Douglas did aspire to the presidency. For popular approval he went out of his way to injure the Latter-day Saints. In fulfilment of the prophecy, he went down in political defeat and died an embittered

⁷*Ibid.*, 33:6; 18:44
⁸*Ibid.*, 5:15; 17:5; 5:25.
⁹*Deseret News*, September 24, 1856, p. 225; *History of the Church*, vol. 5, p. 393.

man. One wonders if he thought then of the prophecy of the Mormon prophet!

In 1832, in the very infancy of the Church, and long before any one thought of a Civil War, Joseph Smith prophesied that war would "shortly come to pass, beginning at the rebellion of South Carolina"; and that "the Southern States shall be divided against the Northern States, and the Southern States will call on other nations even Great Britain for help." Nearly thirty years later in the bloody American Civil War this prophecy was fulfilled to the very letter.

The prophecy went on to say that "the days will come that war will be poured out upon all nations."[10] World Wars I and II, three quarters of a century and more later, were complete fulfilments of this part of the prophecy.

This great and remarkable prophecy still stands as an evidence of Joseph Smith's mighty prophetic power.

In 1842, in the presence of many persons Joseph Smith prophesied that "the saints . . . would be driven to the Rocky Mountains . . . and some of you will . . . assist in making settlements and build cities, and see the saints become a mighty people in the midst of the Rocky Mountains."[11]

At the time that this prophecy was uttered, little was known of the West. Its feasibility for settlement was unknown. The prophecy was uttered before Fremont's reports of his exploration were available. Besides, there were many other places the Saints could go if driven out. American history, dealing with the West, certifies to the fulfilment of this prophecy. The Saints were driven from Nauvoo; they settled in the valleys of the Rocky Mountains, and there have become a mighty people.

Many other like predictions of Joseph Smith could be recited. So far, no prophecy of Joseph Smith has failed. They speak unitedly of a prophetic vision second to none

[10]*Doctrine and Covenants*, Section 87; Nephi L. Morris, *Prophecies of Joseph Smith and Their Fulfillment*, p. 33
[11]Nephi L. Morris, op. cit., p. 124; *History of the Church*, vol. 5, p. 85.

in sacred or profane history. Joseph Smith is fully entitled to be called a Prophet of God.

Students of the life of Joseph Smith cannot lay aside the evidence presented by the fulfilment of these and many other prophecies which rise above mere guesses, since their fulfilment was so improbable or beyond the usual vision of men. The fulfilment of these prophecies alone fully justifies the title *Prophet,* by which Joseph Smith is ordinarily known. But let it always be remembered that the prophetic power of Joseph Smith is most fully illustrated in his revelations and teachings.

The questions that fill every human heart, the wonderment about the past, the hope of the future, and the constant query "What is life for?" were answered by this prophet, simply, clearly, and acceptably to the human soul. Therefore peace and contentment are possessed by Joseph's followers. This is perhaps the foremost reason why we speak of Joseph Smith as a Prophet of God. His prophetic power surpassed human understanding. It came of God to support the work he was called to establish.

CHAPTER 45

THE WORLD-WIDE VIEW

Joseph Smith had a world-wide view of his mission and of the objectives of the Church. He was not building an organization admitting only those of a certain locality and country. He was a fervid believer in the principles embodied in the American Constitution but did not confine his operations to the United States. Rather he urged upon all people of every race and land to accept the gospel of Jesus Christ and become members of the restored Church of Jesus Christ.

He could not do otherwise, for the Savior left the injunction that the gospel should be preached to every kindred, tongue and people.[1] Joseph Smith in his short, turbulent life had the world-sweep of the gospel and left behind him clearly the duty of the Church in this respect.[2]

He declared that the members of the Church were a covenant people,[3] that is, they were under the covenant that the Lord made with Abraham and his children, both as to duties and rewards. How could that be?

Omitting the possibility that some of the members may have had Israelitish blood, he held that the Abrahamic covenant was not only for those of blood descent from Abraham but also for all who accepted the gospel. All such persons underwent a profound change, which made them indeed children of Abraham.[4] In short every one who entered the Church would be by adoption a child of the ancient covenant. This was confirmed in the Book of Abraham which was translated by Joseph Smith:

My name is Jehovah, and I know the end from the beginning . . . and I will make of thee a great nation, and I will bless thee above measure and make thy name great among all nations, and thou shalt be a blessing unto thy seed after thee, that in their hands they shall

---

[1]Revelation 14:6; *Doctrine and Covenants* 1:11
[2]*Doctrine and Covenants*, Section 20; 112:27-28.
[3]*Ibid.*, 42:36.
[4]Joseph Fielding Smith, *Teachings of the Prophet Joseph Smith*, p. 150.

bear this ministry and Priesthood unto all nations, and I will bless them through thy name; for as many as receive this gospel shall be called after thy name, and shall be accounted thy seed, and shall rise up and bless thee as their father.[5]

This view was fortified by the revelations received by the Prophet. In the revelation given as a preface to the Doctrine and Covenants the Lord said:

Hearken ye people from afar; and ye that are upon the islands of the sea, listen together. For verily the voice of the Lord is unto all men, and there is none to escape.[6]

Over and over again this doctrine appeared in his addresses and works; for example, when the question was raised as to the calling of the Twelve Apostles, he ruled that "They are to hold the keys of this ministry, to unlock the door of the kingdom of heaven unto all nations, and to preach the gospel to every creature."[7]

Even a casual examination of the labors of Joseph Smith will show that the practices set up by him for human welfare have world-wide application. While settling local difficulties, building for local needs, all that was decided upon could be used by all people anywhere. His purpose was the conquest of the whole world for the cause of Christ. The restoration which had been effected through his instrumentality must reach every ear so that none would be without excuse. The doctrine of the gospel even in temporal matters, such as have been discussed in an earlier chapter, was universal. Much of the toil of the Prophet can be understood only when this universality of gospel doctrine is understood. It is through this doctrine which actuated all that the Prophet did that he may lay claim to being a world figure.

In the beginning of his work he sent missionaries out into the states of the Union to preach the restoration. Soon thereafter, the missionaries went to Canada, where they found a fruitful field.

---

[5]Abraham 2:8-10.
[6]*Doctrine and Covenants* 1:1-2.
[7]Joseph Fielding Smith, *op., cit.*, p. 74.

Then he ventured across the Atlantic. During the unhappy days of 1837, when an orgy of speculation in the United States led men to new evil deeds which presaged an unusual depression, which indeed did come, the word of the Lord came to Joseph. On June 4, 1837, the Prophet asked Heber C. Kimball, a member of the Council of the Twelve Apostles, to take a mission to Great Britain. Orson Hyde, another member of the Council of the Twelve, volunteered to go along and was accepted. Elder Willard Richards and Joseph Fielding were also called to join the missionary party. This party was to meet three missionaries from Canada, John Goodson, Isaac Russell and John Snyder. This enlarged party of seven then went out to bring the gospel message to the great British nation. They were successful. The way opened before them marvelously.[8] The work in Great Britain prospered exceedingly. So important was this work, that the Prophet incorporated in his journal the reports of the activity of the missionaries and members in Great Britain.

The years that followed were strenuous. Local conditions, the evacuation of the people from Missouri, and the building of Nauvoo, the new city of the Saints, and the complications that arose there kept the Prophet's days fully occupied. However, time and again his mind returned to the duty of the Church to cover the earth with the message of the restoration.

On Tuesday, May 23, 1842, Elder Addison Pratt was "ordained a seventy and blessed and set apart to go to the Society Islands." To accompany him, Elders Noah Rogers, Benjamin Grouard, and Knowlton F. Hanks were set apart and blessed.[9] The work in the Pacific Islands begun by these brethren has likewise been very fruitful.

Had the Prophet lived no doubt other missions would have been opened under his direction; but the work has been carried on to this day by the Prophet's successors.

[8]Richard L. Evans, *A Century of Mormonism in Great Britain*, Chapter 1; Orson F. Whitney, *Life of Heber C. Kimball*, Chapter 14, pp. 103-112.
[9]*History of the Church*, vol. 5, pp. 404-405; Doyle L. Green, *Improvement Era*, 1949 and 1950.

The Prophet's mind swept eternity. In the work of the Lord on earth, he developed a world-wide view, which has given vitality to the Church, as this view has been maintained by officers and members of the Church.

THE NAUVOO TEMPLE
Now destroyed

NAUVOO HOUSE, NAUVOO, ILL.
The foundation only built in the days of Joseph Smith

NAUVOO RESIDENCE OF LORENZO SNOW
Later President of the Church

THE MANSION HOUSE, NAUVOO, ILL.
Home of Joseph Smith

CHAPTER 46

WHAT CHARACTERIZES A PROPHET?

A prophet is a man endowed with priesthood authority who is called by the Lord to leadership in the unfolding
of the plan of salvation. The prophets have been, in their
day and age, the human leaders in the Lord's work. Such
men of the past have been Abraham, Moses, Samuel, Isaiah,
Lehi, and others; of the present dispensation, Joseph Smith,
and his successors in office.

Prophets have a threefold function:

First: The cause of the Lord is divinely organized. It
is the most perfect organization on earth. Competent leaders are necessary in every successful organization. The man
who stands at the head of the organized body of accepted
worshippers to guide its activities and to be God's mouth-
piece is the prophet of that day and group.

Second: The gospel in its purity was given to Adam
and through him to his descendants; but there has been
a constant falling away from the truth. The whisperings
of the tempter lead men into evil deeds. Apostasy has followed apostasy. Consequently successive restorations of the
truth have become necessary. The Prophet restates the
ancient truths and seeks to hold the people to the unchanging laws of the gospel.

Third: Each age has its own peculiar problems. Each
dispensation carried forward into new situations the Lord's
plan for human welfare. Additional revelation from the
Lord is needed to meet the problems of a progressive unfolding plan. Such new truths, emanating from divinity,
come only through the prophet of the day.

These functions of a prophet are well illustrated in
the available histories of the prophets. Each one had been
endowed with the priesthood and therefore spoke with
authority.

Enoch spent his life calling the people to repentance

from their violation of the requirements of the gospel. Abraham became the founder of a people through whom the Lord would accomplish his purposes on earth. Moses led the chosen people into a freedom which would enable them, through obedience, to carry out their high commission. Samuel had the task of guiding Israel until the people chose to be under the leadership of kings. Isaiah and Jeremiah labored to bring the people from a condition of idolatry into paths of purity and truth. Lehi was called to establish the Church on the American continent.

Joseph Smith was commissioned to restore the doctrine, organization, and authority of the Church to a later generation which had lost these fundamentals of the Church of Jesus Christ. His successors have been engaged in carrying forward the restoration, in proclaiming its truth to all the world, and in building securely the Church of Jesus Christ, through which the Lord will soon accomplish his purposes relative to the last days.

All these men were teachers and defenders of the gospel. In addition, each had his special work to do. Each has left behind a message for succeeding generations.

Above all, so prophetic history reveals, each prophet was called to serve the needs of his own generation. His power lay in advancing the unchanging cause of the Lord. In accomplishing this, in admonishing the people to gospel obedience, three major helps and procedures were at his command.

First: The prophet of any age draws upon the records of the past. The keeping of records has ever been enjoined by the Lord upon his people. Each prophet, from the days of the early patriarchs, down the years, has left behind a precious body of teaching and practice, of continuous value. Some have recorded in their messages direct revelations from the Lord. These records are the foundation of all safe gospel teaching. Many have been collected in the volume known as the Holy Bible. Others are found in the Book of Mormon, Doctrine and Covenants, and the Pearl of Great Price. These four books together form the most precious library on earth. There are also compilations of the teachings of modern day prophets, which add to the teaching of those of early days.

The prophet of any time must of necessity draw upon these treasures of the past, in clarifying his own views and in teaching the people.

Second: The great governing principles of truth are unchanging. But the conditions brought about by human activity are forever changing. From sailboat to steamboat to airship, from horse power to steam power, from the grease-soaked wicklight to electric lighting, from the rushing human agent to the telegraph, telephone, and radio— and a multitude of others—we span changes that in the past seemed impossible. Undoubtedly the future holds developments that today are equally inconceivable.

Such changes affect human thinking. New social and economic problems arise. Even the spiritual outlook is invaded. Then it becomes the duty of the prophet to teach how the eternal unchanging laws of the gospel may be applied amidst constant change for the benefit and blessing of humanity. The prophet does not discard new ways for old ones, if truth is preserved. He is not a reactionary, but ever a progressive, holding the new and the old to gospel law. He gives life to that which is new as it blossoms upon the ruins of the old by the constant application to it of principles of truth.

This adherence to and use of the principles of the gospel in an age of changing conditions have characterized the lives of the prophets. It has often been their main responsibility.

Third: The prophet is but a man. He draws heavily upon the past. He seeks inspiration from the Lord for his daily work. There comes at times the need for new knowledge from heaven. Then, if it be the proper time, the Lord speaks. New revelation is given. Pressing problems are solved by a knowledge beyond that of man.

The prophet is never wholly dependent upon the past.

He may always draw upon the fount of truth and wisdom. All the prophets have done this.

By the same token Joseph Smith was a prophet. Like the prophets of old he did well the work assigned to him. That is the test of heaven which make the last ordained elder and the veteran apostle equal before the Lord. In reality his work was greater because of the superhuman task of restoring gospel truths in their purity as given by Jesus Christ when he was upon the earth.

The most important prophet in any age for the people of that age, is the living prophet. The prophets who have gone before have left to us their precious teachings which will be used for the instruction and comfort of mankind. But it is the living prophet who helps us by his teachings, example, and direction to meet and to solve the problems of today, our day. To follow the living prophet, the interpreter of the past, and the foreteller of the future, is the essence of wisdom. The very strength of the Church restored through the instrumentality of Joseph Smith lies in the doctrine of continuing revelation through a living prophet.

Avoiding refinement of definition, a prophet of God performs one or more of three functions. First and foremost, he is a teacher of the gospel of Jesus Christ. Through his teachings he holds the people in the path of truth. Second, a prophet is a seer and revelator of new truth. This is an important function in a changing and increasing world. Third, a prophet may at times foretell future events. This gift is not necessarily the prophet's most important function, but is evidence of his prophetic power.[1]

To an astonishing degree, Joseph Smith was a teacher, revelator, and predictor. He stands among the foremost in the company of historical prophets.

He was a superb teacher. He had a frank and kind manner. His followers flocked to hear him and hung upon his every word. His mind swept the horizons of eternity

---

[1]Amos 3:7; Luke 1:70; *Doctrine and Covenants* 21:1-2; Mosiah 8:13-17.

as he explained the gospel of the Lord Jesus Christ.[2] Strangers were caught by his simple oratory and were left to ponder if he were not indeed dealing with eternal truths.[3]

---

[2]Parley P. Pratt, *Parley P. Pratt Autobiography*, p. 46.
[3]*History of the Church*, vol. 4, pp. 78-79; Josiah Quincy, *Figures of the Past*, p. 381.

CHAPTER 47

DID JOSEPH SMITH SPEAK TO THIS DAY?

The answer to this question is an unqualified "Yes."

The system of truth taught by Joseph Smith is of an eternal and universal nature. Therefore, it must foresee and help solve every human problem of any day. Were it not so, the gospel, which was restored through the Prophet in its fulness, would be incomplete, and insufficient to serve man's every need.

Forgetfulness of the universality of Joseph's commission has led many a man to falter and fail. When problems have arisen, he has sought, of his own power and unsuccessfully, to create or invent solutions instead of looking back upon the unchangeable truths which he might safely apply to present conditions with full assurance of victory. Unwillingness to remember that the business of the day is to use and apply revealed, constant truth to the issues of the day lies at the bottom of much of the world's confusion and unhappiness.

It would be a useful and happy exercise to select any problem, past or present, and to attempt to solve it with the principles of the gospel. Rare, convincing results would follow.

The chief of the world's present issues is a good example. In recent days, fomented by an unprecedented propaganda, is the political, social doctrine that a totalitarian government by dictatorship, is preferable to a democratic government, by the people, of the people and for the people. Even in free countries, many misguided, shallow thinkers as well as would-be power-hungry leaders have fallen for the evil thought that dictatorship is preferable. They have observed occasional errors, growing pains, ripples on the wave in their democracy and have failed to see the great forward, upward movement towards human welfare of peoples who are their own masters.

Right here is the crux of the issue. Shall people be looked upon in the mass and so be treated, which is dictatorship, or shall they be viewed as individuals, and their individuality protected, which is democracy? "The shape of things to come" will depend on the dominance in the world of one or the other of these views.

What is the answer to this query by the gospel restored by Joseph Smith the Prophet? Were he here, he would give a threefold answer:

First: Every man is a person of immeasurable dignity. He has a divine pedigree, extending into the dim eternities before the earth was. His destiny, if he so wills, is to progress eternally to a godlike stature. The generations of men on earth are gods in embryo. That gives them place, position, and rights, compelling deep respect.

Second: Since man rises, with the aid of God, toward his vast future by his own efforts (and there can be no growth otherwise), there must be no interference beyond that of eternal unchangeable law, with the operation of his will, whether to rise or descend. He must remain a free agent to make his own decisions. No one, however high or wise, must attempt to choose for him; others can only teach the better way if they have it. His salvation is strictly individual. There is no place in such a plan for king or potentate, dictator or tyrant, to decide for the free agent. Throughout the whole system revealed through Joseph Smith runs the doctrine of individual salvation, won by each untrammeled free agent, a son of God.

Third: That places an illimitable value upon each human soul. Each man must be looked upon as of potential godlike power. The individual progress of mankind becomes the world's chief responsibility, and by that same token, it leads to the greatest attainable joy. The strength of a chain lies in its weakest link; and the greatness of a generation is determined by the individual conditions of its people. The Lord has said it:

Remember the worth of souls is great in the sight of God . . . And if it so be that you should labor all your days in crying repentance unto this people, and bring, save it be one soul unto me, how great shall be your joy with him in the kingdom of my Father![1]

This is the Prophet's answer to the world's present-day question—clear and practicable. The future happiness of the world rests upon the recognition of the true dignity of man—of each individual, whatever his present lot may be. For the sake of peace and prosperity, the rulers of nations might profitably place this message through the Latter-day Prophet upon their desks for daily reading. It may be added that Joseph's teachings may be applied in the solution of any or every problem arising in our lives. There is divine wisdom in the legacy he left to us.

Joseph Smith did speak to this day. Let those who have ears, hear!

---

[1]*Doctrine and Covenants* 18:10-15.

CHAPTER 48

IS THE HISTORY OF JOSEPH SMITH
TRUSTWORTHY?

The Church of Jesus Christ of Latter-day Saints was commanded on the day of its organization (April 6, 1830) to keep an accurate record of its history. This has been done faithfully to this day. So complete and minute is this record that no existing organization surpasses it.

Frequent moves, stirring events, and ceaseless persecution characterized the early years of the Church. This necessitated frequent changes in recorders and scribes. Now and then an event may have escaped the historians or the record may have been lost. Nevertheless, every effort was made to preserve Church annals of all kinds, even to casual memoranda, correspondence, newspaper accounts of Church affairs, and payments of postage on letters.[1] Besides, Joseph Smith's own journal was kept very regularly.

The Prophet realized that the history of the worldwide movement he had inaugurated would increase in importance with the years. It would be a fundamental document in promoting the work of the Lord. He was urged by an inward force to get the work done well and hastily.

He seemed to have a feeling of impending death, so eager did he seem to get all important matters under way. He declared repeatedly that he would live until his work was finished. But though he feared that his enemies might take his life he defied them to stop the progress of the work he had been commissioned to inaugurate.[2] The many things he did in the last few years of his life were all of a nature to keep the Church going under any authoritative leadership. He did not look upon himself as indispensable. It was the Lord's work destined to go on forever.

----
[1] *History of the Church*, vol. 2, p. 325.
[2] *History of the Church*, vol. 6, p. 592; vol. 5, p. 498.

Early in 1838, the Prophet set about to present the historical events of the Church in connected form. On April 27, 1838, he writes: "This day I chiefly spent in writing a history of the Church from the earliest period of its existence, up to this date."[3] The following Monday, April 30, 1838, he said, "The First Presidency were engaged in writing the Church history."[4] The history so written was under the Prophet's supervision, with the help of his counselors and clerks. This work was continued until the Prophet's death. He manifested great concern about the history. On one occasion he said:

> There are no subjects that I have felt a greater anxiety about than my history, which has been a very difficult task, on account of the death of my best clerks and the apostasy of others, and the stealing of records by John Whitmer, Cyrus Smalling and others.[5]

In 1842 the Church magazine, the *Times and Seasons,* under the editorship of John Taylor, began the publication of the history under the title, *History of Joseph Smith.* The publication of the narrative there ran from June, 1842, to May, 1845. Later the *Millennial Star* republished the series, beginning April, 1852, and ending May, 1863. At length, beginning in 1904, the history was published in modern book form, critically edited, from the beginning to the death of Joseph Smith, forming the first six volumes of the projected full history of the Church.

In successive printings, conflicts of dates were rectified, errors corrected, and later-discovered materials added. The 1904 edition is well annotated. So well has the work been done, and so carefully has the truth been respected, that writers and speakers for and against Mormonism have used it fully as a sound historical document.

The history is really a compilation. It is the journal of the Prophet, interlarded with available, original documents including the revelations to the Prophet. His own comments generally serve to tie the documents together

---

[3]*Ibid.*, vol. 3, p. 25.
[4]*Ibid.*, vol. 3, p. 26.
[5]*Ibid.*, vol. 6, p. 66. It seems Willard Richards and W. W. Phelps did most of the writing.

in historical form. The wealth of original documents makes the volumes of double interest and importance. It is the chief source book of Mormon history.

In some respects this history is a prime evidence of the truth of Mormonism. It recounts intimate family affairs and sometimes apparently trifling Church matters. It sets forth boldly the documents of the day and the faith and opinions of the author. The Prophet and the Church stand in this history free from historical interpretations and other external trappings. There are no arguments for its case. There are no attempts to cover over any event. Here are the naked facts; let every man draw his own conclusions! This challenge to all readers becomes a splendid record of a people who did not fear the truth of its records.

Three kinds of historical occurrences are presented:

First: Events among Church members, and between the Church and the outside world. There were many such. Each one is documented, often with the Prophet's comments. Human nature springs up on almost every page. There has been no refutation of such reported historical facts. Friend and foe have been obliged to accept them as they stand.

Second: Spiritual experiences in the life of the Prophet which were witnessed in part or in full by others. The coming forth of the Book of Mormon is recited in full. His connection with the men who saw the plates is recounted. The visions in the Kirtland Temple were had by the Prophet and Oliver Cowdery. The vision of graded salvation, known as Section 76 in the Doctrine and Covenants, was shared by Sidney Rigdon. Again these stories of spiritual experiences, witnessed by others, are told without argument. The plain telling is enough. Let every man read and judge, seems to be the Prophet's message!

Third: Spiritual manifestations witnessed only by the Prophet. These are also very simply told. At times, under the influence of the divine message, the language rises to great beauty. But there is no argument for their reality. They must speak for themselves. Seekers after truth, who test them properly, will accept them. That is the implied message of the compilation.

These "unwitnessed" revelations have been chosen by enemies of the Church to be targets of attack. However, such critics have failed to take into account that the unquestioned truth of the record in the matters experienced by many persons is an evidence for the truth of the whole record, including the personal, private experiences of the Prophet.

Curiously, the reality of the unseen world has seldom been discussed by these critics. If the existence of an unseen world had been admitted and the possibility of communicating with it, they would have been obliged to examine Joseph's divine messages for the value of their contents. This the many anti-Mormon writers have failed to do. They have not dared to do so, for the system of truth taught by Joseph holds together and answers satisfactorily the deep questions of the human soul. Those who in our day, in the presence of the world's vast knowledge, deny the existence of an unseen world and personalities therein, are but sorry materialists. The world has long since outgrown the folly of materialism.

Therefore, the foiled critics have often resorted to the cheap and unscientific method of declaring the Prophet to be a mendacious deceiver, who invented his revelations, which enemies dare not explore. Desperately, they have thrown dust in the eyes of their readers, to obscure plain truth. For example, the Prophet begins the history with a recitation of his experience in 1820, as a fourteen year old boy. He declares that in a grove near his father's farm, while in the act of prayer, he had a vision of God the Father and God the Son and from them received instructions. Because this First Vision was not published by the Prophet in printed form until after the Prophet began his "history," in 1838, the conclusion has been offered that the whole story is a fabrication, that it did not occur, that it was invented to bolster up the Prophet's claims to revelation. It is much the same as to say that the doings of

Jesus are fiction because the gospels recounting them were not written until after the death of Jesus or that Abraham Lincoln was not a rail-splitter because the story of his youth was not printed until he was a mature man. It is a new and astonishing historical dictum. (See Chapter 14.)

The *History of Joseph Smith*, published by the Church, as to events and dates, may be accepted as an unusually accurate historical document. It will increase in importance with the years and become more and more a proof of the honest sincerity of the founders of the Church in this dispensation.

The history is trustworthy. No flaws have been found in it.

CHAPTER 49

WHY DID JOSEPH SMITH BECOME A MASON?

Nauvoo, Illinois, the city beautiful, was founded by the Latter-day Saints in 1839, nearly ten years after the Church had been organized. During this time the Church had moved from New York State to Ohio, then to Missouri and at last to Illinois. The decade had been one of unreasoning persecution of the members of the Church. The forces of evil seemed to be combined against the restoration of the simple gospel of Jesus Christ.

The Prophet, to save his life, was obliged to flee from Kirtland, Ohio, headquarters of the Church, where a lovely temple had been built and many progressive enterprises had been undertaken. The Saints as a body were expelled from Missouri under an "exterminating" order by the governor of the state, despite several successful settlements by the Church within the state.

In seeking a city of refuge, Nauvoo in the State of Illinois, then a squalid village called Commerce, was founded.

It seems today a marvel that the Church survived under the terrorism that often accompanied the inhuman persecutions of the Church. Perhaps it is better that they be forgotten. Brigham Young, who, while the Prophet was held a prisoner in Liberty Jail, Missouri, led the people out of Missouri, summarized the story in temperate language:

Before the book [of Mormon] was printed—persecution was raised against him [Joseph Smith].—Persecution increased . . . He left the State of New York and went to the State of Ohio. The gospel was preached here, and many received it. A settlement was formed, but Joseph had not the privilege of staying there long before they hunted him so determinedly that he was forced to leave Kirtland and the State of Ohio. He then went to Missouri. . . [He] had not the privilege of staying there more than a few months before the cry was raised against Joseph Smith that he was guilty of high treason.

This aroused the people and the government of the State; and in October [1838] thirty-five hundred of the militia of the State of Missouri were marched against a few of us in Far West. . . But the mob continued until they drove the Latter-day Saints out of Missouri.[1]

The settlement in Nauvoo was effected in the hope that the people might now live in peace to worship the God of heaven in their own way. There they built well, for soon Nauvoo was the most populous and thriving city in Illinois. But soon after the arrival there, neighbors began to question the doctrines of the Church, notably revelation. The prosperity of the industrious Saints also incited jealousy on the part of those who would not pay the price of toil for success or who were speculating in lands and other properties. Persecution began to rise there as in other places.

The Saints knew well enough the sufferings that follow mob persecution. Joseph Smith, the leader, looked about for means to quell the rising tide of opposition.

Many of the Saints were Masons, such as his brother Hyrum, Heber C. Kimball, Elijah Fordham, Newel K. Whitney, James Adams, and John C. Bennett. Those members called attention to the spirit of brotherhood and brotherly love which are supposed to be the foundations of the Masonic fraternity and which characterizes Masonic activities. One writer has said:

On the rolls of Masonry, those lodges will stand highest in which not some few, but each and every member cheerfully gives of his time and labors to make the others happier, not some of the time, but all the time.[2]

This ideal agreed well with the high ideals of the Prophet for his followers. Moreover, it was conceded that many of the prominent and influential men of the state were Masons, who could be friends when needed. Association with such a fraternity might help to avoid the mob persecutions to which the Church had been subjected in Ohio and Missouri. So reasoned the Prophet's advisers.

---

[1] *Journal of Discourses*, vol. 19, p. 60.
[2] Robert C. Wright, *Indian Masonry*, p. 116 as quoted by E. Cecil McGavin, *Mormonism and Masonry*, p. 11.

The people of the Church needed friends. The work in Nauvoo and everywhere would be hindered if opposition to the Church were allowed to grow. The Prophet and his brethren and sisters of the Church had suffered much without cause. They wanted peace. Perhaps Masonry would help. So in the light of history ran the thoughts of the people.

With the acquiescence of the Prophet, Masonic members of the Church petitioned the Grand Master of Illinois for permission to set up a lodge in Nauvoo. In answer they were granted permission, in October, 1841, to hold lodge meetings; but it was March 15, 1842, before authority was given to set up a lodge in Nauvoo and to induct new members. Joseph Smith became a member. His history shows that he was extremely busy at this time with a multitude of Church problems. Lodge matters would have to be left in other hands.

Meanwhile, large numbers of Nauvoo citizens were inducted into the fraternity. Soon the Nauvoo lodge became the largest in the state. In this rapid growth some technical lodge errors appear to have been made. These could easily have been corrected. However, religious prejudice rose above brotherly affection. The attempt to win friends for the sacred cause through Masonry failed, completely failed.

Joseph Smith joined the Masons to promote goodwill towards his people. He was true to his Masonic pledges. But Masonry could not overcome the hatred fired by untruth, when truth raised its banner. The experiment was a failure. The formation of the Nauvoo lodge rather hindered than helped the cause of the Church.

This must not be taken as a charge against Masonry. The Nauvoo affairs were local; therefore, the Masonic order at large could not be blamed for what occurred there.

Joseph had hoped that Masonry would help protect his people from persecution.

CHAPTER 50

THE CONTINUITY OF AUTHORITY

It was the loss of priesthood authority that primarily made necessary the restoration of the gospel in modern times. Had the authority of the priesthood continued unbroken, the leaders of the early Church would have clung to the true doctrines of Jesus the Christ. Or it may be put this way: failure to obey God's commandments caused the loss of divine authority. It amounted to apostasy.

This was to be the last dispensation of the gospel on earth. Therefore, safeguards were set up against priesthood loss. It was equally important that the organization of the Church be preserved as the Lord intended. An unchangeable organization of the Church was necessary and was provided. There was to be no repetition of the events that destroyed the primitive church of Christ.

As the years went on, the Prophet became more and more eager to assure the Church of a continued authorized organization.

First, one man was placed at the head of the Church, as "prophet, seer, and revelator," in whom was vested all priesthood authority and from whom therefore such authority would flow to the members of the Church. On the very day of the organization there came precise words to Joseph Smith:

Thou shalt be called a seer, a translator, a prophet, and apostle of Jesus Christ, and elder of the church through the will of God the Father, and the grace of your Lord Jesus Christ . . . Wherefore, meaning the church, thou shalt give heed unto all his words and commandments which he shall give unto you as he receiveth them, walking in all holiness before me; for his word ye shall receive, as if from mine own mouth, in all patience and faith.[1]

This is the essential doctrine in the organization of the Church.

---

[1] *Doctrine and Covenants* 21:1, 4-5.

That also placed the President or first elder as the deciding authority in all Church affairs. That which he decided could be accepted or rejected by the people, but if his revelations were rejected, the people would become apostates and no longer acceptable members of the Church.

As the Church grew, many new ideas became current among the people. The Latter-day Saints were in general of the ordinary run of men and women. They sometimes, somewhat innocently, fell into error. Then the President would have to act.

Soon after the Church was organized, some persons claimed to have had revelations and wanted to be recognized as revelators for the welfare of the Church. Hiram Page, for example, had in his possession a stone by which he claimed to receive revelations for the doctrine and organization of the Church.[2] A little later a woman pretending to be a prophetess offered revelations for the guidance of the Church.[3]

Such events raised at once the question whether more than one person could or should receive revelations for the Church. It would seem from the authority given the President of the Church that he would be the only one to receive whatever the Lord wanted the Church to have. A revelation to the people of the Church in answer to Joseph's appeal for help settled the matter:

There is none other appointed unto you [Joseph Smith] to receive commandments and revelations until he be taken, if he abide in me. . . None else shall be appointed unto this gift except it be through him; for if it be taken from him he shall not have power except to appoint another in his stead. And this shall be a law unto you, that ye receive not the teachings of any that shall come before you as revelations or commandments; and this I give unto you that you may not be deceived, that you may know they are not of me. For verily I say unto you, that he that is ordained of me shall come in at the gate and be ordained as I have told you before, to teach those revelations which you have received and shall receive through him whom I have appointed.[4]

[2]*Ibid.*, Section 28; *History of the Church*, vol. 1, pp. 109-110.
[3]*History of the Church*, vol. 1, p. 154.
[4]*Doctrine and Covenants* 43:3-7.

This revelation settled the question. Only the President of the Church could receive revelations for the Church.

Nevertheless, another equally disturbing question arose. Joseph Smith was given two counselors, the three forming the First Presidency of the Church. (March 18, 1833.)[5] This was preceded in March 8, 1833 by a revelation declaring that "Through you [Joseph Smith] shall the oracles be given to another, even unto the Church." The pre-eminence of the President of the Church was maintained.[6] The question as to whether the Counselors held the same power as the President was soon debated among the people. What could the Counselors do without direct appointment from the President? These questions were answered in a meeting on January 16, 1836. The Prophet there said, "The Twelve are not subject to any other than the First Presidency . . . *and where I am not, there is no First Presidency over the Twelve.*" In other words were the President taken, the Counselors would have no authority.[7] The Counselors do not possess the power of the President and cannot act in Church matters without direction and consent of the President.

All this defined clearly the position and authority of the President of the Church.

Soon, however, on March 28, 1835, came the great revelation on the priesthood[8] organization of the Church, which confirmed and clarified the previously asked questions and gave further information.

Four administrative groups are authorized to carry on the work of the Church.[9]

The Church is presided over by a President and two Counselors,[10] the First Presidency. In the event of the death of the President, the Council of the First Presidency is dissolved. The Counselors step out.[11]

[5]*History of the Church*, vol. 1, p. 334.
[6]*Doctrine and Covenants*, Section 90.
[7]*History of the Church*, vol. 2, p. 374.
[8]*Doctrine and Covenants*, Section 107.
[9]*Ibid.*, Section 107
[10]*Ibid.*, 107:22
[11]Joseph F. Smith, *Gospel Doctrine*, 1949 edition, p. 175

Then, the Twelve Apostles, equal in "authority and power" would take command[12] and would call a man to be President of the Church. Should the Quorum of the Twelve disappear, by death or otherwise, the First Quorum of the Seventy "equal in authority to that of the Twelve," would assume the leadership of the Church, and reorganize the Church.[13] In the event of the failure of this Quorum of the priesthood to function, the high councils of the Stakes of Zion (including the stake presidencies) would as a body carry out the work of the Church until a reorganization could be effected.[14] Each of these administrative councils, should necessity arise, would restore Church officialdom.

Such a procedure would help hedge about the government of the Church with protection against any intruder who might also become an invader. It is a perfect system of protection of the Church from disaster in the event of the death of the President.

Nevertheless at various times Church members speculated about the future of the Church. One group held that Joseph would live until the coming of the Savior. They held that that coming was near and rested their conclusions on several statements in the revelations to Joseph Smith. Since Joseph was to live until the second coming, there was no need to worry about succession in the Presidency.

The other group, with equal insistence, declared that since the time of the second coming of Christ has not been revealed, it was necessary to provide against the emergencies of daily life.

Joseph apparently did not expect to live on earth to meet the Savior at his second coming. He said at one time:

I was once praying very earnestly to know the time of the coming of the Son of Man, when I heard a voice repeat the following: "Joseph, my son, if thou livest until thou art eighty-five years old, thou shalt see the face of the Son of Man; therefore let this suffice, and trouble me no more on this matter." I was left thus, without being able to decide whether this coming referred to the

---

[12]*Doctrine and Covenants* 107:23-24.
[13]*Ibid.*, 107:26.
[14]*Ibid.*, 107:36-37.

beginning of the millennium or to some previous appearing, or whether I should die and thus see his face.[15]

Both sides seemed to agree that ample and sufficient direction had been provided for action should the President of the Church be taken. Yet the question of succession in the Church Presidency was kept alive by a few who secretly or openly harbored in their hearts ambitions for the position. Therefore the Prophet sought for explicit confirmation of previous revelations.

The answers that came confirmed that which was already known from the revelation known as Section 107 of the Doctrine and Covenants; for example, a revelation dated 1837 states:

> For unto you the Twelve, and those, the First Presidency, who are appointed with you to be your counselors and your leaders, is the power of this priesthood given, for the last days and for the last time, in the which is a dispensation of the gospel, which power you hold, in connection with all those who have received a dispensation at any time from the beginning of creation.[16]

The Prophet seemed to have a presentiment of his early death. He therefore set the Church in order and made every necessary arrangement for the continuity of the priesthood authority of the organized Church, in accordance with the revelations.

On several occasions not long before his death he emphasized the succession of authority to the Twelve in case of his death. This was done especially as the temple endowment was being received, and given to the Twelve.

After the Prophet's martyrdom a meeting of the Apostles, Nauvoo Stake High Council and high priests was held on August 7, 1844. Brigham Young, speaking of the Twelve, said:

> Joseph conferred upon our heads all the keys and powers belonging to the apostleship, which he himself held before he was taken away, and no man or set of men can get between Joseph and the Twelve in this world or the world to come. How often has

---

[15]*Ibid.*, 130:14-16.
[16]*Ibid.*, 112:30-31.

Joseph said to the Twelve "I have laid the foundation and you must build thereon, for upon your shoulders the kingdom rests."[17]

Some years later, January 23, 1848, soon after the Twelve had reorganized the First Presidency, Brigham Young, in a letter addressed to Orson Spencer, then President of the British Mission, said:

Joseph told the Twelve, the year before he died, there is not one key or power to be bestowed upon this Church to lead the people into the celestial gate but what I have given you, showed you, and talked it over to you, the kingdom is set up, and you have the perfect pattern, you can go and build up the kingdom.[18]

President Heber C. Kimball at the trial of Sidney Rigdon said about the same subject:

The Twelve have received the keys of the kingdom, and as long as there is one of them left, he will hold them in preference to any one else.[19]

Parley P. Pratt, in writing a proclamation to the Saints in Great Britain, bore eloquent testimony to this event.

This great and good man [Joseph Smith] was led, before his death, to call the Twelve together, from time to time, and to instruct them in all things pertaining to the kingdom, ordinances, and government of God. He often observed that he was laying the foundation, but it would remain for the Twelve to complete the building. Said he, I know not why; but for some reason I am constrained to hasten my preparations, and to confer upon the Twelve all the ordinances, keys, covenants, endowments, and sealing ordinances of the priesthood, and so set before them a pattern in all things pertaining to the sanctuary and the endowment therein.[20]

Having done this, he rejoiced exceedingly; for, said he, the Lord is about to lay the burden on your shoulders and let me rest awhile; and if they kill me, continued he, the kingdom of God will roll on, as I have now finished the work which was laid upon me, by committing to you all things for the building up of the kingdom according to the heavenly vision, and the pattern shown me from heaven. With many conversations like this, he comforted the minds of the Twelve, and prepared them for what was soon to follow.

‾‾‾‾‾‾
[17]*Millennial Star*, vol. 25, p. 232.
[18]*Ibid.*, vol. 10, p. 115.
[19]Joseph Fielding Smith, *Succession in the Presidency*, p. 83.
[20]*Millennial Star*, vol. 5, p. 151

He proceeded to confer on Elder Young, the President of the Twelve, the keys of the sealing power, as conferred in the last days by the spirit and power of Elijah, in order to seal the hearts of the fathers to the children, and the hearts of the children to the fathers, lest the whole earth should be smitten with a curse.

This last key of the priesthood is the most sacred of all, and pertains exclusively to the First Presidency of the Church, without whose sanction and approval or authority, no sealing blessing shall be administered pertaining to things of the resurrection and the life to come.[21]

Orson Hyde, another member of the original Council of the Twelve, bore his testimony in clear words:

The shafts of the enemy are always aimed at the head first. Brother Joseph said some time before he was murdered, "If I am taken away, upon you, the Twelve, will rest the responsibility of leading this people, and do not be bluffed off by any man."

Before I went east in the 4th of April last, we were in council with Brother Joseph almost every day for weeks, said Brother Joseph in one of those councils, "There is something going to happen; I don't know what it is, but the Lord bids me to hasten and give you your endowment before the temple is finished." He conducted us through every ordinance of the Holy Priesthood, and when he had gone through with all the ordinances, he rejoiced very much, and said, "Now, if they kill me, you have got all the keys, and all the ordinances and you can confer them upon others, and the hosts of Satan will not be able to tear down the kingdom, as fast as you will be able to build it up;" and now, said he, "on your shoulders will the responsibility of leading this people rest, for the Lord is going to let me rest awhile."[22]

Wilford Woodruff, one of the Twelve, in a letter from Salem, Massachusetts, under date of October 11, 1844, declared that he heard the Prophet make this statement:

[Joseph] addressing the Twelve, exclaimed "upon your shoulders the kingdom rests, and you must round up your shoulders and bear it; for I have had to do it until now. But now the responsibility rests upon you. It mattereth not what becomes of me."[23]

This was said by the Prophet Joseph Smith at his last meeting with the Twelve, who at that time were about to start upon their missions to the East.

---

[21]*Ibid.,* vol. 5, p. 151.
[22]*Times and Seasons,* vol. 5, p. 651.
[23]Joseph Fielding Smith, *Succession in the Presidency,* p. 84.

Forty-eight years later, when he was eighty-five years old, Wilford Woodruff confirmed his earlier testimony:

[Joseph said to the Twelve] "I have sealed upon your heads every key, every power, and every principle which the Lord has sealed upon my head," and continuing he said: "I have lived up to the present time, I have been in the midst of this people and in the great work and labor of redemption. I have desired to see this temple [the Nauvoo Temple] built. But I shall never see it completed, but you will. . . I tell you the burden of this kingdom now rests upon your shoulders; You have got to bear it off in all the world, and if you don't, you will be damned."[24]

Several other members of the Twelve confirmed this statement and action of the Prophet; for example, Heber C. Kimball,[25] and Orson Hyde,[26] have borne witness to the truth of Brigham Young's report.

At least three members of the Church not members of the Council of the Twelve have testified that they heard Joseph declare that the Twelve possessed the necessary authority to carry on the work that he had founded. Bathsheba W. Smith, the wife of George A. Smith, stated:

In the year 1844, a short time before the death of the Prophet Joseph Smith, it was my privilege to attend a regular prayer circle meeting in the upper room over the Prophet's store. There were present at this meeting most of the Twelve Apostles, their wives, and a number of other prominent brethren and their wives. On that occasion the Prophet arose and spoke at great length, and during his remarks I heard him say that he had conferred on the heads of the Twelve Apostles all the keys and powers pertaining to the priesthood, and that upon the heads of the Twelve Apostles the burden of the kingdom rested, and they would have to carry it.[27]

At his eighty-seventh birthday anniversary celebration, held at Mesa, Arizona, July 29, 1905, Patriarch Benjamin F. Johnson said:

[24]B. H. Roberts, *Succession in the Presidency of the Church*, appendix; *Millennial Star*, vol. 5, p. 151.
[25]Joseph Fielding Smith, *op.*, *cit.*, p. 83.
[26]*Millennial Star*, vol. 5, p. 151.
[27]Joseph Fielding Smith, *Origin of the Reorganized Church and the Question of Succession*, p. 84.

I speak of things of which I know. I was the business partner of Joseph Smith, from my mission until the time of his martyrdom was as familiar with him as with my brother or my father.

Do I know that Brigham Young was the true successor of Joseph Smith? I knew it before the Prophet was martyred, for Joseph had made it known. I was present when the Prophet gave his charge to the Twelve Apostles, when in council, after solemn prayer, he rose up with the light of heaven shining in his countenance, related his experiences with reference to the beginning of this work, the responsibilities placed upon him, the persecutions and hardships through which he had passed. He declared that God had revealed all the truth necessary to save mankind, had given unto him the keys of the kingdom, and he had carried the weight and load thus far, and then, speaking directly to the Twelve, he said: "I now roll off the burden of this responsibility upon you; I give unto you all the keys and powers bestowed upon me, and I say unto you, that unless you round up your shoulders and bear off this kingdom you will be damned."[28]

Ezra T. Clark, another prominent elder in the Church, said:

Before I left Nauvoo, I heard the Prophet Joseph say he would give the Saints a key whereby they would never be led away or deceived, and that was: "The Lord would never suffer the majority of his people to be led away or deceived by imposters, nor would he allow the records of this Church to fall into the hands of the enemy." I heard Joseph preach many times; heard him in the last sermon he ever delivered, bear testimony to the truth of the work that God had called him to; also that the Lord had never suffered him to be slain by his enemies, because his work had not been done, until a short time ago. He had now laid the foundation of this work, and rolled the burden of the Priesthood upon the Twelve; and having given them their washings and anointings, they would now bear off this work triumphantly, and it would roll on faster than ever before; and, if the Lord was willing to accept him, he was willing to go."[29]

These statements of the Prophet were only confirmations of the directions contained in the various revelations he had received for the Church. But they show clearly that Joseph knew that the chain of authority would carry the Church forward whether he lived or died.

[28]*Ibid.*, p. 85.
[29]*Improvement Era*, vol. 5, p. 202.

Joseph was then at ease about the future of the Church so far as the succession of authority was concerned. There was no question in his mind about Church leadership, and who would possess it properly. His revelations on the subject were and are clear and explicit on that subject. The explanatory words of the Prophet made repeatedly to the Twelve leave no doubt as to the order to be followed whenever the office of President of the Church is vacant. He made these explanations to fasten upon the minds of the Twelve and others how the authority of the Church could be continued unbroken throughout the future. The Twelve stand next to the Presidency and preside over the Church when there is no President. They then have the power to appoint another President, possessing all the powers given to the restored Church.

CHAPTER 51

THE WESTWARD MIGRATION IS PLANNED

From the time that the boy Joseph Smith had his First Vision, some degree of persecution raged around him and his followers. The trail of the Church from New York to Ohio, Missouri and Illinois, was littered with persecutions from enemies, who stooped to every evil and inhuman device to prevent the progress of the work. The claim that God can and does speak to his children on earth begat the fury of hell in the breasts of men whose faith and lives were unsound and often corrupt. It was a thorny and bloody path that the Saints had to follow.

At length the persecuted people found a peaceful haven, as they thought, in Illinois. Through great industry and thrift they reared a beautiful city upon what was an inhospitable marsh. They were good, state-building citizens. Nevertheless, opposition and persecution did not cease. Among neighboring villages, out-distanced by the progress of the city of Nauvoo, hate was fanned into a devouring flame. Reason does not prevail among people governed by intolerance.

That these conditions would ultimately compel another removal of the people became clear to the mind of the Prophet Joseph, the sustained leader of the Church. He had sought in many ways to promote peace, but without success. He began to look for a place to which his people could move and remain relatively unmolested from unfriendly neighbors. The Far West, then being opened on the Pacific Coast, was almost naturally the place to which the Prophet's mind would be directed. No traveler or explorer had as yet suggested settlement in the valleys of the Rocky Mountains or on the surrounding interior deserts. That seemed to be a place where the Saints could live undisturbed, at least for a while. The spirit of revelation confirmed this view.

The Prophet then set about to prepare the people for this coming event. Under date of August 6, 1842, he wrote in his journal:

Passed over the river to Montrose, Iowa. . . I prophesied that the Saints would continue to suffer much affliction and would be driven to the Rocky Mountains, many would apostatize, others would be put to death by our persecutors or lose their lives in consequence of exposure or disease, and some of you will live to go and assist in making settlements and build cities and see the Saints become a mighty people in the midst of the Rocky Mountains.[1]

Anson Call, who was present on that occasion and wrote his recollection of it, says that the Prophet, after uttering this prophecy, began a vivid description of the western country, much as it really is. The Prophet also said that Anson Call, Shadrach Roundy, and others who were present would assist in the building of cities among the Rocky Mountains. He then charged all present to be faithful, so that the priesthood would prevail over all enemies.[2]

More than a year and a half later, on Tuesday, February 20, 1844, the proposed westward movement began to take shape. The Prophet writes:

I instructed the Twelve Apostles to send out a delegation and investigate the locations of California and Oregon, and hunt out a good location, where we can remove to after the temple is completed, and where we can build a city in a day, and have a government of our own, get up into the mountains, where the devil cannot dig us out, and live in a healthful climate, where we can live as old as we have a mind to.[3]

Prompt action was taken to obey these instructions, as shown by the following entry:

At a meeting of the Twelve, at the mayor's office, Nauvoo, February 21, 1844, seven o'clock p.m., Brigham Young, Parley P. Pratt, Orson Pratt, Wilford Woodruff, John Taylor, George A. Smith, Willard Richards and four others being present, called by previous notice, by instruction of President Joseph Smith on the 20th instant,

[1]*History of the Church*, vol. 5, p. 85.
[2]*Ibid.*, vol. 5, pp. 85-86; Orson F. Whitney, *History of Utah*, vol. 4, p. 143.
[3]*History of the Church*, vol. 6, p. 222.

for the purpose of selecting a company to explore Oregon and
California, and select a site for a new city for the Saints.

Jonathan Dunham, Phineas H. Young, David D. Yearsley,
and David Fullmer, volunteered to go; and Alphonso Young, James
Emmett, George D. Watt, and Daniel Spencer were requested
to go.

Voted the above persons to be notified to meet with the
council on Friday evening next, at the assembly room.

Willard Richards, Clerk.[4]

Two days later on the 23rd of February, the Prophet
met with the Twelve concerning the expedition.

I told them I wanted an exploration of all that mountain
country. . . "Send twenty-five men: let them preach the gospel
wherever they go. Let that man go that can raise $500., a good
horse and a mule, a double-barrel gun, one-barrel rifle, and the
other smooth bore, a saddle and bridle, a pair of revolving pistols,
bowie-knife, and a good sabre. Appoint a leader, and let them
beat up for volunteers. I want every man that goes to be a king
and a priest. When he gets on the mountains he may want to talk
with his God; when with the savage nations have power to govern,
etc. If we don't get volunteers, wait till after the election."[5] [The
national election would be held the following November.]

There was no lack of volunteers. Within a week
over twenty men had volunteered.[6] The proposed expedition was widely known. In a letter written to James
Arlington Bennett, March 4, 1844, Willard Richards, under the Prophet's instruction, said: "We are now fitting
out a noble company to explore Oregon and California."[7]
On March 11, the Prophet spoke to the Council about
the desirability of securing "a resting place in the mountains, or some uninhabited region, where we can enjoy
the liberty of conscience guaranteed to us by the Constitution of our country."[8] Anticipating this westward
movement, the Prophet also wrote and sent to Congress,
"An Ordinance for the Protection of the Citizens of the
United States Emigrating to the Territories, and for the

4*Ibid.*, vol. 6, p. 223.
5*Ibid.*, vol. 6, p. 224.
6*Ibid.*, vol. 6, pp. 223-227.
7*Ibid.*, vol. 6, p. 232.
8*Ibid.*, vol. 6, p. 261.

Extension of the Principles of Universal Liberty."[9] This document, which Congress ignored, was clearly designed to protect the migration of the whole people after a suitable location had been found.

During this time while the expedition was being formed, the persecutions of the people reached an unprecedented height. At last, the life of the Prophet was seriously endangered. For his own safety, he left Nauvoo, and intended to go westward himself, to explore the country. He was recalled to Nauvoo before the journey had begun, and, on June 27, 1844, he and his brother Hyrum were foully assassinated.

There can be no question about Joseph Smith's intention to move the Latter-day Saints to some favorable spot among the Rocky Mountains.[10]

Brigham Young in all that he did repeatedly admitted the leadership of Joseph Smith, even in the journey to the Great Salt Lake Valley. For example, this on March 16, 1856:

"The Prophet Joseph has been referred to, and his prophecy that this people would leave Nauvoo and be planted in the midst of the Rocky Mountains. We see it fulfilled . . . it was declared to the people long before we left Nauvoo."[11]

The famous trek from Nauvoo to Salt Lake Valley was a fulfillment of prophecy. Brigham Young repeatedly gave the Prophet proper credit for the westward migration. President Young's loyalty to the Prophet was always unsullied. To him, the Prophet was the great restorer of the Lord's eternal truth.

---

[9]*Ibid.*, vol. 6, p. 275.
[10]B. H. Roberts, *op., cit.*, 2nd edition, pp. 113-117.
[11]*Journal of Discourses*, vol. 4, p. 203; vol. 8, p. 356; *History of the Church*, vol. 5, p. 85; vol. 6, p. 222; Anson Call as cited in Tullidge, *History of Northern Utah and Southern Idaho*, vol. 2, pp. 271-272.

CHAPTER 52

COURAGE TO FACE MARTYRDOM

It was June 22, 1844. Joseph Smith stood on Temple Hill overlooking Nauvoo. Flowers and garden plants were at their best. The city had never looked lovelier. On the drained marshland, homes and business houses had been erected. New dwellings of beauty and dignity had been built. The walls of the Nauvoo House, where travelers would be hospitably entertained, were moving upwards. The temple walls were rising high into the sky. The balmy air of early summer fanned Joseph's cheeks as he surveyed the fruits of six years of toil and faith. He gloried in the picture. Only with the help of the Lord could it have been done!

Then, with a start, he remembered that he and his people would soon have to leave the city and its beauty. Envy, jealousy, political ambition, and above all hate of truth had lifted their heads and spewed poison over the glorious scene. The Saints could not endure the coming persecution. They would have to leave!

He thought of the traitors he had befriended, the unspeakable Bennett, and the ugly group of Higbees, Laws, Fosters, Jackson, Cahoon, Watson, and others who were seeking his overthrow. They had fanned the opposition the Saints had always had to endure into a devouring flame, until many unknown to him in neighboring villages looked upon him as an enemy to human welfare who must be destroyed. He quailed for a moment before human ingratitude but rallied with the assurance that he was in the Lord's work and that he would not let it perish no matter what happened to himself.

His heart warmed when he remembered his faithful people who loved him, cherished him, and who would protect him to the death if need be. How they had given of themselves in building with him this noble city, and its holy temple! His feelings overflowed. He wept just a little.

Now, he knew, the time had come that he and his people would have to leave the city beautiful. The devil whom he had fought so long had won the hearts of evil-minded men. These enemies he knew wanted Joseph first, then they would destroy all who maintained adherence to the Church he had been instrumental in organizing. His people must leave Nauvoo. He had tried every means to prevent the present situation, but had failed.

Had the Lord forsaken his people?

He himself was the appointed leader of the Church on earth. He must go first of all to find another place for his beloved people to dwell, one in the Far West, as the Lord had already told him. A vicious apostate had filed suit against him, of all things, for disorderly conduct! If he answered this unjustifiable call, the removal would be delayed, enemies might even destroy him. He must go in search of the new home! He was the leader appointed by the Lord! He must go now!

Towards the evening of June 22 he called his brother Hyrum Smith. They with the ever faithful Elder Willard Richards clambered into a small boat and Orrin Porter Rockwell rowed them across the Mississippi to Montrose, Iowa. There at last they would be free for a time from their enemies; and also on the way to the West. Safe on the Iowa side of the river, he began to plan for their westward journey. His blood ran warm again. He would yet lead his people to a safe and permanent abiding place.

Then, on the next morning, June 23, men came from the Nauvoo, Illinois, side. They brought letters and messages from supposed friends and one from his wife, Emma, all urging him to return. He was needed in Nauvoo, they said. In the current gossip he was running away from them to save his own skin; he was a coward! So the gossip said.

This stung him to the quick. He had never yet failed his people. Joseph Smith had courage. He was a fearless man. He knew that if he should be destroyed the Lord would find another. The kingdom had been set up for the last time. With sorrow but with courage in his voice he ordered the return. He added, "If my life is of no value to my friends, it is of none to me."[1]

As the evil lives of these enemies had been discovered, Joseph had been obliged to take action against them, as shown in the following letter:

> City of Nauvoo
> Headquarters of the Nauvoo Legion
> April 29th, 1844
> Brigadier-General Charles C. Rich
> Sir:
> Major-General William Law has been suspended for unbecoming conduct, and I hereby order that you take command of said Nauvoo Legion till the result of his case shall be decided by court-martial.
>
> > Respectfully, I have the honor to be
> > your obedient servant,
> > Joseph Smith
> > Lieut-General Nauvoo Legion[2]

Such open charges of their improper behavior made these enemies furious.

Some days before, on June 7, 1844, the Nauvoo city council had declared the *Nauvoo Expositor,* a newspaper dedicated, by these enemies, to the destruction of Joseph Smith, and the Church of Jesus Christ, a nuisance, and had ordered the city marshal to pie the type and destroy the office contents, which was done on June 10, 1844. This action was taken promptly, after the first and only issue of the newspaper. This made the organized enemies of Joseph more furious, and set fire to their purposes. They filed charges against Joseph and Hyrum Smith, who answered that the state or supreme court could determine the legality of the action of the city council. If it were found illegal, damages could be assessed, and paid by the city. This was not satisfactory to the men bent on Joseph's destruction. The governor of the state[3] took a hand in the matter and

---

[1]*History of the Church,* vol. 6, p. 549.
[2]Files of the Daughters of Utah Pioneers
[3]Joseph Fielding Smith, *Essentials in Church History,* p. 373.

asked Joseph to go, under state protection from mobs and lawless groups, to Carthage, seven miles distant to answer the charges made against him.[4]

Joseph Smith knew that the charges would have to be dismissed, but he also knew that the trial was but a part of the plan of his enemies to destroy him. But his friends had prevailed with him until he had promised to face the trial. He therefore decided to meet another trial, such as he had met nearly fifty times before, always with acquittal as judgment.

On June 24, Joseph and Hyrum and his party left Nauvoo for Carthage, the seat of the court. He declared on the journey:

> I am going like a lamb to the slaughter, but I am calm as a summer's morning; I have a conscience void of offense towards God, and toward all men. I shall die innocent, and it shall yet be said of me—he was murdered in cold blood.[5]

They were first installed in the Hamilton House, then on June 26, in Carthage Jail.[6]

On June 27, in the late afternoon, the mob of supposedly orderly men broke into the jail. In the ensuing melee, Joseph and his brother Hyrum were killed and John Taylor severely wounded. The story is told very briefly in the 135th Section of the Doctrine and Covenants:

> To seal the testimony of this book and the Book of Mormon, we announce the martyrdom of Joseph Smith the Prophet, and Hyrum Smith the Patriarch. They were shot in Carthage Jail, on the 27th of June, 1844, about five o'clock p.m., by an armed mob— painted black—of from 150 to 200 persons. Hyrum was shot first and fell calmly, exclaiming: "I am a dead man!" Joseph leaped from the window, and was shot dead in the attempt, exclaiming: "O Lord my God!" They were both shot after they were dead, in a brutal manner, and both received four balls.[7]

Willard Richards, who was with the Prophet, has

---

[4]After Joseph's death the *Expositor* action was declared by a state court to be legal.
[5]Joseph Fielding Smith, *op., cit.,* p. 376.
[6]The story of events, the martyrdom and preceding events are best told by *The History of the Church,* Volume 6; and B. H. Roberts' *Comprehensive History of the Church,* vol. 2, p. 50, and Chapter 55.
[7]*Doctrine and Covenants,* Section 135.

written the most vivid story of the events in Carthage Jail on June 27, 1844:

Possibly the following events occupied near three minutes, but I think only about two, and have penned them for the gratification of my friends.

A shower of musket balls were thrown up the stairway against the door of the prison in the second story, followed by many rapid footsteps.

While Generals Joseph and Hyrum Smith, Mr. Taylor and myself, who were in the front chamber, closed the door of our room against the entry at the head of the stairs, and placed ourselves against it, there being no lock on the door, and no catch that was useable.

The door is a common panel, and as soon as we heard the feet at the stairs head, a ball was sent through the door, which passed between us, and showed that our enemies were desperadoes, and we must change our position.

General Joseph Smith, Mr. Taylor and myself sprang back to the front part of the room, and General Hyrum Smith retreated two-thirds across the chamber in front of and facing the door.

A ball was sent through the door which hit Hyrum on the side of the nose, when he fell backwards, extended at length, without moving his feet.

From the holes in his vest (the day was warm, and no one had their coats on but myself,) pantaloons, drawers and shirt, it appears evident that a ball must have been thrown from without, through the window, which entered his back on the right side, passing through lodged against his watch, which was in his right vest pocket, completely pulverizing the crystal and face, tearing off the hands and mashing the whole body of the watch. At the same time the ball from the door entered his nose.

As he struck the floor he exclaimed emphatically, "I'm a dead man." Joseph looked towards him and responded, "Oh dear Brother Hyrum!" and opening the door two or three inches with his left hand, discharged one barrel of a six shooter (pistol) at random in the entry, from whence a ball grazed Hyrum's breast, and entering his throat passed into his head, while other muskets were aimed at him and some balls hit him.

Joseph continued snapping his revolver round the casing of the door into the space as before, three barrels of which missed fire, while Mr. Taylor with a walking stick stood by his side and knocked down the bayonets and muskets which were constantly discharging through the doorway, while I stood by him, ready to lend any assistance, with another stick, but could not come within striking distance without going directly before the muzzles of the guns.

When the revolver failed, we had no more firearms, and expected an immediate rush of the mob, and the doorway full of muskets, half way in the room, and no hope but instant death from within.

Mr. Taylor rushed into the window, which is some fifteen or twenty feet from the ground. When his body was nearly on a balance, a ball from the door within entered his leg, and a ball from without struck his watch, a patent lever, in his vest pocket near the left breast, and smashed it into 'pie,' leaving the hands standing at 5 o'clock, 16 minutes, and 26 seconds, the force of which ball threw him back on the floor, and he rolled under the bed which stood by his side, where he lay motionless, the mob from the door continuing to fire upon him, cutting away a piece of flesh from his left hip as large as a man's hand, and were hindered only by knocking down their muzzles with a stick; while they continued to reach their guns into the room, probably left-handed, and aimed their discharge so far round as almost to reach us in the corner of the room to where we retreated and dodged, and then I recommenced the attack with my stick.

Joseph attempted, as the last resort, to leap the same window from whence Mr. Taylor fell, when two balls pierced him from the door, and one entered the right breast from without, and he fell outward, exclaiming, "O Lord my God!" As his feet went out of the window my head went in, the balls whistling all around. He fell on his left side a dead man.

At this instant the cry was raised, "He's leaped the window!" and the mob on the stairs and in the entry ran out.

I withdrew from the window, thinking it of no use to leap out on a hundred bayonets, then around General Smith's body.

Not satisfied with this I again reached my head out of the window, and watched some seconds to see if there were any signs of life, regardless of my own, determined to see the end of him I loved. Being fully satisfied that he was dead, with a hundred men near the body and more coming round the corner of the jail, and expecting a return to our room, I rushed towards the prison door, at the head of the stairs, and through the entry from whence the firing had proceeded, to learn if the doors into the prison were open.

When near the entry, Mr. Taylor called out, "Take me." I pressed my way until I found all doors unbarred, returning instantly, caught Mr. Taylor under my arm, and rushed by the stairs into the dungeon, or inner prison, stretched him on the floor and covered him with a bed in such a manner as not likely to be perceived, expecting an immediate return of the mob.

I said to Mr. Taylor, "This is a hard case to lay you on the floor, but if your wounds are not fatal, I want you to live to tell the story." I expected to be shot the next moment, and stood before the door awaiting the onset.[8]

Thus, a great life was ended—two, indeed. The details are well-known. The inherent courage of Joseph Smith was shown by his return from Iowa. He knew that by returning, he was taking his life in his hands, but did so fearlessly. His work on earth was finished. He sealed his testimony with his blood as did his great Exemplar, his real Leader, Jesus the Christ.

---

[8]*History of the Church*, vol. 6, p. 621.

CHAPTER 53

HOW CAN JOSEPH SMITH BE EXPLAINED?

Joseph Smith is the key figure in the restoration of the gospel of Jesus Christ in these latter days. His claims are the foundation of the Church which he was instrumental in restoring to earth. Every doctrine, organization, movement, and achievement of the Latter-day Saints must be attributed directly or indirectly to the latter-day Prophet.

Consequently, opponents to the claims of Joseph Smith have made him, rather than the Church, the subject of specious consideration. A library has grown up around his name, in opposition to his claim that what he gave to the world came to him by revelation from God. The net result of these writings, now covering more than a century, is that before the remarkable history of the Prophet and the results that followed, the authors stand baffled, perplexed, and in disagreement. When they have tried to explain Joseph Smith, the most careful students have been unable to agree in their conclusions.

In reality only three explanations of Joseph Smith have been proposed by those who do not believe in the Prophet's own story. The proponents of each, battle for their own interpretation of his life and work. This difference of opinion, even among mature scholars, is one of the strongest evidences for the truth of the Prophet's claim that he had heavenly visitations and received his revelations from divine sources.

The first, and for some years the favorite, explanation of Joseph Smith was that he was an impostor, deceiver, liar; and that his story of visions and revelations was a concoction of an untruthful, conscienceless mind. This explanation insists that there were no plates from which the Book of Mormon was translated and that he had no spiritual experiences—the whole thing was a hoax of the first order. He attempted, so they say, to foist a horrible untruth upon mankind. Men have scoured the earth wherever the Prophet lived to find evidence of fraudulent, dishonest actions with which to support their explanation of Joseph Smith.

Alexander Campbell,[1] one of the earliest writers against Mormonism, found in the Book of Mormon discussions of every subject on the tongues of people in Joseph's day. Therefore, said he, the Prophet had merely assembled the current talk of the day in the Book of Mormon, and with a lying mouth had invented the supernatural discovery of "golden plates." This is as much as to say that questions concerning life, death, immortality, and others of like nature, were not discussed in antiquity. In view of our historical knowledge, such a statement would be indefensible.

E. D. Howe, the publisher and so-called author of the first book against Mormonism,[2] was so driven to it for proof of Joseph's supposed frauds that he sent the real author of the book, P. Hurlburt of unsavory reputation, to secure blanket affidavits such as may be obtained on any subject, if well-known methods are employed, to the effect that the Smith family were of a lying disposition. Stories of a most farfetched kind, and unproved, concerning Joseph and his dishonesty suddenly sprang into existence. Later writers adopted and circulated such gossip in their muckraking, profit-making books, and magnified it. The reader who begins at the beginning of anti-Mormon literature becomes nauseated with the display of dishonesty on the part of enemies of Mormonism. No one objects to a fair opponent, but every honest man holds an unfair one in contempt. These persecutors, in their despair, when the proof of their case is failing, resort to the ludicrous defense that Joseph was so persistent a liar that at last he came to believe his own lies and thought that he had had spiritual experiences.[3]

---

[1]Alexander Campbell, *Delusions, An Analysis of the Book of Mormon.*
[2]E. D. Howe, *Mormonism Unvailed.*
[3]Fawn M. Brodie, *No Man Knows My History*, pp. 84-85.

The explanation that Joseph Smith was a deliberate deceiver has not satisfied all students. The record of Joseph's life is one of honesty. He taught honesty in all affairs; he insisted that his people be honest; the verified events of his life show him a man always reaching out for honesty. In the face of well-known and documented facts, other opponents have rejected the hypothesis that the Prophet was only a coarse liar, and have sought for a more plausible explanation.

A second method of attack has resulted because his work in its many implications is not shallow, but profound. In doctrine, principle, and organization, it challenges serious thought. This has always been a marvel to candid students of the restored gospel. This, all such investigators agree, could not have come out of the brain of an ignorant youth with a propensity for lying. So opponents of Joseph Smith have concluded that he could not have been the real author of Mormonism. Someone else of maturity and training must have used the Prophet as a blind and hidden behind him. Years of fruitless search for this individual have followed.

It must be acknowledged that Joseph Smith had unusual power to win friends. Strong men like Brigham Young accepted him whole heartedly as a Prophet of God. They loved him. In his life they stood ready to lay down their own lives for him. After his death they composed and sang songs of praise for his work, and devoted their lives to building on the spiritual and temporal truths he taught. There is no evidence however that any of these friends ever participated in the glorious work of translating the Book of Mormon or receiving the commandments such as those found in the Doctrine and Covenants, Pearl of Great Price, and elsewhere.

In their defeat, but unwilling to abandon the theory, and leaping over existing facts, the only real victim of these searchers has been Sidney Rigdon. This man was an earnest seeker after truth, associated with Alexander Campbell, of the Christian Church; he had some education above that commonly enjoyed in that day and was an eloquent speaker. When he read the Book of Mormon, he became convinced of its truth, accepted the restored gospel, and became a leader in the building of the restored Church of Jesus Christ.

Proof has been sought that Rigdon knew the young Joseph Smith and chose him to be a blind for his own doctrine. Rigdon has been made an absurd, shadowy figure, known to no one, who came and went while training Joseph for a career of perfidy. Every doctrine of consequence in the Church has been said by some to come from the mind of Sidney Rigdon through the mouth of Joseph Smith. Every principle of organization, it is claimed, was Rigdon's. Joseph Smith appears to such students only a willing pawn in Rigdon's hands.[4]

These detractors of the Prophet's claims also make Rigdon responsible for the Book of Mormon. They say that a Reverend Solomon Spaulding had written an Indian story which fell into the hands of Sidney Rigdon. He edited and improved it and sent it out through the hands of Joseph Smith as the Book of Mormon.[5]

Unfortunately, for these gropers in the dark, the life of Sidney Rigdon is well known. He was not a man to hide behind others. Indeed the Prophet often had to curb Rigdon's desire for primacy.[6]

There is also the fact that the Reverend Spaulding's manuscript story of ancient America was found in 1884. It has been published and bears no resemblance to the Book of Mormon. Drawn by stern necessity to prove their thesis, they who hold that Joseph Smith was an impostor who used the ideas of Rigdon are now of the opinion that there is another Spaulding manuscript, another Indian story from which the Book of Mormon was created. "A man convinced against his will is of the same opinion still." These attempts to catch shadows on the wall are not only laughable but also ridiculous.

---

[4]W. A. Linn, *The Story of the Mormons.*
[5]See chapters 13 and 14.
[6]*History of the Church,* vol. 4, p. 283.

The final and conclusive act in this drama of proving that Joseph Smith was only the tool of others, came towards the end of Sidney Rigdon's life. During his long career Sidney Rigdon never hinted that he knew Joseph Smith before he saw the Book of Mormon. On the contrary he recited the prophetic office of Joseph Smith over and over again. When his son, John W. Rigdon, asked him if he had anything to do with the Book of Mormon before it was handed to him in Kirtland, Sidney Rigdon testified again that he had had nothing to do with the founding of the Church,[7] that he first saw the Book of Mormon when it was printed and handed to him by Parley P. Pratt.[8] Thus falls the second explanation of Joseph Smith.

The third explanation rejects the other two. Under this last explanation Joseph was the real author of Mormonism; but he was self-deceived; he did not try to deceive others. This explanation rests upon the hypothesis that Joseph Smith suffered from mental disease, epilepsy, and the like. When he was in a seizure by the malady, so these people say, he actually saw the visions and heard the words which he later, when he was well again, communicated to his followers. The Prophet, therefore, was not a deceiver, but a poor soul who suffered from hallucinations, brought on by a deranged mind, was self-deceived, and involuntarily misled others. It is a perfect whitewash of the Prophet. One author, a psychologist, has written a whole book on the subject.[9] He has examined the Smith progenitors and because they were God-fearing people, who at times had dreams and told about them, as do many other people, they were all classed as mental cases. Moreover, the author blandly concludes that it was only natural that Joseph Smith by inheritance would suffer mental aberrations. At times it seems to the author of this explanation that the Prophet was actually demented.

---

[7]*History of the Church,* vol. 1, pp. 122-123.
[8]See chapter 14.
[9]I. Woodbridge Riley, *The Founder of Mormonism.*

Under this explanation, the revelations to Joseph Smith, the existence of the "golden plates," everything that he did was a succession of psychological phenomena. If the Prophet was not in a trance, then "automatic writing" was called into service. Apparently, so these theorists would have us believe, Joseph Smith was never free from unsound mental behavior.[10]

Unfortunately for this pretty theory, the facts do not sustain it. Whatever issues from a deranged mind is usually disorderly and illogical. The structure reared upon the revelations to Joseph Smith is essentially orderly in organization and logical in doctrinal development. The doctrine and organization of the Church of Jesus Christ of Latter-day Saints, apart from its origin through the instrumentality of Joseph Smith, appeal to every competent person as of unusual order and logical structure. Many persons, in many books, have commented on the excellence of the organization of the Church and its doctrinal coherence. It is the one characteristic of Mormonism agreed upon by all reputable writers on the subject.

After examining the various explanations there is only one that satisfies the rational mind, and that answers all questions arising from the life of Joseph Smith: that is his own explanation. He, a boy untaught in worldly learning, had communion with Heavenly Beings and was instructed by them; he received and translated the plates of the Book of Mormon by divine aid and organized the Church under divine authority and command. All that he did for the building of the latter-day kingdom of God came in like manner. As fact after fact is examined, Joseph Smith's own explanation of himself and his labors—simple, supported by witnesses, of logical wholeness and affecting a great people for good—is the only one that the rational mind can accept. Pure water does not flow from an impure source. Good never results from evil.

The "doctors" continue to disagree about Joseph Smith. Therefore, Latter-day Saints have no need to worry

---

[10]See chapter 15.

about any other explanation than the one given by the Prophet himself. In this matter the Church organized through his instrumentality stands on a firm and stable foundation. The perplexity of the enemies of Mormonism becomes a source of amusement to his followers and members of the restored gospel of Jesus Christ.

LIEUTENANT-GENERAL JOSEPH SMITH
Of the Nauvoo Legion

JOSEPH SMITH
Addressing the Nauvoo Legion

CHAPTER 54

THE SOURCE OF JOSEPH SMITH'S GREATNESS

It would not be fair to close this book without saying something about Joseph's character, which made him serviceable in the Lord's work. He received a magnificent education from divine sources, during the decade from the First Vision to the organization of the Church. But this education was possible because of the innate qualities of his character. Even the Lord needs good material, if a good and great man is to be formed.

From his boyhood Joseph Smith's character displayed the elements of greatness. It is the verdict of the years that in his life labors and endeavors there was greatness, which is a product of many causes. Like the mighty flowing river, it is fed and made possible by thousands of mountain rivulets. Even so with Joseph Smith.

Using another figure, the reflections from innumerable facets of his character make up the glowing picture of his greatness. That he was great, measured against the men of his and earlier days, has become the judgment of the passing years, in the mouths of all honest students of the Prophet's life and contributions to man's progress.

Five qualities among others made him great. They were human but never wavering. They appear in his every act. They form the cornerstones of his character.

First, he had unchanging faith and trust in God. Second, he was in love with truth and believed that God would help every searcher after truth. Third, he was humble; he took little honor to himself. Fourth, he loved his fellow men. For them he toiled; for them he died. Fifth, he was obedient. God's law was always his law. These qualities always lead to greatness. Without them there is no true greatness.

Joseph's faith in God, his existence, reality, and relationship to man was superb. He took God at his word, as in the First Vision; and throughout life he took counsel with the Almighty and did not try to act alone upon his own judgment. The striving of his life was to grow towards God's likeness. He said:

If you wish to go where God is, you must be like God, or possess the principles which God possesses, for if we are not drawing towards God in principle, we are going from Him and drawing towards the devil. . . Search your hearts, and see if you are like God. I have searched mine, and feel to repent of my sins.[1]

His love of truth was the beginning of his search; to possess truth was the end of his inmost desire. Truth was the measuring stick of his conduct and teaching. Joseph's story begins with his petition for truth, which led to the First Vision. The concluding, sober paragraph of that recital is the foundation of his life's achievements:

I had now got my mind satisfied so far as the sectarian world was concerned, that it was not my duty to join with any of them, but to continue as I was until further directed. I had found the testimony of James to be true, that a man who lacked wisdom might ask of God, and obtain, and not be upbraided.[2]

A jubilant note is sounded in his reply upon his return from the divine interview, to his mother's solicitous concern:

Never mind. All is well—I am well enough off. I have learned for myself that [your church] is not true.[3]

In the midst of the Nauvoo tribulations of the Church, James Arlington Bennett proposed himself to be the Prophet's "right hand man", and to give the necessary help in those strenuous days. Courteously, the offer was declined and in ringing words, like blows upon an anvil, Joseph declared his certain dependence upon truth:

I combat the errors of ages; I meet the violence of mobs; I cope with illegal proceedings from executive authority; I cut the

---

[1]*History of the Church*, vol. 4, p. 588.
[2]*Ibid.*, vol. 1, p. 8.
[3]*Ibid.*, vol. 1, p. 6.

Gordian knot of powers; and I solve the mathematical problems of universities, with truth—diamond truth—and God is my right hand man.[4]

The possession of truth made him fearless, with a lion-like courage. When the people of Palmyra and vicinity, during the printing of the Book of Mormon, held a mass meeting and passed a resolution against his venture, his only reply was to guard the manuscript of the book more carefully.[5]

There was no disloyalty to truth, no retreat from it. He could not exchange truth for popular approval. So he not only published the Book of Mormon, but he also restored the Lord's Church that challenged the popular errors and superstitions of the centuries.

Facing the terrors of Nauvoo, he wrote to the commander of the legion: "Let every man's brow be as the face of a lion; let his breast be as unshaken as the mighty oak."[6]

To remove untruth from its pedestal is an unhonored task. The Prophet and his companions during the Missouri persecutions were sentenced to be shot. Joseph inquired why they were "thus treated", and added that he "was not aware of having done anything worthy of such treatment." General Wilson's answer echoed the eternal hate that untruth bears for truth: "I know it, and that is the reason why I want to kill you, or have you killed."[7] Such hate followed the Prophet, but all the while truth nestled in his bosom and gave him courage.

Joseph Smith was a humble man. He recognized that he was only an instrument in God's hands. He took no glory to himself. In a meeting with Saints who had just arrived in Nauvoo he spoke noble words:

I told them I was but a man, and they must not expect me to be perfect; if they expected perfection from me, I should expect it from them; but if they would bear with my infirmities and the in-

---

[4] *Ibid.*, vol. 6, p. 78.
[5] *Ibid.*, vol. 1, p. 76
[6] *Ibid.*, vol. 5, p. 94.
[7] *Ibid.*, vol. 3, pp. 190-191.

firmities of the brethren, I would likewise bear with their infirmities.[8]

On one occasion he characterized himself:

I am like a huge, rough stone rolling down from a high mountain; and the only polishing I get is when some corner gets rubbed off by coming in contact with something else, striking with accelerated force against religious bigotry, priestcraft, lawyer-craft, doctor-craft, lying editors, suborned judges and jurors, and the authority of perjured executives, backed by mobs, blasphemers, licentious and corrupt men and women—all hell knocking off a corner here and a corner there. Thus I will become a smooth and polished shaft in the quiver of the Almighty, who will give me dominion over all and every one of them, when their refuge of lies shall fail, and their hiding place shall be destroyed, while these smooth-polished stones with which I come in contact become marred.[9]

Courageous he was but always humble. Only humble men can climb the slopes to greatness.

Joseph Smith loved his fellow men. He did not hesitate to tell them so or to show his love by his acts. The end of a letter to Jared Carter reads:

I love your soul, and the souls of the children of men, and pray and do all I can for the salvation of all.[10]

It was through Joseph that the Lord revealed anew the true dignity of man. Men are begotten spirit children of God. That makes all men of the race of Gods, with godlike destinies. In the light of this divine origin and destiny of man, he understood the word of the Lord:

Remember, the worth of souls is great in the sight of God and if it so be that you should labor all your days in crying repentance unto this people, and bring, save it be one soul, unto me, how great shall your joy be with him in the kingdom of my Father.[11]

This joy the Prophet sought throughout his years.

Throughout the pages of his journal runs a spirit of love for his fellow men. He cherished his friendships and

---

[8]*Ibid.*, vol. 5, p. 181.
[9]*Ibid.*, vol. 5, p. 401.
[10]*Ibid.*, vol. 1, p. 339.
[11]*Doctrine and Covenants* 18:10, 15

spoke of them with a love so tender as to melt the heart. When he was urged to go to Carthage where he was martyred, he said, "If my life is of no value to my friends, it is of none to myself."[12] In the cause that he represented, he forgot himself and thought only of others.

Joseph Smith was an obedient man. Humility always breeds obedience. Moreover, the revelations he received from God made obedience to truth the main issue of a happy gospel life. He declared that "if a person gains more knowledge and intelligence in this life through his diligence and obedience than another, he will have so much the advantage in the world to come."[13] From him came also the compelling statement that "there is a law, irrevocably decreed in heaven before the foundations of this world, upon which all blessings are predicated. And when we obtain any blessing from God, it is by obedience to that law upon which it is predicated."[14] That placed obedience to truth the first active principle in his life's success.

His life was an example of obedience. He was shown the Book of Mormon plates; he knew where they were; yet despite his natural eagerness to possess them, he obediently saw them for four years only once a year, as commanded. Obediently, as the Lord directed, he went from place to place, built temples in the midst of his people's poverty, subjected himself to trials and toils, accepted plural marriage in the face of his training for monogamy—and in every manner throughout his life showed obedience to the Lord's will. As did Abraham of old, his all could be laid on the altar of the Lord. By these tests, as by many others, Joseph Smith was a great man.

Faith in God, love of truth, genuine humility, sincere love of our fellow men, and unwavering obedience to truth are always distinguishing marks of greatness. That applies not only to Joseph, but also to all his followers now living.

These qualities also answer those who would have the Church restored through Joseph Smith, make this or

[12]*History of the Church*, vol. 6, p. 549.
[13]*Doctrine and Covenants* 130:19.
[14]*Ibid.*, 130:20-21.

that change, set up this or that new practice. The Church as an organization must never fail to appeal to God or go beyond the bounds of truth but must look upon itself as a mere instrument to accomplish God's purposes, and in all of its work it must be a blessing to mankind.

CHAPTER 55

THE STORY SUMMARIZED

Among the many religious leaders since the days of the Christ, Joseph Smith stands a solitary unique figure. His claims and work were such that there is no other like him. He alone, over the centuries, received his commission, knowledge and authority directly from the Lord, in actual converse with the Supreme Ruler of the Universe.

This claim has caused the furious, malicious and malignant opposition to him and his work. It has been the cause of the bitter, shameful persecution of his followers.

His subsequent claim that personages out of the unseen world waited upon him has only added to the fury of the opposition and persecution.

Yet thousands upon thousands of Joseph Smith's followers, intelligent men and women, have testified to the truth of his claims. They declared that the claims can be fully verified by a careful and prayerful study of the life of the Prophet, and by the consistent use of his teachings. The evidences are all in the Prophet's favor. They themselves rejoice to know that their religion rests upon God's own words. They have used in their search the divine formulas from the Prophet Moroni:

And when ye shall receive these things, I would exhort you that ye would ask God, the Eternal Father, in the name of Christ, if these things are not true; and if ye shall ask with a sincere heart, with real intent, having faith in Christ, he will manifest the truth of it unto you, by the power of the Holy Ghost.[1]

Thus each truth seeker may have his own "First Vision."

Above all, Joseph Smith was a humble searcher after truth. Therefore the Lord could use him. Truth must be placed above all else, otherwise it cannot be found. If truth is lost at any cost, it may easily be found.

---

[1]Moroni 10:4.

Joseph Smith, seeker after truth, was commissioned to re-establish on earth the Church of Jesus Christ. To do so he needed authority from Jesus the Christ, the Head of the Church. From the beginning such authority has been given successively by the laying on of hands by those who themselves have received priesthood authority. In other churches, in Joseph Smith's day and since, the line of authority from Jesus Christ has been broken. Men ordained one another upon their own authority, not that of Jesus the Christ. They admit it and make no claim to divine communication.

So that no question could be raised, Joseph's authority was given him by ancient men, resurrected men, who in their day received the priesthood from Jesus the Christ himself. They appeared, laid their hands upon the heads of Joseph Smith and his companion, Oliver Cowdery, and conferred upon them the priesthood needed to carry out the divine commission of restoration.

Never before, since the days of the Christ and his immediate successors, had such certainty of divine authority been given mortal men. It places the Prophet and his followers in a group peculiar to themselves differing from all others.

Joseph Smith claimed nothing new. He was simply a restorer of that which had been lost from the gospel of the Lord Jesus Christ. He promulgated no new doctrine. He assembled and put together the fragments of truth scattered among man-made religions, and added that which was revealed to him. The resulting authoritative and complete gospel of Jesus Christ becomes a clear, comprehensive, logical and understandable philosophy of man's existence. It traces man's history and destiny, under an eternal purpose, from the dim eternity of the past, into the waiting, endless future. He showed the place of the gospel in a happy and successful human life.

It was this discovery and consolidation of forgotten truth that honest-thinking men, who observe the gaps of missing truth in existing religions, have sought and longed for throughout the centuries. In the multitude of incomplete faiths, often made by man in his helpless search for truth, the restored gospel stands as a complete offering. It explains that which has mystified man, and shows the way to greater truth possession. Truth seekers who can lay aside inherited dogmas were and are glad when the restored truth reaches them.

The restored gospel, thus presented to the world by Joseph Smith, when examined is found to be strictly Biblical. Every doctrine, including those that seemed new because they had been forgotten, or superseded by man-made philosophies, could be defended by the Bible. The Biblical type of opposition to Joseph's teachings has long since been laid aside. The newfound truths of the restoration are thoroughly in harmony with the teachings found in the Bible.

Then the Prophet found ways and means of using the gospel in meeting the many human needs of the present day. It was not only a gospel for life hereafter that he presented, but one designed to foster human welfare on earth in every age. That was a new conception of the gospel to people of Joseph's day. The nature of man is complex. He has many faculties which need development in the pursuit of happiness. Joseph Smith showed how the gospel develops man's innate powers, and how it may be made useful in the daily lives of men. He taught that it should not only prepare men for a joyous hereafter but should be a caretaker of a person's daily joy. The gospel gives life to all periods of life, and light to solve all the problems of life. Light and truth were the watchwords of the restored gospel.[2] This came as lightning in the sky to a world steeped in dark and narrow lifeless religions which promised joy in heaven and accepted misery as man's portion on earth.

Honest men who dare to think for themselves first marvel at the wealth of truth delivered by Joseph Smith, and then marvel still more to think that the mighty restoration of lost truth should come through a youth, untrained

---

[2] *Doctrine and Covenants* 93:1-2, 9, 29, 37-40.

in the learning of the world. It is an evidence of the truth of
the restoration that could not well be gainsaid. The whole
thing becomes "a marvelous work and a wonder."

Admittedly the most remarkable and challenging
evidence to searchers after the truth in Joseph Smith's
story is the fact that he received most of his major spiritual
experiences in the presence of others who shared the
events with him. These men became his witnesses. Such
witnesses are not found elsewhere in ecclesiastical history.
The great religious teachers who claimed spiritual manifestations received them in forests, caves, deserts, or in
their study rooms, but always alone. These leaders brought
no witnesses with them.

Joseph Smith was alone in the sacred grove when
he received his First Vision. No other human eyes or ears
than his own saw and heard the divine, world-changing
drama there enacted. He was also alone in his repeated
contacts with the angel Moroni, who taught him his mission, and brought him the plates from which the Book of
Mormon was translated. At the time of these early manifestations, the Church was not organized nor did he have
fellow laborers to share his experiences.

With these two exceptions the major extraordinary
spiritual experiences of Joseph Smith, including visitations
from the unseen world, were witnessed by other living
men, who never failed to testify of their spiritual experiences though some became later disaffected through ambition or other causes.

The Book of Mormon plates were seen and handled,
at different times, by eleven competent men, of independent minds and spotless reputations, who published a
formal statement of their experience.

Oliver Cowdery, whose reputation for honesty has
never been questioned, was with Joseph Smith when
John the Baptist came to restore the authority of the
Aaronic Priesthood,[3] and when Peter, James and John appeared to restore the Melchizedek Priesthood,[4] and also

---

[3]*Doctrine and Covenants*, Section 13.
[4]*Ibid.*, 27:12; 128:20.

when the foundation-laying revelations from spiritual beings, given at the time of the dedication of the Kirtland Temple were received.[5] Of all these joint experiences Oliver Cowdery often bore testimony.

Sidney Rigdon who was with Joseph Smith when the revelation called the Vision[6] was received bore testimony in diverse places, to the glimpse at that time, with Joseph Smith, of heavenly personages, including the Lord himself.

Many of the revelations of Joseph were received in the presence of other human, living persons, who saw and heard the manifestations at the time that they were given. Some of these witnesses have recorded their experiences in print.[7]

At one time, [Oct. 29, 1831] in a public meeting held in Orange, Cuyahoga County, Ohio, Joseph called upon the witnesses to the Book of Mormon to bear their testimonies to the conference. [All but three of the twelve witnesses were present.] This they did in the presence of a large group of people.[8]

All these witnesses, of unchallenged honesty in the affairs of life, remained true to their testimonies throughout their lives without deviation or variation.[9]

This body of witnesses—there are many of them—must be accepted in any fair study of Joseph Smith. It would be preposterous to ignore them. They form a powerful evidence for the truth of Joseph's claims, and a safe bulwark against the unfriendly attacks upon his integrity. The fact that others besides Joseph communicated with personages from the "other world," confirms the claims of Joseph's experiences when he was alone, and floods all of his claims and teachings with the light of truth.

In short, on the testimony of reliable witnesses who shared the experiences with him, some of which he recounts in his "history," Joseph Smith had spiritual experiences,

---

[5]*Ibid.*, Section 110.
[6]*Ibid.*, Section 76.
[7]Parley P. Pratt, *Parley P. Pratt Autobiography*, p. 62.
[8]*History of the Church*, vol. 1, p. 220; "History of Luke Johnson," *Millennial Star*, vol. 26, p. 835; Far West Record 12, 16.
[9]See flyleaf of the Book of Mormon, also Preston Nibley, *Witnesses to the Book of Mormon*.

including the actual visitations of personages from the unseen, the spiritual, the "other world." The revelations which have received most condemnation from his enemies were shared by others.

This succession of witnesses to the fundamental experiences in Joseph's life have been stumbling blocks, and so remain, to the unbeliever. They cannot be explained away by saying that Joseph fooled or hypnotized all these people. That would be pure nonsense. They told the truth. They stand as evidences of the truth of his story. Evidences may as properly be used in religion as elsewhere.

The most powerful witness of Joseph's truth comes from the testimony of the Holy Ghost to earnest seekers after truth. That witness must be placed first. However, living men as witnesses under God's direction help greatly to establish the truth of any claim.

There is a notable openness about Joseph's career. Whether his experiences were spiritual or temporal he laid them open to his people. Thus his friendly followers participated in nearly all his experiences.

Of course a Christian cannot with good grace deny the power of God to show himself to human beings, his children, nor the possibility of personages of the great unseen world, to appear to men on earth. There is no need for argument there.

Joseph Smith's frequent association with heavenly beings and eternal truths as revealed to him naturally reacted upon his very nature and changed his manner of life. Such changes are well known and understood. Indeed the change of a man for good in his walk and talk when he accepts truth is of itself the strongest evidence of the presence of truth.

Joseph was but a man with a human nature and the weaknesses of human beings, but he was in communication with heavenly influences. He sought mightily from his youth for truth, heavenly truth. Therefore he rose above many of the frailties of man. He was constantly in a process of growth. He recognized his human weaknesses, but sought to overcome them. Modestly, as already quoted, he compared himself to the rough stone which rolling down a mountain side is rounded and smoothed by coming in contact with other stones.[10] Thus Joseph Smith became a great man, great in noble qualities.

After the desire for truth, the love of his fellow men and respect for them became his foremost characteristics. For them as for himself the plan of salvation had been formulated. They were the very children of God, with a godlike destiny. To all men he showed courtesy, charity and forgiveness such as a true leader should manifest. He sought learning eagerly. He must know more and more. Yet he found time to play with children, who loved him. He asked nothing of his followers that he would not do himself. As new revelations came to him, he shared them with the people. All that he did was known to all. He made no pretense of hidden doctrine or plans.

He grew in spiritual stature as revelations were received. As his commission progressed he rose in nobility of action. He became a powerful teacher and leader of men. There lingered about him a majesty recognized by all who met him, friend or foe. Those about him felt the divine influences which radiated from him.

His bitterest enemies could find no fault with the walk of his life. His own people almost to a man loved him, revered him, obeyed him, and followed his teachings, before and after his death. The warmth of his nature comforted all who became acquainted with him, whether in person or by study.

His life was a great contribution to human welfare. His teachings as accepted will in time make the earth a pleasant place in which to dwell. His career on earth lifts him to a towering place among men, second to none since the days of the Lord Jesus Christ. He stands on the pages of history a majestic figure.

He sought truth; he found it. He used truth for man's

[10]See chapter 54.

eternal progressive welfare. Thus he won from God the prophetic title.

Joseph Smith is himself the best evidence of the truth of his message to the world.

Joseph Smith the truth seeker was a prophet of God.

CHAPTER 56

THEY KNEW JOSEPH

Many persons who knew Joseph, believers and unbelievers in his spiritual claims, have set down in writing the impression he made upon them. With very few exceptions he has been described by those who met him personally as a fine-looking man of gentlemanly demeanor, who told simply and without flourish the story of the coming forth of the Book of Mormon and the organization of the Church. The uniformity of these reports is a proof of their correctness.

The few, and very few, who have reported otherwise have been professed enemies of the Prophet. They have been chiefly ministers of other churches who resorted to anything to destroy the teachings of Joseph Smith. In the face of the numerous testimonies to the contrary, the statements of these enemies have no confirmatory value.

In the following pages are presented extracts from friends and foes of Joseph Smith, who knew him personally.

FROM AVOWED ENEMIES

Enemies could of course see nothing good in Joseph Smith, inwardly or outwardly. Yet most of them have admitted his personal attractiveness, which has led many to ascribe to him a hypnotic power by which he was able to do his work.

The irrational, hateful extremes to which a few enemies have gone in their description of Joseph Smith are really proofs of their vindictiveness. The coarsest, issuing from a supposed cultured and honest man, comes from Reverend Henry Caswall, a transparent lover of a lie to win a case. He called at Nauvoo in 1842, in a valiant but unsuccessful attempt to win the Saints from their faith. He met the Prophet:

He [Joseph Smith] is a coarse plebeian sensual person in aspect, and his countenance exhibits a curious mixture of the knave and the clown. His hands are large and fat, and on one of his fingers he wears a massive gold ring upon which is an inscription. His dress was of coarse country manufacture, and his white hat was enveloped by a piece of black crepe as a sign of mourning for his deceased brother, Don Carlos Smith, the late editor of the "Times and Seasons." His eyes appear deficient in that open and straightforward expression which often characterizes an honest man.[1]

From Neutral Non-Members of the Church

Mr. John S. Reed, lawyer by profession, was employed by Joseph Smith to help him in some of his early law suits. Mr. Reed on May 17, 1844, said in an address in Nauvoo:

. . . The first acquaintance I had with General Smith was about the year 1823. He came into my neighborhood, being then about eighteen years of age, and resided there two years, during which time I became intimately acquainted with him. I do know that his character was irreproachable, and that he was well known for truth and uprightness; that he moved in the first circles of the community, and he was often spoken of as a young man of intelligence and good morals, and possessing a mind susceptible of the highest intellectual attainments.

I early discovered that his mind was constantly in search of truth, expressing an anxious desire to know the will of God. . .[2]

Matthew S. Davis, member of Congress, heard the Prophet speak in Washington, D.C., on February 6, 1840. He wrote a report of the meeting to his wife, in which he says:

He is not an educated man; but he is a plain sensible, strong minded man. Everything he says, is said in a manner to leave an impression that he is sincere. There is no levity, no fanaticism, no want of dignity in his deportment. He is apparently from forty to forty-five years of age, rather above the middle stature, and what you ladies would call a very good looking man. In his garb there are no peculiarities; his dress being that of a plain, unpretending citizen. He is by profession a farmer, but is evidently well read. . .[3]

---

[1]Henry Caswall, M.A., *The City of the Mormons; or, Three Days at Nauvoo,* in 1842, p. 35.
[2]*History of the Church,* vol. 1, p. 94.
[3]*Ibid.,* vol. 4, p. 78.

Josiah Quincy, distinguished scholar, author, and
Massachusetts leader, who visited Joseph Smith in May,
1844, says:

> Preëminent among the stragglers by the door stood a man of
> commanding appearance, clad in the costume of a journeyman
> carpenter when about his work. He was a hearty, athletic fellow,
> with blue eyes standing prominently out upon his light complexion,
> a long nose, and a retreating forehead. . . A fine looking man is
> what the passerby would instinctively have murmured upon meet-
> ing the remarkable individual. . . One could not resist the impres-
> sion that capacity and resource were natural to his stalwart person.
> . . . Of all men I have met, these two, [Elisha R. Potter of Rhode
> Island and Joseph Smith] seemed best endowed with that kingly
> faculty which directs, as by intrinsic right, the feeble or confused
> souls who are looking for guidance.[4]

From Members of the Church

Numerous members of the Church who knew the
Prophet intimately have left their description of his person,
always in loving words. These have been best summarized
by President George Q. Cannon, who in his boyhood knew
the Prophet:

> President Cannon, then 15 years old, first saw the Prophet in
> 1842 in Nauvoo. A large company of emigrants, chiefly from Eng-
> land, were met at the ship's landing by a large group of welcoming
> Church members. Nearly every prominent man in the community
> was there. Familiar with the names of all, and with the persons
> of many of the prominent elders (I) sought, with a boy's curiosity
> and eagerness, to discover those whom (I) knew, and especially
> to get sight of the Prophet, and his brother Hyrum, neither of
> whom (I) had ever met.
> When (my) eyes fell upon the Prophet, without a word from
> anyone to point him out, or any reason to separate him from others
> who stood around, (I) knew him instantly. (I) would have
> known him among ten thousand. There was that about him which
> to the boy's eyes distinguished him from all the men he had ever
> met."[5]

In mature life, drawing upon his personal knowledge,

---

[4]Josiah Quincy, *Figures of the Past*, 1901 edition, pp. 380-381.
[5]George Q. Cannon. *Life of Joseph Smith*, p. 26.

and that of many who had known the Prophet, President Cannon wrote:

> He was more than six feet in height, with expansive chest and clean cut limbs—a staunch and graceful figure. His head, crowned with a mass of soft wavy hair, was grandly poised. His face possessed a complexion of such clearness and transparency that the soul appeared to shine through. He wore no beard, and the full strength and beauty of his countenance impressed all beholders at a glance. He had eyes which seemed to read the hearts of men. His mouth was one of mingled power and sweetness. His majesty of air was natural, not studied.[6]

Parley P. Pratt, who knew the Prophet from the early years of the Church, wrote:

> President Joseph Smith was in person tall and well built, strong and active; of a light complexion, light hair, blue eyes, very little beard, and of an expression peculiar to himself, on which the eye naturally rested with interest, and was never weary of beholding. His countenance was ever mild, affable, beaming with intelligence and benevolence; mingled with a look of interest and an unconscious smile, or cheerfulness, and entirely free from all restraint or affectation of gravity; and there was something connected with the serene and steady penetrating glance of his eye, as if he would penetrate the deepest abyss of the human heart, gaze into eternity, penetrate the heavens, and comprehend all worlds.
>
> He possessed a noble boldness and independence of character; his manner was easy and familiar; his rebuke terrible as the lion; his benevolence unbounded as the ocean; his intelligence universal, and his language abounding in original eloquence peculiar to himself—not polished—not studied—not smoothed and softened by education and refined by art; but flowing forth in its own native simplicity, and profusely abounding in variety of subject and manner. He interested and edified, while, at the same time, he amused and entertained his audience; and none listened to him that were ever weary with his discourse. I have known him to retain a congregation of willing and anxious listeners for many hours together, in the midst of cold or sunshine, rain or wind, while they were laughing at one moment and weeping the next. Even his most bitter enemies were generally overcome, if he could once get their ears.
>
> I have known him when chained and surrounded with armed murderers and assassins who were heaping upon him every possible

---

[6] *Ibid.*, pp. 25-26.

insult and abuse, rise up in the majesty of a son of God and rebuke
them, in the name of Jesus Christ, till they quailed before him,
dropped their weapons, and on their knees, begged his pardon,
and ceased their abuse.

. . . In him the characters of a Daniel and a Cyrus were won-
derfully blended. The gifts, wisdom and devotion of a Daniel
were united with the boldness, courage, temperance, perseverance
and generosity of a Cyrus. . . As it is, his works will live to endless
ages, and unnumbered millions yet unborn will mention his name
with honor, as a noble instrument in the hands of God, who, during
his short and youthful career, laid the foundation of that kingdom
spoken of by Daniel, the Prophet, which should break in pieces all
other kingdoms and stand forever.[7]

Brigham Young, successor to Joseph Smith in the
Presidency of the Church, said:

When I first heard him preach, he brought heaven and earth
together; and all the priests of the day could not tell me anything
correct about heaven, hell, God, angels, or devils; they were as
blind as Egyptian darkness. When I saw Joseph Smith, he took
heaven, figuratively speaking, and brought it down to earth; and
he took the earth, brought it up, and opened up in plainness and
simplicity, the things of God; and that is the beauty of his mission.[8]

. . . When he preached to the people—revealed the things of
God, the will of God, the plan of salvation, the purposes of Jehovah,
the relation in which we stand to him and all the heavenly beings,
he reduced his teachings to the capacity of every man, woman, and
child, making them as plain as a well-defined pathway. . .[9]

John Taylor testified:

I testify that I was acquainted with Joseph Smith for years. I
have traveled with him; I have been with him in private and in
public; I have associated with him in councils of all kinds; I have
listened hundreds of times to his public teachings, and his advice
to his friends and associates of a more private nature. I have been
at his house. I have seen him then under these various circumstances, and I testify before God, angels, and men, that he was a
good, honorable, virtuous man—that his doctrines were good,
scriptural, and wholesome. . .[10]

Wilford Woodruff confirmed these statements:

[7]Parley P. Pratt, *Parley P. Pratt Autobiography*, p. 45.
[8]John A. Widtsoe, *The Discourses of Brigham Young*, p. 458.
[9]*Ibid.*, p. 463.
[10]G. Homer Durham, *The Gospel Kingdom*, p. 355

When I look at the history of Joseph Smith, I sometimes think that he came as near following the footsteps of the Savior—(although no more so than His disciples)—as anyone possibly could.

I have heard the Prophet Joseph pray when the power of God rested upon him, and all who heard him felt it; and I have seen his prayers answered in a marvelous manner almost immediately.

Joseph Smith was what he professed to be, a Prophet of God, a seer and revelator. He laid the foundation of this Church and Kingdom, and lived long enough to deliver the keys of the Kingdom to the elders of Israel, unto the Twelve Apostles. . .[11]

Lorenzo Snow, who saw the Prophet before joining the Church, says:

Few men now living were so well acquainted with Joseph Smith the Prophet as I was. I was with him oftentimes. I visited him in his family, sat at his table, associated with him under various circumstances, and had private interviews with him for counsel. I know that Joseph Smith was a Prophet of God; I know that he was an honorable man, a moral man, and that he had the respect of those who were acquainted with him. . . The Lord has shown me most clearly and completely that he was a Prophet of God, and that he held the Holy Priesthood and the authority to baptize people for the remission of their sins and to lay hands upon them for the reception of the Holy Ghost. . .

. . . I shall never forget the first time I saw Joseph Smith. It was in Father Johnson's house, in the township of Hiram, in the State of Ohio, about twenty-five miles from Kirtland. It was near Father Johnson's where the mob tarred and feathered him. When I saw him he was standing in the doorway. Before him was a small bowery occupied by about a hundred and fifty or two hundred men and women. There for the first time I heard his voice. When I heard his testimony in regard to what the Lord had revealed to him, it seemed to me that he must be an honest man. He talked and looked like an honest man. He was an honest man.[12]

Joseph F. Smith, although a boy, knew the Prophet.

I bear my testimony to you and to the world, that Joseph Smith was raised up by the power of God to lay the foundations of this great latter-day work, to reveal the fulness of the gospel to the world, by which men may act in the name of the Father, and

[11]G. Homer Durham, *The Discourses of Wilford Woodruff*, pp. 32-34.
[12]*Conference Reports*, October, 1897, to October, 1902, *Semi-Annual Conference Report of Lorenzo Snow*, 1900, p. 61.

of the Son, and of the Holy Ghost, and it will be accepted of God. . .

I testify to you, as I know and feel that I live and move and have my being, that the Lord raised up the boy prophet, Joseph Smith, and endowed him with divine authority, and taught him those things which were necessary for him to know that he might have power to lay the foundation of God's Church and Kingdom in the earth. Joseph Smith was true to the covenants that he made with the Lord, true to his mission, and the Lord enabled him to accomplish his work, even to the sealing of his testimony with his shed blood. . .[13]

In 1892 President George Q. Cannon, then editor of the *Juvenile Instructor,* published upwards of fifty reminiscences which all together confirm the summary descriptions of the preceding. Note these brief extracts from these brethren and sisters.

Elder Lyman O. Littlefield:

I first beheld him (Joseph Smith) a tall, well proportioned man, busily mingling with the members of Zion's Camp, shaking hands with them, meeting them with friendly greetings and carefully seeing to their comforts. His familiar, yet courteous and dignified manner, his pleasant and intelligent countenance, his intellectual and well-formed forehead, the expressive and philanthropic facial lineaments, the pleasant smile and the happy light that beamed from his mild blue eyes; all these were among the attractive attributes that at once awakened a responsive interest in the minds of every kindly beholder, which increased in intensity as the acquaintance continued.

With his most familiar friends he was social, conversational and often indulged in harmless jokes; but when discoursing upon complicated topics that pertained to the welfare of individuals or the progressiveness of communities, his lucidations were clear and so full of common sense and genuine philosophy that the candid and fair-minded felt interested by his views, though they might decline to entertain or promulgate all of the self-evident truths he originated.

Such is a brief though imperfect pen picture of this celebrated man; he was all this when I first beheld him in this traveling camp, and it is any wonder that I, so young in years, should be filled with sensation and intense pleasure and respect for him when I first met him?[14]

[13]Joseph F. Smith, *Gospel Doctrine,* pp. 168-169.
[14]*Juvenile Instructor,* vol. 27, pp. 56-57.

Elder Wiley Payne Allred:

On first sight I thought he was the most noble man I ever saw in my life. I know that he was a prophet, seer and revelator of God.

I thought he had a very noble appearance, very kind and affectionate. I visited the camp several times while they were stopping at my Uncle James Allred's farm.

I have played ball with him many times in Nauvoo. He was preaching once, and he said it tried some of the pious folk to see him play ball with the boys.[15]

Sister Margarette McIntire Burgess:

The Prophet Joseph was often at my father's house. Some incidents which I recollect of him made deep impressions on my child-mind. One morning when he called at our house, I had a very sore throat. It was much swollen and gave me great pain. He took me up in his lap, and gently anointed my throat with consecrated oil and administered to me, and I was healed. I had no more pain nor soreness.

Another time my older brother and I were going to school, near to the building which was known as Joseph's brick store. It had been raining the previous day, causing the ground to be very muddy, especially along that street. My brother Wallace and I both got fast in the mud, and could not get out, and of course childlike, we began to cry, for we thought we would have to stay there. But looking up, I beheld the loving friend of children, the Prophet Joseph, coming to us. He soon had us on higher and drier ground. Then he stooped down and cleaned the mud from our little, heavyladen shoes, took his handkerchief from his pocket and wiped our tear-stained faces. He spoke kind and cheering words to us, and sent us on our way to school rejoicing.[16]

Elder John W. Hess:

At that time Joseph was studying Greek and Latin, and when he got tired studying he would go and play with the children in their games about the house, to give himself exercise. Then he would go back to his studies as before. I was a boy then about fourteen years old. He used to take me up on his knee and caress me as he would a child.

I relate this to show the kindness and simplicity of his nature. I never saw another man like Joseph. There was something heavenly and angelic in his looks that I never witnessed in

15*Ibid.*, vol. 27, pp. 255-256.
16*Ibid.*, vol. 27, pp. 66-67.

the countenance of any other person. During his short stay I became very much attached to him, and learned to love him more dearly than any other person I ever met, my father and mother not excepted.[17]

Elder Edwin Holden:

In 1838 Joseph and some of the young men were playing various out-door games, among which was a game of ball. By and by they began to get weary. He saw it, and calling them together he said: "Let us build a log cabin." So off they went, Joseph and the young men, to build a log cabin for a widow woman. Such was Joseph's way, always assisting in whatever he could.[18]

Elder James Leech:

After arriving in Nauvoo we were five or six weeks looking for employment, but failed to get any. One morning I said to my brother-in-law, "Let us go and see the Prophet. I feel that he will give us something to do." He considered a short time, then consented to go. On arriving at his house we inquired for the Prophet. We were told he was over the road. So we went over, and found him in a little store selling a lady some goods. This was the first time I had had an opportunity to be near him and get a good look at him. I felt there was a superior spirit in him. He was different to anyone I had ever met before; and I said in my heart, he is truly a Prophet of the most high God.

As I was not a member of the Church I wanted Henry to ask him for work, but he did not do so, so I had to. I said, "Mr. Smith, if you please, have you any employment you could give us both, so we can get some provisions?"

He viewed us with a cheerful countenance, and with such a feeling of kindness said: "Well, boys, what can you do?"

We told him what our employment was before we left our native land.

Said, he, "Can you make a ditch?"

I replied we would do the best we could at it.

"That's right, boys," and picking up a tape line he said, "Come along with me."

He took us a few rods from the store, gave me the ring to hold, and stretched all the tape from the reel and marked a line for us to work by.

"Now, boys," said he, "can you make a ditch three feet wide and two and half feet deep along this line?"

---

[17]*Ibid.*, vol. 27, pp. 302-303.
[18]*Ibid.*, vol. 27, p. 153.

We said we would do our best, and he left us. We went to work, and when it was finished I went and told him it was done.

He came and looked at it and said, "Boys, if I had done it myself it could not have been done better. Now come with me."

He led the way back to the store, and told us to pick the best ham or piece of pork for ourselves. Being rather bashful, I said we would rather he would give us some. So he picked two of the largest and best pieces of meat and a sack of flour for each of us, and asked us if that would do. We told him we would be willing to do more work for it, but he said, "If you are satisfied, boys, I am."

We thanked him kindly, and went on our way home rejoicing in the kindheartedness of the Prophet of our God.[19]

Louisa Y. Littlefield:

I will speak of a prominent trait of his character which was perhaps more marked in his early career than was the case after public cares and responsibilities multiplied upon him from so many sources. I mean his natural fondness for children. In Kirtland, when wagon loads of grown people and children came in from the country to meeting, Joseph would make his way to as many of the wagons as he well could and cordially shake the hand of each person. Every child and young babe in the company were especially noticed by him and tenderly taken by the hand, with his kind words and blessings. He loved innocence and purity, and he seemed to find it in the greatest perfection with the prattling child.[20]

Daniel D. McArthur:

To me he seemed to possess more power and force of character than any ordinary man. I would look upon him when he was with hundreds of other men, then he would appear greater than ever.[21]

James Worthington Phippen:

I was favorably impressed with his noble mien, his stately form and his pleasant, smiling face and cheerful conversation.[22]

Bathsheba W. Smith:

My first impressions were that he was an extraordinary man —a man of great penetration; was different from any other man

[19]*Ibid.*, vol. 27, pp. 152-153.
[20]*Ibid.*, vol. 27, p. 24.
[21]*Ibid.*, vol. 27, pp. 128-229
[22]*Ibid.*, vol. 27, p. 24.

I ever saw; had the most heavenly countenance, was genial, affable and kind, and looked the soul of honor and integrity.[23]

Jesse N. Smith:

Incomparably the most Godlike man I ever saw. . . . I know that by nature he was incapable of lying and deceitfulness, possessing the greatest kindness and nobility of character. I felt when in his presence that he could read me through and through. I know he was all that he claimed to be.[24]

John Lyman Smith who lived for several months with the Prophet when a boy:

In my early years I used to often eat at the table with Joseph the Prophet. At one time he called us to dinner. I being at play in the room with his son Joseph, he called us to him, and we stood one on each side of him. After he had looked over the table he said, "Lord, we thank Thee for this Johnny cake, and ask Thee to send us something better. Amen." The corn bread was cut and I received a piece from his hand.

"Before the bread was all eaten, a man came to the door and asked if the Prophet Joseph was at home. Joseph replied he was, whereupon the visitor said, "I have brought you some flour and a ham."

Joseph arose and took the gift, and blessed the man in the name of the Lord. Turning to his wife, Emma, he said, "I knew the Lord would answer my prayer."[25]

Mercy R. Thompson:

We listened with joy and profit to the words of instruction and counsel which fell from the inspired lips of Joseph Smith, each word carrying to our hearts deeper and stronger convictions that we were listening to a mighty Prophet of God. And yet there was not the slightest appearance of ostentation of conscious power on his part; he was as free and sociable as though we had all been his own brothers and sisters, or members of one family. He was as unassuming as a child.[26]

Daniel Tyler's impression of the Prophet's character was, as he states:

---

[23]*Ibid.*, vol. 27, pp. 344-345.
[24]*Ibid.*, vol. 27, pp. 23-24.
[25]*Ibid.*, vol. 27, pp. 172-173.
[26]*Ibid.*, vol. 27, pp. 398-400.

That he was a meek, humble, sociable and very affable man, as a citizen, and one of the most intelligent of men, and a great Prophet.[27]

Such was this man of God to those who knew him personally. To those who loved his memory and cherished his great life-work he is truly a great and sincere seeker after truth. Indeed, he has left us a great heritage of truth. Seekers for truth continue to marvel at his solutions of the many problems of life. He kept close to the Lord. Revelations flowed to him. Though but a man, he rose mightily above the men of his generation. He had enough faith and humility to be called by God to an office, transcending any other in his day. As he died he exclaimed, "O Lord, my God." To Him he had always gone for help and all his followers must do likewise.

[27]*Ibid.*, vol. 27, pp. 93-95.

CHAPTER 57

THE SUCCESSION

Joseph Smith had provided for the continuation of the Church in the event of his death, as shown in Chapter 49. Should he pass away the Twelve would take over.

The revelations to the Prophet and his well authenticated statement are indisputable proofs of the validity of this order.

At the time of the assassination of Joseph and Hyrum most of the Twelve were in various parts of the country campaigning for the Prophet's candidacy for the Presidency of the United States. Upon their return, the Twelve followed the order set up by the Prophet. On August 8, 1844, a little more than a month after the Prophet's death, they called the people together in a general conference of the Church. The question of succession in the presidency of the Church was there presented to the people. By a practically unanimous vote, the people confirmed the order set up by Joseph Smith, that when the First Presidency is dissolved, the authority is held by the Council of Twelve Apostles.[1]

In the discussion, Brigham Young as the President of the Quorum declared that he did not care who led the Church, provided it was done with the approval of the Lord. The Apostles were following strictly the word of the Lord and had no other ambition. The action taken settled the question of succession. That occasional individuals, fired by ambition or other purposes, set themselves up as proper president, could only be expected. That story is interesting, but only that. The faithful people followed the Twelve. They preferred to obey the voice of the Lord.

It was understood in Joseph's day that in all probability persecution would soon compel the Saints to leave Nauvoo. Therefore the Prophet, shortly before his death,

[1]Doctrine and Covenants 107:58.

prepared to move the people westward into a place that others did not want. (See Chapter 50.) He was on the way to find a place when recalled from Montrose to Nauvoo, and eventually to his death.

When the people had acted, the Twelve set out to prepare for the evacuation of Nauvoo. The bitterness and hostility of the countryside were increased daily. The murder of the Prophet and his brother did not satisfy those who hated the mission of the Latter-day Saints. The situation was becoming intolerable. At length the Twelve under Brigham Young's leadership agreed with their persecutors that the Church would move out of Illinois.

Many possible locations were considered by the Twelve and the people. At last the decision was taken to follow the plan of the martyred Prophet. They studied diligently all available information concerning the West, then really unexplored. Fremont's reports of his trips into the West had just been published. Brigham Young, a loyal follower of the Prophet, looked upon the Far West as a desirable abiding place for the Church. It was felt that in that unknown land, the Lord would speak when the right place was found. So, it was decided to move westward.

From that time on earnest preparations were made for the removal and the leaders hoped to be in readiness by the spring. But the vicious persecutions of their enemies forced their removal in mid-winter whether or not they were ready. Therefore on February 4, 1846,[2] the evacuation of Nauvoo began. It was a bitter cold month. Ice covered the Mississippi, but the people, loyal to the great Cause of the Lord, undertook the journey which in poetry and prose has been hailed as the world's greatest recorded successful trek of a whole people. Over plains, deserts and mountains they rode behind oxen or pulled and pushed their handcarts, or walked, over two thousand miles. Thousands laid down their lives by the side of the trail. But, in the end they won. Faith in the Cause with the Lord's help was the motive power that led the people to tremendous success. By con-

---

[2] E. Cecil McGavin, *Nauvoo the Beautiful*, 1946 edition, pp. 221-222.

quering the unfriendly, intermountain West, they made our land one from ocean to ocean. They were truly empire builders.

It was a grievious sorrow to the Saints that Emma Smith with her children refused to go westward with the body of the Saints. She with Joseph's brother William, who was not in good standing in the Church, preferred to remain in Nauvoo. Since that was her decision, the Church under the leadership of Brigham Young made ample provision before they left, for her and the members of Joseph's family.

In the afternoon of August 2, 1845, when preparations were being made for the westward trek, President Brigham Young and Heber C. Kimball and the bishops of Nauvoo rode out in the new Church carriage to look at two [city] blocks belonging to Emma Smith which she agreed to sell for $550.00. They selected blocks ninety-six and ninety-seven, and authorized their purchase. They then drove to Mother Smith's home (the Prophet's mother) and asked her to choose which of the two blocks she would like to have deeded to herself and her daughters. She chose block ninety-six and asked that the Church build on it a house like President Kimball's. She also asked for the carriage they were riding in with a horse and a double carriage harness. The use of the carriage was given her during her lifetime.[3] They also gave Emma $1,500.00 in cash; the Cleveland farm, and another farm of three hundred and twenty acres; and other items. She also possessed the property of her martyred husband.[4]

Emma never became reconciled in her feelings to those who crossed the plains to Utah; she, therefore, remained, after her husband Prophet's death, estranged from the Church founded through his efforts.

Benjamin F. Johnson, the Prophet's intimate friend who had a deep respect for Emma, says:

[3]*Journal History*, August 2, 1845, p. 1.
[4]*History of the Church*, vol. 7, p. 194 (July 17, 1844); also hand-written memorandum authorized by Brigham Young and Heber C. Kimball.

I was appointed with Bishop N. K. Whitney to visit Sister Emma for the last time, and if possible persuade her to remain with the Church. Nearly all night we labored with her, and all we could learn was that she was willing to go with the Church on condition that she could be the leading spirit. So we left her, and she did lead all who would follow her so long as she lived.[5]

Emma Smith, who played so vital a part in the life of Joseph Smith, is difficult to understand. She loved the Prophet and was loyal to him. She felt assured that he translated the Book of Mormon by a power beyond his own.[6] Her faith may have been tested beyond her strength by the hardships that she was obliged to undergo in the early strenuous history of the Church. The strain may have been too great for her nature. She may have been thrown back upon the false doctrine that if this were the Lord's work he would not permit such persecutions as they had to endure.

It was a shock to the Latter-day Saints that shortly after the death of the Prophet she married Major Lewis C. Bidamon, not a member of the Church nor a believer in the divine calling of Joseph Smith. She held herself aloof from the Church. This condition may have rooted in her unwillingness to face further hardships in the unbroken west, or in her love for her family, whom she wanted to lead the Church, or in her dislike of Brigham Young and his associates, the men her husband loved, and who were ever the Prophet's defenders. Uncontrolled ambitions and personal dislike are deadly in their effects.

These things, however, would have been of little consequence had her faith been valiant and strong. She will stand before the bar of God to answer for whatever she did contrary to the light given her. We of a later age are not her judges.

On the other hand, and by contrast, the widow of the martyred patriarch Hyrum Smith, Mary Fielding Smith, who was no less tried and bereft by her tragic loss, joined the westward trek of the Church. With her two

---

[5]Benjamin F. Johnson, *My Life's Review*, p. 107.
[6]Kirkham, *op., cit.*, p. 195.

children and the two from her husband's former marriage, she faced the strenuous hardships of the western journey, and toiled with the others amidst great hardships to the valley of the Great Salt Lake. She did not remarry, but remained faithful to the memory of her husband the Patriarch Hyrum Smith. She was true to the Church which was restored by the martyred Prophet. She died five years after their arrival in what is now Salt Lake City. Her descendants have been protectors of the restored Church. Some have held high offices in the Church.

A CHRONOLOGY FEATURING POLITICAL HIGHLIGHTS
IN THE CAREER OF JOSEPH SMITH
(1805-1844)[1]

By Dr. G. Homer Durham[2]

—1805—

December 23. Born, Sharon, Windsor County, Vermont, son of Joseph and Lucy Mack Smith.

—1814—

Moved to Palmyra, New York.

—ca. 1818—

Moved to Smith farm (Manchester) near Palmyra.

—1820—

Spring. Had the Vision of the Father and the Son in the grove of trees on the Smith farm.

—1823—

September 21. Existence of the Nephite record revealed by Angel Moroni.
September 22. The record's location discovered in the Hill Cumorah near the Smith farm.

—1825—

October. Hires out to work for Josiah Stoal in Harmony, Pennsylvania.

—1827—

January 18. Marries Emma Hale of Harmony, and leaves Stoal to work on his father's farm in New York.
September 22. Receives from the angel custody of the golden plates containing the Nephite record.
December. Goes to home of his wife's father, Isaac Hale, in Harmony, Pennsylvania, to avoid neighborhood difficulties and commences translation of the plates.

—1828—

February. Martin Harris takes copies of characters from the plates to New York where Charles Anthon and Samuel E. Mitchell pronounce them authentic.
April 12. Martin Harris returns and works as scribe.
June 14. Martin Harris loses 116 pages of completed manuscript while Joseph visits in New York.
July. Joseph returns to Harmony and operates a small farm purchased from Isaac Hale.

—1829—

April 5. Oliver Cowdery, Palmyra school teacher, comes to Harmony to inquire about the plates.
April 7. Oliver Cowdery begins as scribe, recommencing the work.
May 15. John the Baptist appears, confers authority of the Aaronic priesthood.
May-June. Peter, James, and John confer the apostleship and Melchizedek priesthood.
June. Leaves Harmony for Peter Whitmer's farm, Fayette, New York. Early baptisms subsequently performed.
August 25. Contract signed with E. B. Grandin to print 5,000 copies of the Book of Mormon for $3,000.

—1830—

Book of Mormon published by Grandin press. Palmyra, March, 26.
April 6. Church of Jesus Christ of Latter-day Saints organized at Peter Whitmer's home, Fayette, New York.
June. Arrested "for setting the country in an uproar and preaching the Book of Mormon." Tried and acquitted.
August. Removes family from Harmony to Fayette.
October. Oliver Cowdery, Parley P. Pratt and Ziba Peterson sent on a mission to the American west.

---

[1]Selection based on political and legal considerations as revealed in his journal.
[2]From G. Homer Durham, *Joseph Smith Prophet-Statesman*.

Agents missionize large colony at Kirtland, Ohio.

December. Sidney Rigdon and Edward Partridge come from Kirtland to see the new prophet, who commences revision of the English Bible and decides to go to Ohio, gaining Rigdon's services as scribe.

—1831—

January-February. Moves to Kirtland. Organizes Rigdon's "Family" society into flourishing Mormon community.

June 19. Starts on first journey to Missouri "wherein it was promised the place for the New Jerusalem should be revealed."

Middle of July. Arrives in Jackson county, (western) Missouri. Proclaims it to be Zion.

August 2. Colesville branch (New York) arrives from the east and forms Mormon settlement, Kaw Township, Jackson county.

August 3. Dedicates spot for Temple at Independence, Missouri.

August 9. Returns to Kirtland, arriving on the 27th.

September 12. Moves from Kirtland to Hiram, Portage county, Ohio, and resumes revision of Bible.

—1832—

January. Goes on preaching mission through Ohio towns with Sidney Rigdon.

January 25. Sustained and ordained President of the High Priesthood at Amhurst, Ohio.

March 24-25. Mobbed, tarred, and feathered, by frontiersmen at Hiram.

April 2. Starts second visit to "Zion" in Missouri, removing family from Hiram to Kirtland.

April 24. Arrives at Independence; organizes an order to manage affairs both at Kirtland and in Zion.

April 26. Acknowledged as President of the High Priesthood. Tours Missouri settlements.

May 6th. Leaves Missouri for Kirtland.

June. Arrives Kirtland and spends summer with Bible revision and general affairs.

November 8. Attracts visitors from Vermont: Brigham Young, Joseph Young, Heber C. Kimball and others.

December 25. Records revelation and prophecy on war.

—1833—

January 4. Writes Seaton letter to Rochester, N. Y.

February 2. Completes "translation and review" of the New Testament.

February 27. Revelation of the Word of Wisdom.

March 8-18. Organizes First Presidency of the Church.

June 25. Plat of Zion and items of instruction on economic development sent to Missouri.

July 20. Mobs in Jackson county, Missouri, destroy store, printing press, other Mormon properties.

July 23. Mormons agree to leave Jackson county. Oliver Cowdery hurries to Kirtland with news.

August. Oliver Cowdery arrives Kirtland. Orson Hyde and William W. Phelps sent to Missouri.

September 28. Mormons petition Daniel Dunklin, Governor of Missouri.

October 5. Goes on mission to Canada.

October 31. Armed attacks on Mormons in Missouri, who flee to banks of the Missouri river.

November 4. Returns from Canadian mission.

November 25. Orson Hyde returns from Missouri and reports; Prophet ponders group problem in Missouri.

—1834—

February 17. Organizes a high council to stabilize Church government at Kirtland, while he goes to Missouri.

February 26. Begins organization of Zion's Camp, relief expedition to Missouri.

May 5. Leads Zion's Camp from Kirtland to give military support, if necessary, to Missouri saints.

June 23. Arrives at Clay county, Missouri, and begins to organize affairs.

July 3. A Missouri high council organized. Zion's Camp formally discharged.

July 9. With local Church government stabilized, returns to Kirtland, arriving about August 1.

September 1. Labors with own hands in Ohio stone quarry to help build Kirtland temple.

September 24. Heads committee to arrange "the items of the doctrine of Jesus Christ for the government of the Church."

—1835—

February 14. Twelve Apostles called and ordained at Kirtland. Expansion of general, central Church government.
February 28. The Seventy called and ordained.
July 3. Visited by Michael Chandler, interprets his papyrus rolls and spends remainder of month "arranging a grammar of the Egyptian language as practiced by the ancients" then goes on brief mission to Michigan.
August 17. The book of Doctrine and Covenants, "carefully selected from the revelations of God and compiled by Joseph Smith, Jr., Oliver Cowdery, Sidney Rigdon, and Frederick G. Williams, Presiding Elders of the Church," accepted by conference vote at Kirtland.
August 23. Arrives home (Kirtland) from Michigan.
September 24. Covenants with Kirtland high council to re-occupy Jackson county and "to struggle for this thing [liberty], until death."
November 20. Oliver Cowdery brings him a quantity of books from New Yory City, including Hebrew and Greek grammars, lexicons, and a copy of Webster's English dictionary. Spends winter of 1835-36 translating book of Abraham, building temple, and attending Joshua Seixas' lectures on Hebrew.

—1836—

March 27. Dedicates completed temple at Kirtland.
July 25. Goes by water and rail to Albany, thence to New York City, Providence, R. I., Boston, and Salem.
August. Rents house in Salem, Massachusetts, and lives there about a month with Sidney Rigdon, Oliver Cowdery, Hyrum Smith, Brigham Young, and Lyman Johnson.
September. Returns to Kirtland.
November 2. Kirtland Safety (banking) Society organized.
December. Missouri legislature grants

Mormon petition to organize Caldwell county, "a fresh impetus . . . to the gathering, and the county grew like Jonah's gourd."

—1837—

January 2. New articles for the Kirtland Banking Society framed.
May-June. Panic of 1837 strikes Kirtland.
ca. June 1. Heber C. Kimball called to undertake a mission to England.
ca. July 7. Joseph resigns from Kirtland Safety Society.
July 27. Makes second trip to Canada.
September 18. Back in Kirtland. Conreference appoints him and Sidney Rigdon to solve the Missouri gathering problem.
September 27. Leaves on fourth journey to Missouri, arriving there about November 1, spending ten days.
ca. November 10. Leaves Far West, Missouri, arriving in Kirtland ca. December 10 to find turmoil in the Church.

—1838—

January 12. Flees from Kirtland with Sidney Rigdon "to escape mob violence."
January 16. Joined by family, proceeds overland in covered wagons on fifth journey to Missouri, crossing the Mississippi at Quincy, Illinois, on this journey.
March 14. Enters Far West and issues "The Political Motto of the Church."
April 12-13. Oliver Cowdery and David Whitmer excommunicated.
May 18. Begins personal exploration and development of sites for additional communities, Adam-ondi-Ahman and others.
July 4. Impressive Independence Day ceremonies at Far West, including laying of corner stones for temple, which incites reaction and subsequent organization among anti-Mormon elements.
August. Efforts under way to prevent or discourage Mormons from voting at the election of August 6.
August 7. Goes to Gallatin, Daviess county, to investigate news that Mormons were killed at polls previous day. Men wounded only. Disturbances spread through Daviess, Clay, and Carroll counties.

August 30. Governor Boggs holds Missouri militia in readiness in view of "civil disturbances."

September 3-4. Communicates with General David R. Atchison and A. W. Doniphan retaining them as "our counsel in law." Begins study of law, with Sidney Rigdon, under Doniphan and Atchison, with ambition of gaining admission to bar "in twelve months."

September 7. Submits to trial on counsel's advice, to test judicial remedy for Mormon position. Bound over on $500 bond; no trial.

September 8. Armed hostilities break out at Adam-ondi-Ahman.

October 2. Kirtland Camp arrives in Far West, having been organized in Kirtland July 5.

October 4. Saints at DeWitt, Missouri, return fire of attackers.

October 6. Tries to make peace at DeWitt. John Taylor sustained as an apostle at Far West.

October 11. DeWitt evacuated.

October 15. Far West militia organizes under Lt. Col. George M. Hinkle.

October 25. Battle of Crooked River. David W. Patten, Patrick O'Banion, Gideon Carter, killed.

October 27. Governor Lilburn W. Boggs issues "exterminating order. Atchison withdraws from militia.

October 30. Haun's Mill massacre.

October 31. Missouri militia surrounded Far West, send truce flag to city; accepted by Hinkle who surrenders Mormon leaders for trial and punishment. S. D. Lucas orders execution of Joseph Smith.

November 1. A. W. Doniphan refuses to execute Lucas's order. Joseph Smith carried away, prisoner, to Richmond, Missouri.

November 13. With numerous others, tried at Richmond.

November 28. All Mormon prisoners taken November 1, released except Joseph Smith, Lyman Wight, Caleb Baldwin, Hyrum Smith, Alexander McRae, and Sidney Rigdon. These sent to Liberty jail, to stand trial for "treason and murder." Parley P. Pratt and others, meanwhile, imprisoned at Richmond.

—1839—

February 6-7. Stephen Markham starts for Quincy, Illinois, with the prophet's family, followed by Brigham Young on the 18th.

February 25. The Democratic Association of Quincy meets and approves a resolution friendly to Mormon settlement in Illinois.

March 15. After almost five months in chains and prison, Joseph petitions judges of the Supreme Court of Missouri for release; meanwhile directs activities from Liberty Jail.

April 6. Moved as prisoner to Gallatin, Daviess county.

April 9. Tried before a drunken court and indicted by Daviess county grand jury, presumably for "treason and murder."

April 15. En route to Boone county, under guard, makes escape and proceeds towards Illinois.

April 22. Arrives at Quincy, reports having spent $50,000 in lands and cash for legal counsel in Missouri, which partially explains his subsequent application for bankruptcy.

May 1. Arranges land purchases at future site of Nauvoo.

May 9. Removes to a log hut in Commerce, thereafter Nauvoo, Illinois. Commences building a new city.

July 4. Parley P. Pratt and other brethren escape from jail, Columbia, Missouri.

October 20. Decides to personally present the Mormon case before the 26th Congress and President Martin Van Buren.

October 29. Leaves Nauvoo for Washington, D.C., with Sidney Rigdon, Elias Higbee, Orrin Porter Rockwell, and Dr. R. D. Foster.

November 18. Leaves all but Higbee in Columbus, Ohio, and proceeds to Washington.

November 28. Arrives in the nation's capitol; the Twenty-sixth Congress is about to convene.

November 29. Interviews President Martin Van Buren in the White House.

December 6. Meets with the Illinois congressional delegation at the capitol, on Mormon claims bill, totaling $1,381,044. Calls on Henry Clay, John C. Calhoun, and others.

December 21. Visits Philadelphia on a branch-visiting and preaching tour, while Congress recesses for Christmas.

December 29. At Monmouth, New Jersey.

—1840—

January 9. Back in Philadelphia, touring branches in that region. Meets companions left in Columbus, Ohio.

January 27. Returns to Washington with Rockwell, Higbee, and Foster, leaving Rigdon in Philadelphia.

February 5. Preaches in Washington, D.C.

ca. February 20. Leaves the capital for Dayton, Ohio, with Foster.

March 4. Arrives in Nauvoo. In Washington the Senate judiciary committee discharges itself from the Mormon claim ruling that "It can never be presumed that a state (Missouri) either wants the power or lacks the disposition to redress the wrongs of its own citizens . . . whether they proceed from the lawless acts of her officers or any other persons." This view accords with a Supreme Court ruling of 1833.

April 8. General conference at Nauvoo goes on record that it considers the Senate report "unconstitutional and subversive to the rights of a free people."

April 15. Dispatches Orson Hyde to Palestine to dedicate that land for the return of the Jews.

October 4. General conference votes to draft a bill of incorporation for Nauvoo. Plans laid for establishing stakes of Zion throughout the area. People pouring in.

November 28. Elias Higbee and R. B. Thompson re-present the prophet's petition to the Congress.

December 16. The Nauvoo charter passes the Illinois legislature, is signed by Governor Thomas Carlin. A young legislator named Abraham Lincoln comes forward and cordially congratulates the Mormon managers on their bill's successful passage.

—1841—

February 1. First municipal election, Nauvoo. Joseph elected member of the City Council.

February 3. Presents ordinances establishing Nauvoo Legion and University. State legislature amends Nauvoo charter to permit "any citizen of Hancock county . . . [to] attach himself to the Nauvoo Legion. . . ."

February 4. Elected Lieut.-Gen. Nau-

voo Legion. (Commissioned formally by the Governor, March 10.)

February 20. The Legion, by rule of its court-martial, makes all residents aged 18-45 subject to military service.

February 27. Nauvoo Agricultural and Manufacturing Association chartered by the legislature.

May 24. Joseph calls upon the Saints to concentrate at Nauvoo.

June 4. Trouble afoot, visits Governor Carlin at latter's Quincy home.

June 5. Surprise arrest, on Carlin's order, granting extradition to Missouri.

June 9. Tried before Judge Stephen A. Douglas at Monmouth, Illinois court.

June 10. Douglas orders release. Returns to Nauvoo to regulate affairs and build up the city.

December 14. Moves into his new brick store.

December 24. Plans an immigration agency to be established for Mormon immigrants, in England.

—1842—

January 4. Joseph Duncan. Whig candidate for governor, makes bitter attack on Mormon charters. Joseph subsequently names his favorite horse "Joe Duncan" and supports Thomas Ford, Democrat, for Governor of Illinois.

March 1. Begins publishing the Book of Abraham in the Times and Seasons. Writes John Wentworth, editor and proprietor of the Chicago Democrat.

March 2. Is visited by Governor Dudley of Connecticut.

March 17. Organizes the Female Society.

March 27. Baptizes 107 persons in the Mississippi.

April 18. Commences bankruptcy proceedings under a new federal law.

May 4. Inaugurates endowment ceremonies in the private office of his Nauvoo store.

May 19. Elected Mayor in the place of John C. Bennett who resigned May 17.

May 22. Issues statement disavowing complicity in attempt on life of ex-Governor Boggs in Missouri.

June 1. Attends a political meeting "in the grove" and approves list of candidates for public office in Hancock county, with exception of the candidate for sheriff.

July 4. In an Independence Day address, declares the purpose of the Legion "to yield obedience to the institutions of our country, and protect the Saints from mobs."

July 5. Approves ordinance making it illegal to remove any citizen from the city without privilege of investigation before the Municipal Court of Nauvoo and the writ of habeas corpus. (A Missouri dragnet, aided by extradition in Illinois, is after the prophet.)

August 6. In Montrose, Iowa, at installation of Rising Sun Lodge, York rite Masons, prophesies removal of the Mormon people to the Rocky Mountains.

August 8. Arrested as accessory to the attempt on Bogg's life, by extradition proceedings. Released on habeas corpus issued by the Nauvoo Municipal Court. Seeks seclusion. City Council passes supplementary ordinance bolstering habeas corpus procedure.

August 11. Hides upstream on the Mississippi.

August 16. Considers further flight, perhaps to the west.

August 17. Hiding place discovered; removes to Carlos Granger home in Nauvoo.

August 19. Returns to his own home, but resumes secluded life shortly.

September 3. Attempt to arrest renewed unsuccessfully.

October 2. Governor Carlin having previously issued a proclamation for the arrest of Joseph Smith, a reward of $500 is now posted for his capture, $300 of it by Governor Reynolds of Missouri.

December 8. Thomas Ford, inaugurated as Governor of Illinois, at the polls, recommends modification in the Mormon charters.

December 9. Bills introduced into the Illinois legislature to repeal the charters.

December 26. With Ford in the governor's chair, Joseph submits to friendly arrest under Carlin's proclamation, by Wilson Law. His wife Emma delivers a still-born son.

December 27-30. Goes to Springfield for extradition trial, arraigned before a U. S. Circuit Judge.

—1843—

January 1-7, at home of James Adams in Springfield. Trial before Judge Pope. Illinois' prosecutors challenge jurisdiction of the federal court, but are overruled. Pope orders release and Ford advises Joseph to "refrain from all political electioneering." The prophet tells him the Mormons vote as they please.

January 7-10. Returns to Nauvoo from the Illinois capital.

January 18. John C. Bennett begins operations to revive the Missouri charges and Joseph warns Ford that "before I would be troubled any more by Missouri, I would fight."

February 3. Begins study of German (and continues same until the end of his life).

February 6. Re-elected mayor unanimously.

March 2. Reads law, Blackstone and Phillips, in connection with his duties as chief justice of the municipal court.

March 3. Bills in the legislature come to vote. Lower house votes repeal of charter by 58-33.

March 4. Charter saved in the upper house by narrow margin of 17-16, refusing to consider. Repeal measure tabled.

May 1. Translates a portion of certain brass plates discovered at Kinderhook, Iowa.

May 11. Appoints a mission to the Pacific Isles.

May 12. Purchases half-interest in Mississippi steamboat, Maid of Iowa.

May 18. Dines with Stephen A. Douglas and tells that gentleman he will aspire to the U. S. Presidency. Douglas, aged 30, acknowledges that the Prophet has read his ambitions correctly.

June 10. Plans an arsenal for the Legion.

June 16. Word from Springfield indicates that Ford is about to yield to pressure and comply with Missouri request for extradition.

June 21. At Dixon, Lee county, some 200 miles from Nauvoo, visiting Emma's relatives with his family.

June 23. Arrested without due process at Dixon by Joseph H. Reynolds, sheriff of Jackson county, Missouri, and Harmon T. Wilson, constable of Carthage, county seat of Hancock (Nauvoo) county. Resists, is manhandled, but succeeds in filing counter-suit of false arrest.

June 24. Retains Cyrus Walker, Whig candidate for Congress (same district as Nauvoo) in August election, on forced promise to give Walker his vote. Sets writ of habeas corpus from Master of Chancery of Dixon, "returnable to the nearest court having jurisdiction." and proceeds under arrest to Quincy for trial.

June 25. Wilson Law, Charles C. Rich, and 175 men ride from Nauvoo to assist the Prophet.

June 29. Steers his captors towards Nauvoo instead of Quincy, to get protection of municipal court.

June 30. Triumphal entry into Nauvoo. Reynolds refuses to recognize the city court but Joseph gets his writ anyway and is delivered into the hands of his city marshal. Reynolds and Wilson go to Carthage to organize a posse to take their intended captive.

July 4. Declares he never tells any man how to vote, but explains why the Mormons voted for Ford rather than Duncan at last election.

July 12. Records the revelation on eternity of the marriage covenant, including a plurality of wives.

July 29. Visited by Joseph P. Hoge (Democrat) and Cyrus Walker (Whig), rival candidates for Congress, climaxing their campaign.

August 6. Election eve. Says "The Lord has not given me a revelation concerning politics. I have not asked Him for one. I am a third party and stand independent and alone." Declares, then, that he will vote for Walker but advises large meeting that Hyrum has had a testimony that the people should vote for Hoge, and that Hyrum's revelations are seldom wrong.

August 7. Votes for Walker, as pledged; but Hoge is overwhelmingly elected to Congress.

August. Increasing friction between the governmental authority of the city of Nauvoo and that of Hancock county (seat, Carthage). Tax collections controlled by the county.

September 4. The New York Sun calls him "one of the great men of this age."

September 5. The first of a series of formal anti-Mormon meetings convenes at Carthage and appoints committees of correspondence to take suitable action against those who yield "implicit obedience" to "this latter-day would-be Mahomet." Resolution to blacklist any political party or leader that goes to Nauvoo to "truckle . . . for their influence."

September 9. Nauvoo Legion in general training and maneuvers. Plans opened to get their portion of state arms.

September 13-14. Attends a series of lectures on socialism and has them answered by John Taylor.

September 15. Opens the Mansion House as a hotel.

September 23. At Dixon, Reynolds and Wilson's trial for falsely arresting Joseph postponed six months.

September 24. Preaches against folly of "common stock" and favors individual stewardships and control of property.

October 1. Times and Seasons asks, editorially, "Who shall be our next President?"

November 4. Writes letters to leading presidential candidates, Martin Van Buren, Lewis Cass, Johnson, Henry Clay, and John C. Calhoun, asking their attitude towards Mormon claims.

November 15. Speaks of writing a proclamation to the kings of the earth.

November 25-29. Waited upon by agent of John C. Calhoun, who agrees to have Senator Rhett of South Carolina push Mormon claim, and who composes a model "petition" to be presented.

November 29. Tells council he will no longer use his influence, as heretofore, to prevent Mormons from fighting when mobbed.

December 7. Ford about to give in to anti-Mormon pressure, Nauvoo petitions him to reject Missouri requisitions.

December 8. Calls on City Council "to make preparations for any invasion from Missouri." Ordinance for the extra case of Joseph Smith passed, imposing penalty of life imprisonment for anyone attempting requisition of the Prophet in Nauvoo. Plans to harness Mississippi river for navigation and industrial purposes.

December 12. Nauvoo police force increased by forty men.

December 14. Ford breaks with the Mormons.

December 18. Joseph orders out a company of 100 Legionnaires to apprehend Levi Williams of Carthage, for the kidnapping of Mormon brethren and attempting to take them to Missouri. Williams retaliates by organizing a company at Warsaw.

December 19. The Legion mobilized.

December 21. A memorial dispatched to Congress asking that Nauvoo be clothed with authority of a federal district; that the Legion be accounted as federal troops under the city's control.

—1844—

January 2. Writes scorching letter to Calhoun, disagreeing with his restricted view of the national power under the Constitution.

January 4. Schism with Laws and Higbees flares openly.

January 29. Meets with the Twelve to consider the coming 1844 election and determines on his own candidacy for the office of U. S. President. Begins work on the Views on the Powers and Policy of the Government of the United States.

February 3. Niles' Register publishes Smith-Calhoun correspondence.

February 7. Completes writing the Views.

February 12. Recommends repeal of the "extra ordinance" and sends Orson Pratt and Orson Hyde to Washington with specific instructions for dealing with the Illinois delegation, John Quincy Adams, and the Massachusetts delegation.

February 17. The anti-Mormon convention at Carthage considers ways and means of expelling the Mormons from Illinois.

February 20. The Twelve instructed to send out an Oregon and California exploration company to locate a new home for the Church. Carthage convention sets date for a "wolf hunt."

February 24-27. Fifteen hundred copies of the Views come from the press and are mailed to the President, supreme court justices, cabinet officers, congressmen, postmasters, and others.

March 26. Petitions Congress for permission to raise and equip 100,000 men "for the protection of the citizens of the United States emigrating to the territories, and for the extension of the principles of universal liberty."

March 27. Joseph H. Jackson and others organize in Nauvoo to take the prophet's life.

April 5. Attends dedication of Nauvoo Masonic temple, erected under direction of Lucius N. Scovil.

April 6. Tells the general conference that all of America is Zion and is to be built up.

April 10-29. R. D. Foster, F. M. and C. L. Higbee, Wilson and William Law, excommunicated. Joseph is threatened with drawn weapons April 26. C. C. Rich supplants Wilson Law as executive officer of Legion.

May 7. An "opposition" printing press arrives at R. D. Foster's in Nauvoo.

May 8. The Hancock county court and the municipal court of Nauvoo engage in legal battle, Joseph securing habeas corpus and discharge from order of the county court to appear "on the first day of the next term."

May 10. Prospectus for a new paper, the Nauvoo Expositor, circulated throughout the city. A jury in Lee county awards Joseph $40 damages against Wilson and Reynolds for false arrest and imprisonment.

May 12. Hyrum Smith receives a threatening letter, presumably from Joseph H. Jackson and the apostate Mormons.

May 13. Joseph receives Orson Hyde's reports conveying intelligence of Fremont's explorations and surveys of the inland west and outlining a route to Oregon.

May 15. Charles Francis Adams and Josiah Quincy call to see the Nauvoo Prophet.

May 17. A state political convention, in Nauvoo, endorses the Prophet's candidacy for President.

May 20. The circuit court convenes at Carthage, and issues a summons for Joseph Smith.

May 21. A process-server from Carthage fails to find Joseph in Nauvoo.

May 23. A grand jury, impaneled in Carthage, returns two indictments against the Prophet, for polygamy, and for false swearing.

May 25. (In what I believe to be an effort to secure grounds for transfer to a federal court in event of future arrest), urges agents in Washington to use pressure on Hoge and others to gain him the Nauvoo postmastership in lieu of Rigdon. Rigdon resigns and recommends Joseph Smith as his successor.

May 27. Goes to Carthage with a body of men, "thinking it best to meet my enemies before the circuit court." Open attempts on his life expected. Returns safely.

May 30. Sitting as chief justice of the Nauvoo court, releases Jeremiah Smith on habeas corpus, in face of a federal order and warrant issuer by Nathaniel Pope, judge of the United States circuit court, T. B. Johnson, acting federal marshal, threatens to bring U. S. troops from an Iowa garrison to get Jeremiah. Joseph writes Pope, introducing Jeremiah as one of the "brethren of the mystic tie."

May 31. Issues a warrant for the arrest of T. B. Johnson for "threatening the peace of the city with United States dragoons."

June 1. Plans development of a coal mine on Rock river.

June 8. Considers subject of the *Nauvoo Expositor* in city council. Polk's nomination made known. William Clayton says that William Law has offered Joseph H. Jackson $500 to kill the prophet.

June 10. Orders the destruction of the Expositor as a "nuisance." Orders executed by city marshal.

June 11. Issues proclamation asking assistance of all citizens in preserving public order. Receives intelligence of a forthcoming indictment by a federal grand jury at Springfield for his action in the Jeremiah Smith case.

June 12. Arrested by David Bettisworth on a justice's writ (Hancock county) to answer for destruction of the Expositor. Obtains habeas corpus from the Municipal Court.

June 13. Hyrum Smith and others arrested by Bettisworth on same circumstances. Joseph orders release and issues habeas corpus as chief justice. Mob of 300 armed men assemble at Carthage. Mass meeting at Warsaw asks Ford to intervene in behalf of the law as interpreted at Carthage.

June 14. Sends the Mormon side of the story by carrier to Ford, supported by a mass of documents.

June 15. Arms and munitions arrive at Carthage. The mob drills.

June 16. Sends agents to surrounding towns to disabuse the public mind.

June 17. Attempts to solve the problem by having himself arrested by Joel S. Miles and submitting to hearing before a friendly but non-Mormon justice of the peace, Daniel H. Wells, at Nauvoo. Subject: the Expositor. Wells discharges the prisoner. Legal position of the Prophet strong. Orders Legion in readiness, as Carthage acknowledges that he is beyond the reach of law, but not beyond powder and ball.

June 18. Places Nauvoo under martial law. Calls "God and angels to witness that I have unsheathed my sword with firm and unalterable determination that this people shall have their legal rights . . . or my blood shall be spilt upon the ground like water."

June 19. Iowa volunteers for the Legion arrive (from outlying Mormon settlements). Roads into Nauvoo picketed. Mississippi patrolled.

June 20. Studies countryside and devises plan for defense of city. Recalls the Twelve from their mission fields. Urges Hyrum to take his family and go to Cincinnati.

June 21. Governor Ford calls a council of both sides. John Taylor and John M. Bernhisel sent to represent the Mormon view.

June 22. Invites Ford to Nauvoo. Ford writes that it was illegal to suppress the Expositor under the law governing nuisances. Invites Joseph to Carthage under guarantee of safety; threatens militia if non-compliance. Joseph plans to cross river, go west, sending his family to Cincinnati, and W. W. Phelps to Washington as emissary.

June 23. On the Iowa side of the river. A posse appears in Nauvoo to arrest the Mayor. Emma sends Reynolds Cahoon, her relative L. D. Wasson, and Hiram Kimball, a well-to-do Nauvoo host, to persuade Joseph to return. Under pressure, he returns.

June 24. In custody of Ford's posse. Countersigns Ford's order disarming Nauvoo Legion. Says "I am going like a lamb to the slaughter."

June 25. In Carthage. Another writ, for treason, served. Arraigned before Justice R. F. Smith on charge of riot and is bound over to the circuit court for trial. Imprisoned on a false commitment at 11:30 p.m.

June 26. Asks change of venue to Quincy. Sends repeated messages to Ford, who comes to Carthage jail for interview at 9:27 a.m. and again promises protection from violence. Taken again to courtroom for a justice's examination, same postponed until next day and is returned to jail. Meanwhile a military council, including Ford, decides to march the restless troops to Nauvoo next day, to return the day following. Joseph's trial to be further postponed until June 29. A few men to be left to guard the jail.

June 27. With some modifications, the council's plan proceeds. With John Taylor, Willard Richards, and Hyrum, Joseph is guarded in the jail by a small detachment of Carthage Greys. Ford goes to Nauvoo with the remnants of the militia. The rest are disbanded. The stage is set for the drama of the afternoon. At four p.m. the guard is changed to eight men. At five p.m. a mob with painted faces and disguises storm the jail. Joseph Smith, with his brother Hyrum, are killed by gunfire shortly after 5:15 p.m.

—1845—

ca. January 25. Nauvoo charter is repealed by the Illinois legislature, followed by severe persecution in Hancock county.

April 6. The Twelve issue the proclamation to the "rulers of all nations."

—1846—

February 4. Mormons evacuate Nauvoo and cross Mississippi en route to the Great Basin. It is 1846, "the year of decision." The Mormons are on the march to build Zion in America.

BIBLIOGRAPHY

I. LATTER-DAY SAINT SCRIPTURES:

The Bible (King James translation).
The Book of Mormon (1920 edition).
The Doctrine and Covenants (1921 edition).
The Pearl of Great Price (1921 edition).

II. HISTORIES AND BIOGRAPHIES:

Bancroft, Hubert Howe, *Native Races*, Volume 2, 1883.

Cannon, George Q., *The Life of Joseph Smith*, 1888.

Corrill, John, *A Brief History of the Church of Latter-day Saints*, 1839.

Cowley, Matthias F., *Life of Wilford Woodruff*, 1909.

Davis, Inez Smith, *The Story of the Church*, 1948.

Documentary History of the Church of Jesus Christ of Latter-day Saints, Seven Volumes to 1848. (Edition beginning 1902).

Evans, John Henry, *Joseph Smith, An American Prophet*, 1933.

Evans, Richard L., *A Century of Mormonism in Great Britain*, 1937.

Jenson, Andrew, *Encyclopedic History of the Church*, 1941.

Jenson, Andrew, *Church Chronology*, 1914.

Journal History (In Historian's Office) 1830 to and including March, 1943.

Lang, P. W., *History of Seneca County*, 1880.

Linn, W. A., *The Story of the Mormons*, 1902.

Meyer, Edward, *Ursprung und Geschichte der Mormonen*, 1912.

Nibley, Preston, *Joseph Smith, the Prophet*, 1944.

Pratt, Parley P., *Autobiography*, 1888.

Rigdon, Mrs. John W., *Life of Sidney Rigdon* (Historian's Office).

Roberts, B. H., *Comprehensive History of the Church*, Six Volumes, 1930.

Smith, Joseph Fielding, *Life of Joseph F. Smith*, 1938.

Smith, Joseph Fielding, *Essentials of Church History*, 1947.

Smith, Lucy Mack, *History of the Prophet Joseph*, 1850, 1902 and 1945 editions.

Tullidge, Edward, *History of Northern Utah and Southern Idaho Biographical Supplement*, Volume 2, 1889.

Tullidge, Edward, *Joseph Smith the Prophet*, 1879.

Wayne County, History of, 1877.

Whitney, Orson F., *History of Utah*, Four Volumes, 1892-1904.

Whitney, Orson F., *Life of Heber C. Kimball*, 1888.

III. NEWSPAPERS AND PERIODICALS:

Contributor, The, Volume 4, 1882-1883.
Cowdery, Oliver, *Messenger and Advocate,* 1835.
Campbell, Alexander, *Millennial Harbinger,* February 7, 1831.
Crowley, Ariel L., "The Anthon Transcript," *Improvement Era,* Volume 45, March 1942.
Deseret News, January 20, 1894.
Elders' Journal, July 1838.
Evening and Morning Star, 1832.
Bennett, Archibald F., "The Ancestry of Joseph Smith the Prophet," *Utah Genealogical and Historical Magazine,* Volume 20, 1929.
Journal of Discourses, 1853-1886.
Juvenile Instructor (The), 1866-1949.
Kimball, Heber C., *Journal of Discourses,* Volume 6, 1857.
Littlefield, Lyman O., "Discussion with Joseph Smith 3rd (Reorganite)" *Deseret News,* April 2, 27, May 5, 16, 29, Sept. 5, 6, 1883.
Messenger and Advocate, 1834.
Millennial Star, 1840-1950.
Relief Society Magazine, Volume 6, "A Centenary of Relief Society," 1919.
Richmond (Missouri) Conservator, March 25, 1881.
The Saints' Herald, Volume 31, 1884.
Smith, George A., *Journal of Discourses,* Volume 12 (1869), Volume 13 (1871), Volume 11 (1867).
Smith, William, *Deseret News,* January 20, 1894.
Times and Seasons, 1839-1845.
Widtsoe, John A., "Where was the Garden of Eden?" *Improvement Era,* January, 1950.
Woman's Exponent, Volumes 13, 14, 1884-1885.
Young Woman's Journal, Volume 31, 1920.

IV. SPECIAL WORKS:

Adams, George J., *A Letter to His Excellency John Tyler,* 1844.
Adams, J. T., *The Epic of America.*
Allen, J. Edward, *The Second United Order Among the Mormons,* 1936.
Appleby, W. L., *A Dissertation on Nebuchadnezzar's Dream,* 1844.
Arbaugh, G. B., *Revelation Among the Mormons* (Revelation in Mormonism, 1932).
Barker, James L., *The Protesters of Christendom,* 1946.
Batchelor, Origen, *Mormonism Exposed,* 1838.
Bays, Doris H., *Doctrine and Dogmas of Mormonism,* 1897.
Berry, John, *Plain Facts Against Latter-day Saints,* 1844.

Booth, *Letters,* 1834 (E. D. Howe, *Mormonism Unvailed*).

Bowen, A. E., *The Church Welfare Plan,* Sunday School Lessons, 1946

Brewster, James Colin, *Mormon Money Diggers,* 1843.

Brodie, Fawn M., *No Man Knows My History,* 1945.

Campbell, Alexander, *An Analysis of the Book of Mormon,* 1832.

Campbell, Alexander, *Delusions,* 1832.

Caswall, Henry, *The City of the Mormons or Three Days at Nauvoo in 1842.*

Caswall, Henry, *The Prophet of the Nineteenth Century,* 1843.

Chase, Daryl, *Joseph, the Prophet,* 1944.

Chase, Daryl, *Sidney Rigdon, Early Mormon,* (unpublished thesis University of Chicago, 1931.)

Clark, J. Reuben, Jr., *On The Way to Immortality and Eternal Life,* 1949.

Clark, Rev., John A., *Gleanings by the Way,* 1842.

Dickinson, Ellen, *New Light on Mormonism,* 1885.

Durham, G. Homer, (The) *Discourses of Wilford Woodruff,* 1946.

Durham, G. Homer, *Joseph Smith, Prophet Statesman,* 1944.

Flagg, *The Far West, A Tour Beyond the Mountains,* 1838.

Ford and Crowther, *My Life and Work,* 1922.

Frost, S. E., *The Basic Teachings of the Great Philosopher,* 1945.

Geddes, Joseph A., *The United Order Among the Mormons,* 1924.

Greene, J. P., *Facts Relative to the Expulsion of Mormons from Missouri,* 1839

Greene, John P., *Facts Relative to the Expulsion of the Mormons or Latter-day Saints from the State of Missouri under the Exterminating Order,* 1839.

Haining, Samuel, *Mormonism Weighed in the Balance of the Sanctuary and Found Wanting,* 1840.

Harris, William, *Mormonism Portrayed,* 1841.

Haynard, John, *The Religious Creeds and Statistics of Every Christian Denomination in the United States and British Provinces,* 1836.

Howe, E. D., *Mormonism Unvailed,* 1834.

Hunter, Milton R. and Ferguson, Thomas Stuart, *Ancient America and the Book of Mormon,* 1950.

Hunter, Milton R., *The Gospel Through the Ages,* 1945.

Hunter, Milton R., *Pearl of Great Price Commentary,* 1948.

Johnson, Benjamin F., *My Life's Review,* 1947.

Johnson, J. Edwin, *Joseph Smith.*

Kennedy, J. H., *Early Days of Mormonism,* 1888.

Kidder, Daniel F., *Mormonism and the Mormons,* 1842.

Kimball, Heber C., *Missouri Pamphlet,* 1882.

Kimball, Heber C. and Woodruff, Wilford, *The Word of the Lord to the Citizens of London.*

Kirkham, F. W., *A New Witness for Christ in America,* 1943.

Livesey, Richard, *Exposure of Mormonism,* 1838.

Lundwall, N. B., *Masterful Discourses and Writings of Orson Pratt,* 1946.

McChesney, James, *An Antidote to Mormonism,* 1838, New York Supplement, 1939.

McNiff, William J., *Heaven on Earth,* 1940.

Mill, John Stuart, *The Subjection of Women* (1853) Everyman's Library #825.

Morish, W. J., *The Latter-day Saints and the Book of Mormon,* 1840.

Morris, Nephi L., *Prophecies of Joseph Smith and their Fulfillment,* 1920, 1926.

Nibley, Preston, *Exodus to Greatness,* 1847.

Nibley, Preston, *Life of Joseph the Prophet,* 1944

Nibley, Preston, *The Witnesses of the Book of Mormon,* 1946.

Onley, Oliver H., *The Absurdities of Mormonism Portrayed,* 1843.

Orr, Dr. Adrian, *Mormonism Dissected,* 1841.

Patterson, Robert, *Who Wrote the Book of Mormon,* 1882.

Pratt, Orson, *Absurdities of Immaterialism,* 1849.

Pratt, Orson, *Journal of Discourses.*

Pratt, Orson, *Remarkable Visions,* 1840.

Quincy, Josiah, *Figures of the Past,* 1901 edition.

Reynolds, Arch S., *The Urim and Thummim,* 1950.

Reynolds, Arch S., *How did Joseph Smith Translate?,* 1950.

Riley, I. Woodbridge, *The Founder of Mormonism,* 1902.

Roberts, B. H., *New Witness for God,* 1895, 1909.

Roberts, B. H., *Defense of the Faith,* Volume 2, 1907.

Roberts, B. H., *Succession in the Presidency of the Church,* 1894.

St. Clair, D. L., *To the Followers of the Latter-day Saints,* October 14, 1840.

Shook, Charles A., *The True Origin of the Book of Mormon,* 1914.

Simons, John, *A Few More Facts,* 1840.

Sjodahl, J. M., *Introduction to Study of Book of Mormon,* 1927.

Smith, Joseph Fielding, *Succession in the Presidency,* 1907.

Smith, Joseph Fielding, *Teachings of the Prophet Joseph Smith,* 1946.

Smith, Joseph Fielding, *Blood Atonement and the Origin of Plural Marriage,* 1905.

Smith, Joseph F., *Gospel Doctrine,* 1949.

Sperry, Sidney B., *Our Book of Mormon,* 1947.

Stenhouse, T. B. H., *Rocky Mountain Saints,* 1873.

Stevenson, Edward, *Reminiscences of Joseph the Prophet*, 1893.

Talmage, James E., *Articles of Faith*, 1950.

Taylor, John, *The Gospel Kingdom*, 1944.

Tucker, Pomeroy, *Origin, Rise and Progress of Mormonism*, 1867.

Turner, J. B., *Mormonism in all Ages, or the Rise, Progress and Cause of Mormonism*, 1842.

Whitmer, David, *An Address to all Believers in Christ*, 1887.

Widtsoe, John A., *Discourses of Brigham Young*, 1925, 1941.

Widtsoe, John A. and Leah D., *The Word of Wisdom*, 1938, 1950.

Widtsoe, John A. and Harris, F. S., Jr., *Seven Claims of the Book of Mormon*, 1936.

Winchester, B., *The Spaulding Story*, 1840.

Winchester, B., *Biography of Dr. Hurlburt*, 1838.

Winebrenner, John, *History of Religious Denominations in the United States*, 2nd edition, 1849.

Wollastonecraft, Mary (Godwin), *The Rights of Woman*, 1792, Everyman's Library #825.

Woodruff, Wilford, *Leaves from My Journal*, 1881.

Wright, Robert C., *Indian Masonry*.

Young, Brigham, *The Resurrection*, 1944 edition.

INDEX

A

AARONIC Priesthood, conferred, 112, 125, 126
Aaron, rod of, 260
Abraham, book of, 254
Acts, book of, 28
Adam and Eve, 158-161
Adams, James, 238, 299
Adams, James Truslow, 196n
Administrative work, of Church, 129
Adult education, 224
Adultery, Hurlburt excommunicated for, 76
Administration, of sick by women, 185
Affidavits, 76, 77
Affidavits, regarding plural marriage, 239
Ages, of Church organizers, 123-124
Alcohol, 198
Alger, Fannie, plural wife, 237
Allen, Edward J., 192n
Allred, Wiley Payne, describes prophet, 350
American government, 217-219
American Revolution, 100
Ancestry, of Joseph Smith, 99-107
Ancient writing, on plates, 61-62
Angel, 27, 28, 29, 30
Anthon, Dr. Charles, 39
Anthropomorphism, 5
Apostles, 100, 114, Council of the Twelve, 304, 312-314; 355-359
Apostleship, 304, 305, 310
Arbaugh, J. B., cited, 19n
Archaeology, American, 62-63
"Articles and Covenants" of the Church, 117
Atheism, 5
Atom bomb, 149
Atonement, doctrine of, 160-161
Attorney, 54
Authenticity, of Book of Mormon, 60-66, of Church History, 293ff
Authority, 8, of the Church, 105-132, succession and continuity, 301-310, 355-359
Authorship, of Book of Mormon, 82-89

B

BABEL, Tower of, 60
Bancroft, H. H., 62n
Bank, Kirtland, 195
Baptism, revealed, 112ff, 124, 125, 164, 180, 181
Baptist, 1

Barker, James L., 115n
Basic doctrine of Church, 118
Batchelor, Origen, 92
Bays, Doris H., 23n
Bennett, A. F., cited, 99n
Bennett, James Arlington, 313, 330
Bennett, John C., 95-96, 299
Bible, influence in restoration of gospel, 105-107, necessary use leads to revision effort, 139-140, translation and revision, 251, mentions Urim and Thummim, 265
Bibliography, 261-265
Bidamon, Major Lewis C., married Emma, 358
Billings, Titus, 136
Bishop, Gladden, 238
Blind obedience, repugnant doctrine, 166
Book of Commandments, 251-253
Book of Mormon, and prophet's persecution, 17; storm center, 20; translated 38ff; printed in English, 42; publication and copyrighted, 43; evidences for, 60-66; language of (vocabulary) 67-71; Rigdon-Spaulding theory, 76; authorship issue, 82ff; influence in proselyting, 135-136ff
Books, produced by prophet, 250ff
Bowen, Albert E., 192n
Breastplate, 37
Brick store, endowment at, 246-247
British Mission, 137
Briton, D. G., 63n
Brodie, Fawn M., cited, 77n, 232n
Buddha, 61
Buel, J. W., 245n
Burgess, Margareth M., describes Prophet, 350

C

CAFFEINE, 201
California, 313
Call, Anson, 312
Campbell, Alexander, 82, 83, 90-91, 136, 323, 323n, 324
Campbellites, 83, 136
Canada, 24; mission to, 137
Canadaigua, N. Y., first missionary activity, 134
Cannon, George Q., 238n, 260n, 267n, 345n, 349; describes Prophet, 345-346
Carthage Jail, 318
Cash, $1,500 given Emma, 357

JOSEPH RECEIVES THE PLATES

CUMORAH

THE THREE WITNESSES